ABORIGINAL
Land Claims
IN CANADA

ABORIGINAL
Land Claims
IN CANADA

A REGIONAL PERSPECTIVE

edited by

KEN COATES
University of
Northern British Columbia

Copp Clark Pitman Ltd.
A Longman Company
Toronto

ISBN: 0-7730-5196-1

Editor: Curtis Fahey
Design: Kyle Gell
Cover: The Blackfoot Treaty, 1877. Painting by A. Bruce Stapleton.
          Photo supplied by Glenbow Museum, Calgary, Alberta, No. 13, 186.
Illustration: Christopher Griffin
Typesetting: Marnie Morrissey
Printing and binding: Friesen Printers

Canadian Cataloguing in Publication Data

Main entry under title:
Aboriginal land claims in Canada

Includes bibliographical references.

ISBN 0-7730-5196-1

1. Native peoples – Canada – Claims.* 2. Native peoples – Canada – Land tenure.* 3. Native peoples – Canada – Land transfers. I. Coates, Kenneth, 1956– .

KE7718.A37 1992   346.7104'32'08997   C92-094115-X

Copp Clark Pitman Ltd.
2775 Matheson Blvd. East
Mississauga, Ontario
L4W 4P7

Associated companies:
Longman Group Ltd., London
Longman Inc., New York
Longman Cheshire Pty., Melbourne
Longman Paul Pty. Auckland

Printed and bound in Canada

1 2 3 4 5   5196-1   96 95 94 93 92

Contents

Introduction

Ken Coates

Debate about aboriginal land rights has engulfed Canada. From Innu protests in Labrador to the complex land settlement negotiated by the Council of Yukon Indians, native groups across this country have voiced their anger over years of government inattention to their legitimate grievances. Governments and the non-native majority in Canada have reacted in different ways to aboriginal assertions of land ownership and demands for compensation. Some groups, chiefly those from the churches and the political left, have allied themselves with native claimants, but many other Canadians have expressed objections to the very concept of aboriginal land settlements.

For decades, non-native Canadians paid little attention to aboriginal demands for redress of outstanding land claims. Although native organizations from the Maritimes to British Columbia and north to the Arctic repeatedly placed their claims before the policy makers, governments had the power and the Eurocentric sense of superiority necessary to shelve most of the requests for settlements. Treaties were signed, particularly the Robinson Treaties in Ontario and the Numbered Treaties that spanned the region from James Bay to the Mackenzie River valley, but these originated primarily in response to the desire by non-native settlers that all impediments to development be cleared away. With respect to aboriginal peoples living in economically undesirable areas—Labrador, the Yukon, the Arctic—the federal government refused to budge.

Although the non-native majority assumed that the demands would disappear as indigenous peoples were absorbed into the dominant society, the aboriginal cultures proved to be both resilient and determined. The land issue did not evaporate, as successive non-native governments clearly hoped, but instead remained vital to the First Nations. Aboriginal peoples found few allies through much of their struggle, but they were not deterred.

The land-claims issue erupted in earnest in the 1960s, when the political and social turmoil of that decade generated support for aboriginal causes. A number of church groups, struggling to overcome the guilt they felt for their efforts at cultural and social assimilation, threw their weight behind native claims. Many other politically active Canadians, newly alerted to the nature and consequences of the dispossession of indigenous peoples, likewise rallied to the aboriginal cause. While in some quarters this support emerged as a new form of paternalism—in that some non-native activists "knew" better than the native groups what was best for the First Nations—a more general sympathy for aboriginal rights did develop. The transition was not immediate, nor was it comprehensive. Many Canadians came to share a concern for the relative poverty of aboriginal communities but drew the line at supporting claims for vast quantities of land and large sums of money.

The federal government, saddled with a fiduciary responsibility for indigenous peoples that it reluctantly accepted as a burden of leadership, lagged behind the native and non-native activists on this issue. When Pierre Elliott Trudeau was elected as leader of the Liberal Party in 1967 and swept to power in the "Trudeaumania" election of the following year, many assumed that the Liberals' concept of the "Just Society" incorporated renewed power for indigenous peoples. Although the Liberal government engaged in a highly publicized series of consultations with aboriginal leaders, the subsequent White Paper on Indian affairs (1969) proved to be a bitter disappointment. The government's agenda included a rejection of the natives' demands and a thinly disguised attempt to assimilate native people into the Canadian mainstream.

The aboriginal response to the White Paper, combined with the shifting intellectual waters of the Canadian judiciary, provided the foundation for the contemporary era of land-claims negotiations. Native leaders from across Canada united in rejecting the federal government's vision of the aboriginal future, and instead articulated a strikingly different agenda. At the same time, some aboriginal groups had resorted to the court system in an attempt to force governments to recognize their demands. One case, the famous Calder lawsuit argued before the Supreme Court of Canada by Thomas Berger, forced the government's hand. The Calder case focused on the demands of the Nisga'a of northwest British Columbia for a settlement of their longstanding land claim. While the Nisga'a lost their 1973 case on a technicality, the Supreme

Court did concur with Berger's argument that aboriginal title to traditional lands had not yet been resolved. The Trudeau administration was forced to rethink its opposition to native demands, and in 1973 as well it accepted the claim tabled by the Yukon Native Brotherhood for a settlement of the land question in the Yukon Territory.

Over the last twenty years, the land-claims process has expanded in scope and complexity. To an existing backlog of claims and court cases have been added literally hundreds of demands and challenges by native people. The contested territories range enormously in size, from the massive Dene claim in the Mackenzie valley and the Inuit territories in the eastern Arctic to relatively small pieces of reserve or treaty lands in British Columbia, Quebec, Nova Scotia, and elsewhere. All provinces and territories in Canada now find themselves addressing native demands of greater or lesser complexity. Once submerged within the federal Indian Affairs bureaucracy and kept from public view primarily by a compelling lack of interest on the part of the non-native population, the land-claims question has now emerged at the forefront of contemporary Canadian political life.

Even a brief reflection on the question of land rights illustrates how pervasive, and how crucial, this issue has become in Canada. In Labrador, the Innu blocked airfields and challenged a NATO air-training plan, demanding immediate attention to their land claims. The Mohawk near Montreal and the Cree of northern Quebec have each garnered much attention by their controversial and provocative attempts to resolve their land rights and claims. And so the struggle continues, ranging from the tense stand-offs involving the Teme-Augama Anishnabai in Ontario and the Lubicon Cree in northern Alberta to the campaigns of the persistent Nisga'a of British Columbia and the outspoken Dene of the Northwest Territories. It includes the desperate disappointment of the Gitskan-Wet'suwet'en when they lost their court challenge before the British Columbia Supreme Court, and the cautious optimism of the James Bay Cree when they negotiated an agreement with the province of Quebec and the government of Canada. The highly publicized contests, of course, tell only part of the story. For every stand-off, road blockade, and other such public conflict, there are literally dozens of low-profile demands, negotiations, and controversies across the country. Further, the regional complexity of the land-claims issue has not yet received its due. Western Canadians hear very little about aboriginal land protests in Nova Scotia and New Brunswick, just as people in Quebec rarely hear about the localized land struggles that have broken out across British Columbia.

Aboriginal Land Claims in Canada is an attempt to bring the complex and multifaceted land-claims issue into focus. This matter has, of course, attracted its share of commentators in the past, and they have done much to chart its national character. Michael Asch's *Home and Native*

Land, for example, is a fine survey of land claims in Canada (although it has been rendered somewhat dated by rapid legal and political changes) and provides a useful overview of the major legislative stages and national concerns that affect native land rights in Canada. *Aboriginal Land Claims in Canada,* however, starts from a different premise—that it is misleading to consider such an important issue from a national point of view, and that a regional perspective helps to clarify a complex process.

Although even the most cursory consideration of the First Nations in what is now Canada reveals striking cultural variations across the country, commentators have often ignored the fundamental importance of regional identities. This applies equally to the non-native population. From the earliest days of European occupation, Canada developed as a series of related but distinct regions. New France/Quebec has, perhaps, the most obvious claim of the newcomer societies to the appellation of "distinct," but it is clear that each of the regions has its own history, culture, and political agenda. The legal and administrative histories of the various regions of the country provide compelling proof of the value of a regional approach to the discussion of aboriginal land claims in Canada.

One of the most profound ironies of the land-claims question is that the matter has not yet taken on a truly aboriginal perspective. Although indigenous peoples would clearly wish to have the land question based on aboriginal principles, the debate in Canada has not even approached this plane. Rather than focus on native concepts of occupation, ownership, and transference of control, land-claims discussions have remained within the constraints of the British/Canadian legal system. This oddity has attracted surprisingly little attention, partially because of the ability of aboriginal leaders to debate the land issue on Euro-Canadian terms. (One wonders at how well the enormous battery of non-native politicians, administrators, lawyers, and judges would do if the tables were turned and they were forced to operate within aboriginal systems of diplomacy and negotiation. The evidence, based on such incidents as the Gitskan-Wet'suwet'en court case, is that the cultural chasm might well prove insurmountable for non-native participants.) What this means, of course, is that the land-claims question is being debated (and ultimately resolved) on the basis of Canadian legal and political traditions, and with precious little consideration of the unique traditions and values of the many First Nations in Canada.

The aboriginal land-claims process in Canada is obviously nearing a crossroads. The settlement of major land claims in the Canadian north, where the federal government has a relatively free hand, signals that non-native Canadians are anxious to resolve this issue. There is reason to believe that the previously intractable position of the British Columbia government will be abandoned by the newly elected New Democratic Party administration. But at the same time, it is difficult to be overly optimistic. The Council of Yukon Indians' claim, for example, took over seventeen years to negotiate—and it is now counted as a sign of the success of the federal approach to negotiations. The inflexibility of the federal and provincial governments in the Oka controversy, the continued struggle of the Lubicon Cree for a settlement of their claim, and a myriad of other complaints, challenges, and controversies suggests that the issue will drag on for many years.

Recent public opinion polls suggest that most Canadians are anxious to settle aboriginal land claims, and demands have increased that federal and provincial politicians redouble their efforts in this quarter. But this is not the first time that Canadian political leaders have run behind public opinion, and support for aboriginal claims is sufficiently shallow that relatively few non-native Canadians are prepared to go out of their way to support native demands. Furthermore, although the future is uncertain, there is little doubt (as the essays collected here illustrate) that the cost and pain of delay is borne disproportionately by the First Nations. In many areas of the country, development proceeds while native people attempt to secure control of traditional lands and some compensation for resources and territory already taken from them. As Canada's fiscal crisis deepens, it is possible that non-native Canadians will be less keen about settling the expensive and complex claims brought forward by aboriginal groups.

The first six essays in this book consider native land claims in the main regions of the country—the Maritimes, Quebec, Ontario, the Prairie provinces, British Columbia, and the Yukon and Northwest Territories. The remaining contributions examine two important contemporary issues: the claims brought forward by the Metis people in Canada—a subject complicated by a variety of political, legal, and social issues—and the historical background of the Oka controversy. The conflict at Oka, perceived by many Canadians to be a modern-day struggle, is in fact deeply imbedded in the history of native-newcomer relations in this country and reveals the profound shortcomings of the federal government's land-claims process.

This book is designed to be an introduction to native land claims in Canada. The land-claims debate has been clouded in misunderstanding and misrepresentation, and has often been seen as a contest between aboriginal and non-aboriginal rights. As the essays in this book illustrate, the land-claims issue is both longstanding and complex; it cannot be easily summarized nor is it likely to be easily resolved. To facilitate discussion of aboriginal land claims, and to provide readers with some of the raw data necessary to judge the complexity of the issues for themselves, this book includes extensive selections of original documents. These materials, covering both historical and contemporary situations, set out native and non-native positions at different points in the negotiation process. The documents represent a select sample from a vast array of position papers, claims documents, government legislation, and third-party commentary. Together with the essays, they underline the complexities of the land-claims question and the important regional variations on what is all too often perceived as a singular, national issue.

The contributors to this volume come from across the country—from Saint John's, Newfoundland, to Victoria, British Columbia—and from a variety of academic disciplines. They bring to the task at hand a scholarly understanding of the issues surrounding aboriginal land claims in their particular region of the country. Adrian Tanner is a professor of anthropology at Memorial University and a leading expert in the field of aboriginal land use; his co-author for this volume, Sakej Henderson, is a lawyer of Micmac ancestry with a detailed background in aboriginal law in the Maritimes. Toby Morantz, professor of anthropology at McGill University, has published widely in the field of aboriginal–white relations and on the indigenous peoples of northern Quebec; she has also been an active participant in contemporary debates over aboriginal rights in the province. Dr David McNab was formerly with the Native Affairs Secretariat of the Province of Ontario, and has examined the land-claims process both as an academic historian interested in the early treaty processes and as a government official. Thomas Flanagan, professor of political science, University of Calgary, has published extensively on native and Metis issues in the Prairie west, and has contributed to a variety of legal cases related to aboriginal land rights. Frank Cassidy, of the Department of Public Administration, University of Victoria, has had an extensive career with aboriginal organizations, government offices, and academic units; he is widely regarded as one of the foremost experts on aboriginal land claims in British Columbia. W.R. Morrison, director of the Centre for Northern Studies, Lakehead University, is one of Canada's leading historians of the north; he has published many studies on the role of government in the Yukon and the Northwest Territories and on the evolution of aboriginal land claims there. D.N. Sprague, who contributed the essay on Metis claims, teaches in the Department of History, University of Manitoba. He is an acknowledged expert in the field of Metis history and has been actively involved with Metis efforts to secure government attention to their outstanding land claims. J.R. Miller, Department of History, University of Saskatchewan, is the author of *Skyscrapers Hide the Heavens: A History of Native–White Relations in Canada*, and a regular commentator on native affairs in Canada; he has been working on a historical study of the Oka controversy.

Aboriginal Land Claims in Canada does not seek to be the definitive work on the land-claims question. As indicated, the issue is too complex, with too many historical, legal, and political variations, to be easily summarized. The goal, instead, is to provide a short introduction to the subject and to alert students of native issues to the many regional variations in the aboriginal land-claims debate. Through the analytical essays and the documents, readers will encounter the emotions, the historical

nuances, the political dimensions, and the legal complexity of the aboriginal land-claims process in Canada. One hopes that the persistence of
the aboriginal peoples also comes through, for it is their conviction and
determination to attain just settlements that has kept the land-claims
issue alive in the face of many non-native attempts to brush it aside. This
book seeks to contribute to the discussion, and to provide the insights
necessary for participants and students to understand one of the most
important issues facing Canada today.

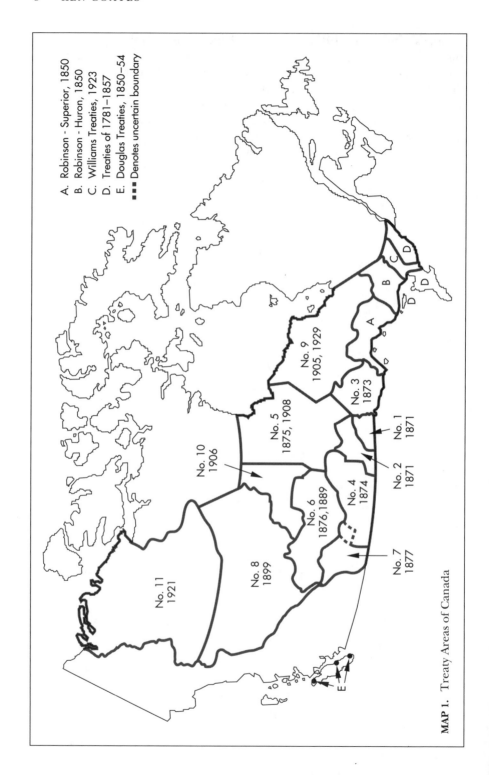

A. Robinson - Superior, 1850
B. Robinson - Huron, 1850
C. Williams Treaties, 1923
D. Treaties of 1781–1857
E. Douglas Treaties, 1850–54
▪▪▪ Denotes uncertain boundary

No. 11
1921

No. 10
1906

No. 8
1899

No. 5
1875, 1908

No. 9
1905, 1929

No. 6
1876,1889

No. 3
1873

No. 4
1874

No. 1
1871

No. 2
1871

No. 7
1877

MAP 1. Treaty Areas of Canada

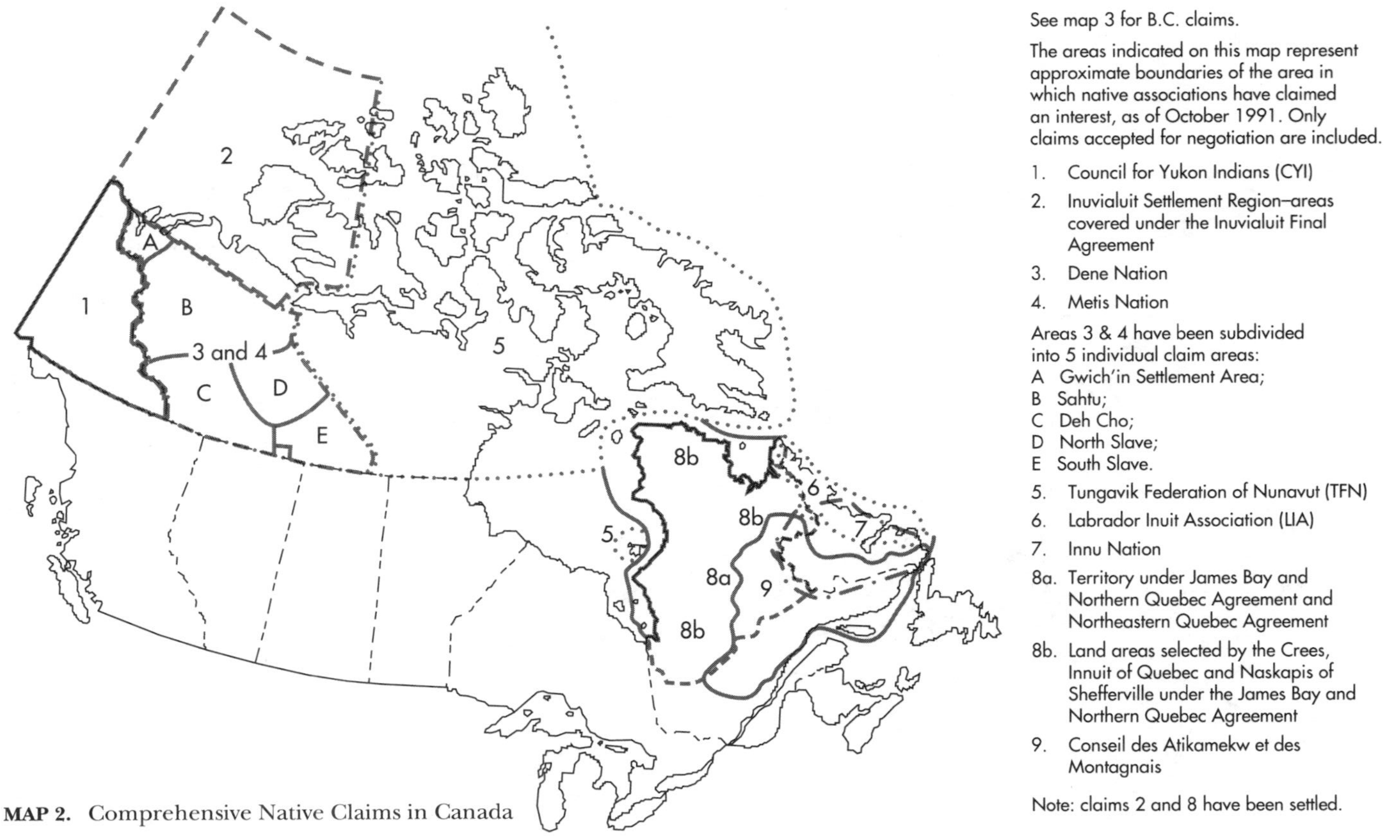

See map 3 for B.C. claims.

The areas indicated on this map represent approximate boundaries of the area in which native associations have claimed an interest, as of October 1991. Only claims accepted for negotiation are included.

1. Council for Yukon Indians (CYI)
2. Inuvialuit Settlement Region—areas covered under the Inuvialuit Final Agreement
3. Dene Nation
4. Metis Nation

Areas 3 & 4 have been subdivided into 5 individual claim areas:
A Gwich'in Settlement Area;
B Sahtu;
C Deh Cho;
D North Slave;
E South Slave.

5. Tungavik Federation of Nunavut (TFN)
6. Labrador Inuit Association (LIA)
7. Innu Nation
8a. Territory under James Bay and Northern Quebec Agreement and Northeastern Quebec Agreement
8b. Land areas selected by the Crees, Innuit of Quebec and Naskapis of Shefferville under the James Bay and Northern Quebec Agreement
9. Conseil des Atikamekw et des Montagnais

Note: claims 2 and 8 have been settled.

MAP 2. Comprehensive Native Claims in Canada

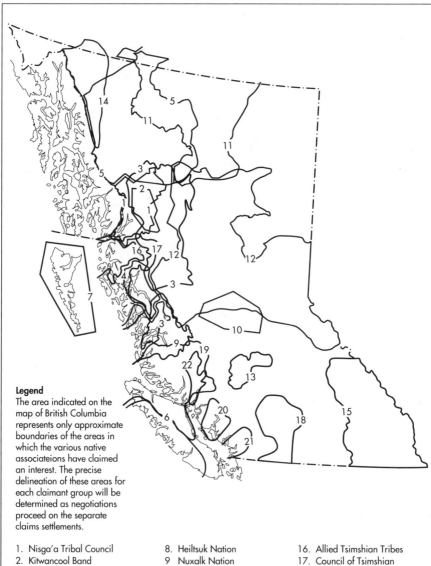

Legend
The area indicated on the map of British Columbia represents only approximate boundaries of the areas in which the various native associateions have claimed an interest. The precise delineation of these areas for each claimant group will be determined as negotiations proceed on the separate claims settlements.

1. Nisga'a Tribal Council
2. Kitwancool Band
3. Gitksan-Wet'suwet'en Tribal Council
4. Haisla Nation
5. Association of United Tahltans
6. Nuu-Cha-Nulth Tribal Council
7. Council of Haida Nation

8. Heiltsuk Nation
9. Nuxalk Nation
10. Nazko-Kluskus Bands
11. Kaska-Dena Council
12. Carrier-Sekani Tribal Council
13. Alkali Lake Bank
14. Taku Tlingit (Atlin)
15. Kootenay Indian Area Council

16. Allied Tsimshian Tribes
17. Council of Tsimshian Nation
18. Nlaka'pamux Nation
19. Kwakiutl First Nations
20. Sechelt Band
21. Musqueam Band
22. Homalco Band

MAP 3. Comprehensive Claims in British Columbia

Aboriginal Land Claims in British Columbia

Frank Cassidy

The aboriginal land question is a centrepiece in the historical development of the province of British Columbia. Because of its historical and economic dimensions, it is of immense political importance and indeed may well become, at one point or another, the issue that shapes the future of the province.

If the aboriginal land question is of such significance, then one may justifiably ask: What are the roots of this matter? What are the specific issues to which it gives rise? How is it perceived by various aboriginal peoples and what do they really want to have done about it? What are governments doing in response to the challenges it poses? Where is the issue going and how might it be resolved? These are the questions that will be addressed in this chapter.

Unfinished Business

No one knows the exact number, but there are somewhere around 150 000 aboriginal people in British Columbia today. Before contact with Europeans, the most recent estimates puts the aboriginal population in the area now known as British Columbia at 300 000 to 400 000.[1] This population was diverse, with more than thirty tribal groupings.

Many different languages and dialects were spoken, and coastal peoples followed very different patterns from those of interior peoples. Nevertheless, there were active trade, family, and political networks among the different tribes.

Russian and Spanish explorers were the first Europeans to reach the coast in the middle of the eighteenth century. But it was not until 1778, with the arrival of England's Captain James Cook, that much interest was expressed by the outside world in the region. Cook found that there was great demand in China for sea-otter furs, and the next quarter-century saw the development of a thriving maritime fur trade in which the coastal native people were expert participants. By 1825 the maritime trade had faded and, under the auspices of the Hudson's Bay Company, the era of the land-based trade had begun. What did not change, however, was the continued interest of native people in the fur trade—and their importance to it.

That trade, whether in its maritime or land-based forms, did not cause any major disruptions to the aboriginal people's way of life; in fact, it brought much new wealth to the region. Yet the rise of the fur trade also meant that the economic pursuits of aboriginal peoples became part of a commercial framework which had an external dynamic.

The British were not the only whites interested in the fur trade. The Americans were also keenly interested. In 1849 the imperial government decided that it had to establish Vancouver Island as a colony in order to confirm its assertion of British sovereignty in the region. The colony was granted to the Hudson's Bay Company by a royal charter. Shortly thereafter, in 1851, James Douglas, the company's chief factor at Fort Victoria, was appointed governor. Douglas was also to become governor of the mainland colony when it was brought into existence in 1858. At that time he gave up his position with the company, and he continued as governor of both colonies until 1864. In 1866 the colonies were merged. In 1871 the united colony entered Confederation as the Province of British Columbia.

Gradually, settlers came to the colony. They did not need the aboriginal people as the fur traders had, and many of the newcomers grew to fear and despise people who seemed to pose a constant danger and who stood in the way of the orderly—from a colonial point of view—settlement of the land. Douglas responded to the needs and fears of the settlers by attempting to follow the customary British practice of purchasing aboriginal rights to the land in order to clear the crown's underlying title of any proprietory rights that might interfere with its settlement and development.

Between 1850 and 1854, Douglas made fourteen treaties with the First Nations living around Victoria, Nanaimo, and Fort Rupert on Vancouver Island. His intentions were clear. In exchange for the colony's undisputed ownership of and control over the land, the First Nations involved were to have their village sites and the surrounding islands reserved for their use. Each family was also given some minimal monetary compensation. In addition, they could hunt over unoccupied territories and fish as before. To date, the Douglas treaties remain the only treaties in British Columbia, with the exception of Treaty 8 which covers an area of northeastern British Columbia.

The Douglas treaties did not bring an end to the land question for the First Nations involved. Whereas the colonial government saw the treaties as a final and lasting surrender of native lands, the First Nations viewed them as mutual arrangements of a much more limited nature. As more newcomers settled on Vancouver Island, relations between these aboriginal peoples and white settlers became increasingly troubled. This was generally so throughout the colony and, eventually, the province. Nevertheless, settlement continued to accelerate.

Douglas made efforts to protect reserve lands from encroachment, but even his government could not always resist the urge to expropriate aboriginal land for its uses. In fact, ten acres of reserve land in Victoria were taken so that government offices could be established on the site. As Robin Fisher notes: "There is undoubtedly something symbolic about the fact that the legislative buildings of British Columbia stand on land that perhaps rightfully belongs to Indian people."[2]

Douglas soon ran out of funds to make more treaties, and the imperial government refused to grant him any additional monies for the purpose. As a result, the short treaty-making era in British Columbia came to an end. By the time the province entered Confederation, its policy on the matter was one that ignored aboriginal title and any requirement to make treaties. The Terms of Union provided for Ottawa to assume responsibility for "the Indians, and the trusteeship and management of the lands received for their use and benefit."[3]

Ottawa expressed some discontent with the province's Indian policy at first. It disallowed the British Columbia Crown Lands Act on the basis that a cessation of aboriginal title had not been obtained, although it later backed away from this position. In fact, Ottawa gradually came to accept British Columbia's policy and to work with the province in consistent attempts to focus aboriginal people on more limited and manageable issues relating to reserve lands rather than those that centred upon questions about the basic ownership of and control over the land. What Ottawa accepted, the aboriginal peoples of British Columbia were never to accept. For them, the land question, as it came to be known, was a matter of increasing concern as settlers, miners, and others began to encroach more and more on their lands.

In 1877 war almost broke out in the south-central interior over the aboriginal land issue. In 1890 the first Nisga'a land committee was organized and in 1913 the Nisga'a petitioned the crown for recognition of their rights. Earlier, in 1906, a delegation had been sent to London by the Squamish, Shuswap, and other tribes. Another delegation, representing twenty Indian nations, went to England in 1909. There was no satisfaction as a result of any of these efforts.

In 1910, during a pre-election campaign visit to Kamloops, Prime Minister Wilfrid Laurier received a "Memorial" from the chiefs of the Shuswap, Okanagan, and Couteau tribes. In this document, the chiefs pointed out that their peoples had originally treated the "whites" as guests but had come to feel a sense of betrayal:

> When they first came amongst us . . . they found the people of each tribe supreme in their own territory, and having tribal boundaries known and recognised by all. . . . We waited for treaties to be made, and everything settled. . . . Gradually . . . they little by little changed their policy towards us, and commensed to put restrictions on us. Their government or chiefs have taken every advantage of our friendliness. . . . They treat us as subjects without any agreement to that effect, and force their laws on us without our consent. . . . They "have stolen our lands and everything on them." . . . The queen's law which we believe guaranteed us our rights, the B.C. government has trampled underfoot.[4]

Sharing these sentiments with other First Nations, the Shuswap, Nisga'a, and several other tribes joined to form the Allied Tribes of British Columbia in 1916, the first native organization on a provincial level. The Allied Tribes proceeded, over the next eleven years, to oppose the extension and modification of the reserve system as the "answer" to the land question. In 1926 the organization presented its grievances to the federal parliament. A special joint Senate–House committee was established to hold hearings and make recommendations. The province refused to participate.

The joint committee unanimously rejected all of the grievances of the Allied Tribes. It suggested that the British Columbia Indians should receive an annual allotment of $100 000 "in lieu of" treaty payments. This was done and the sum became known as the "B.C. Special." More significantly, one of the committee's recommendations led to an amendment to the Indian Act prohibiting anyone from raising funds, providing money, or working with any tribe or band to pursue matters pertaining to the land question. Shortly thereafter, the Allied Tribes ceased to exist. As Paul Tennant notes, the amendment had a striking effect:

> Without the Minister's approval, no Indian or other person . . . could now request or receive from any registered Indian any fee for legal or other service or any money for postage, travel, advertising, hall rental, refreshments, research expenses, legal fees, or court cases. The amendment quite simply made it impossible for any organization to exist if pursuing the land claim was one of its objectives. . . . From the white perspective, the Indian land question in British Columbia had been resolved.[5]

With the same force of authority on the national level that had been exerted on aboriginal territories at the provincial level for many years, the federal government now joined with the provincial government to suppress the campaign by First Nations for a just resolution of the land question. The aboriginal peoples in British Columbia were never to let the question die; in the late 1960s, the Nisga'a brought their case before the courts in *Calder* v. *Attorney General of British Columbia*.

In the Supreme Court of Canada in 1973, six judges ruled, in response to *Calder*, that aboriginal title had existed in British Columbia. Three said that it was still in existence and three ruled that it had been extinguished by general land legislation in the colonial period. The seventh did not express any opinion on the merit of the claim and ruled on a procedural matter. Shortly thereafter the federal government established the Office of Native Claims to negotiate settlements in non-treaty areas, including British Columbia.

Since 1973 the federal government has accepted nineteen claims from First Nations for negotiation. Three others are under review. Much of the land mass of British Columbia remains the subject of unresolved claims. The aboriginal land question is unfinished business. Aboriginal peoples are still unrecognized in their own territories, while logging, mining, and other economic pursuits change the face of these lands, perhaps forever.

The Issues

The aboriginal land question in British Columbia raises many cultural, economic, and political issues.[6] The overarching issue concerns the matter of aboriginal title to the land, the current status of this title, and its content. Those who challenge the existence of aboriginal title, such as the provincial government, put forward several arguments. They question the coherence and, in some cases, the existence of aboriginal land-use and tenure systems before contact. They assert, as the special joint committee did in 1927 and part of the Supreme Court did in the 1973 Calder ruling, that if aboriginal title ever did exist it was implicitly extinguished by pre-Confederation land legislation. Moreover, they argue that aboriginal peoples have abandoned whatever inherent rights they had by accepting, in fact if not in principle, the reserve system and various federal and provincial laws, regulations, and programs. As Douglas Sanders has observed: "None of these arguments has been authoritatively ruled on by the Canadian Courts. No one can deny they are substantitive legal and factual questions."[7]

The extent of aboriginal title is as debated a question as its existence. Some argue that aboriginal title is limited to the use of the land in traditional ways. From this perspective, aboriginal title means that native people have the right to hunt, fish, and gather on particular lands as they did before contact. Others argue that title is more than just use rights, that it represents a limited form of what might be termed, for the lack of a better word, ownership, which is subject to the underlying title of the crown. Still others, in the now famous words of the late Nisga'a leader James Gosnell, assert that aboriginal peoples own the province, "lock, stock, and barrel." The concept of aboriginal title, as it has historically been expressed by aboriginal peoples in British Columbia, has always reflected a strong sense of stewardship with regard to the land. In non-aboriginal terms, such a concept might be translated to express full ownership and control of the land and its resources.

The dispute over the existence and extent of aboriginal title is, in many ways, a debate between different cultures. As many aboriginal leaders in British Columbia point out this dispute at its heart is not about money or power. Rather, it is rooted in the need for mutual recognition and respect. The two cultures need to understand, value, and respect one another and the different ways in which they view the land and their relations with it.

This does not mean that money or power are not important aspects of the aboriginal land question. On the contrary, the question has several economic dimensions. As the Premier's Council on Native Affairs observed in 1990:

> It is distressing to see that most aboriginal communities have not been able to participate fully in the economic activity that has taken place in this Province in recent years. . . . [We] still see aboriginal unemployment at well over 50 percent in many parts of British Columbia. The consequence of unemployment is widespread poverty. . . . The life expectancy of aboriginal people is still 10 years shorter than for other British Columbians. The incidence of suicide, family violence, and substance abuse is more than double that of the general population.[8]

Most First Nations in British Columbia perceive the land question to be the key to renewed prosperity, since its resolution, they hope, will provide their communities with much needed economic resources.

These economic resources must come from somewhere. Someone will have to bear the costs of settlements. Who will do so is another key issue. This is a matter of longstanding dispute on the part of the federal and provincial governments, with each arguing that the other should bear the costs. No matter which does or whatever share either takes, eventually the costs will be borne by taxpayers and by those working in economic sectors where resources and resource rights will be reallocated from non-aboriginal to aboriginal interests.

For some, the possibility of land-claims settlements is extremely threatening. As a senior vice-president of one of the largest forest companies in British Columbia observes, the economy in the province is a "zero-sum game, for there are no uncommitted lands and resources that have economic value."[9] Fears about economic dislocation are most strongly held in the forestry, the non-renewable resources, and, in particular, the fishing sectors. The Prince Rupert Fisherman's Cooperative, for instance, notes that "our fishermen have been alarmed for some time about the desire of some civil servants and politicians to settle land claims on the backs of British Columbians and fishermen in particular."[10]

The cost of land settlements will be significant. If previous land-claims agreements are used as guideposts, the settlement of the land question could cost as much as $10 billion or more. This part of the issue has another dimension, for it is not just a matter of how much it will cost to resolve outstanding claims. It is increasingly becoming recognized that there is a substantial cost to *not* resolving the land question. In a confidential report prepared by Price Waterhouse for the federal government in 1990, it was established that the cost of not settling claims might add up to close to $1 billion. According to the study, 70 per cent of the companies that were surveyed and that planned major capital projects on land most likely to be affected by claims, expect delays or cancellations because of unresolved claims.[11]

These costs are the result of the uncertainty that surrounds the land question. As the British Columbia Chamber of Commerce has asserted: "Native land claims are creating uncertainty among native Indians and among the population at large and the uncertainty is having a detrimental effect on possible industrial and commercial projects."[12] The Council of Forest Industries of British Columbia is even more specific: "The political and legal debate surrounding Indian land claims and aboriginal title in BC has already had serious consequences for the BC forest industry. . . . Since 1985, a growing number of companies in BC have faced disrupting of logging operations, suspension of logging activities, the need to pursue costly litigation to protect harvesting rights and growing uncertainty about the security of long-term tenure and access to crown-owned timber."[13]

The aboriginal land question is very much about the pace and direction of the economy in British Columbia. Because of this, it is not only an economic question. It is also a political one. Some observers and business interests, in particular, worry about the possibility that government's regulatory role might grow massively as a result of land settlements. They are concerned about a rapid increase in the incidence of environmental- and social-impact assessment processes and a proliferation of rules governing the rate and timing of resource extraction. In general, various stakeholders in resource management and development are concerned about what their roles might be in regulatory decision making once claims are resolved.

Comprehensive-claims settlements in other parts of Canada have given rise to a range of new bureaucratic structures such as project-review boards and sectoral as well as integrated resource-management units. Many of the interests which will be most directly touched by claims, whether they be aboriginal or non-aboriginal, are concerned that their activities and their communities will be "bureaucratized" as a result of such measures. Alongside this concern is a more general one that resource conflicts will continue as before, with the only real change being that they will be institutionalized and perpetuated.

One of the most significant political issues that surrounds the aboriginal land question concerns aboriginal self-government. For First Nations in British Columbia, self-government and the land question cannot be detached: they are one and the same. The resolution of the land question, they assert, must provide the economic base for real political autonomy. More generally, the land question, they argue, is a self-government question because it involves not just the ownership but also the control of land and resources. And, if aboriginal peoples are going to exercise such control, they maintain that they must have the real jurisdictional authority to do so. They must have a recognition of their inherent and independent jurisdiction.

Such perspectives elicit concerns from several quarters. The federal and provincial governments fear that some of their powers will be eroded and that the complex web of competing jurisdictions that results will stifle the governing process and lead to political gridlock. Members of the general public and representatives of specific interests wonder about their political concerns and how these will be protected and asserted in relation to more fully empowered aboriginal governments.

One final set of political issues that characterizes the aboriginal land question revolves around the nature of the negotiation process. Many third parties—those who are neither aboriginal nor the representatives of governments—want to be represented actively at the negotiating table. In some instances, they actually want to be at the table. As the president of one mining company has put it: "Our company feels very strongly that so called 'third parties' which can have a substantial stake in land claims should be part of any negotiation that does proceed. In short, negotiations solely between native groups and the federal government would not in our opinion be acceptable."[14]

First Nations object to such proposals on the grounds that it is the role of the federal and provincial governments to represent their citizens. They have other concerns about the negotiation process, concerns that are shared by many others. Given that there may well be twenty or more claims to resolve, there are genuine and legitimate fears that it may take years upon years to reach agreements. As a result, many environmental, economic, and social issues could become stalled. Excessive amounts of resources might be consumed in the negotiating process and, eventually, efforts might be made by governments to push through settlements that resolve little or that fail to recognize the great diversity among aboriginal peoples across the province. If this were the case, the many issues involved in the land question could continue to plague the province well into the twenty-first century.

An Enduring Position

In many respects, the aboriginal peoples of British Columbia share a common perspective on the land question. All assert that their title to the land is not something that was given to them by English or Canadian law, but, rather, is a gift of the Creator. All seek a large amount of self-governing power. All want to be economically self-sufficient and to ensure that the environment is respected and protected. To one degree or another, all are willing to share the land and other resources with other British Columbians. Beyond these broad, enduring positions, however, aboriginal peoples have taken a range of approaches to the land question because of differing historical, political, and economic influences.

No people have asserted their rights for a longer period or with more force than the Nisga'a. The Nisga'a Tribal Council (NTC) represents approximately five thousand people whose homeland is the Nass River watershed in northwestern British Columbia. Over the past thirty years, the Nisga'a have expressed strong concerns about the fate of the natural resources in their territory. This has been particularly so with regard to their land-claims goals. "Since 1958 when logging operations first reached the Nass Valley," the Nisga'a "have watched the destruction of [their] forests." Soil and water quality have been seriously disrupted. Fish and wildlife habitats have been destroyed. "The Nass valley has changed from a rich forested area to a sea of rotten stumps."[15]

The Nisga'a are not opposed to development. "We are for orderly, rational development," they assert, "which is in tune with our culture, economic interests, and long-term survival."[16] The Nisga'a have no intention of taking back the small amount of land in the Nass valley that has been alienated for private ownership. Yet they do expect to be compensated for the loss of land and for resources extracted prior to a negotiated settlement. Such a settlement must recognize Nisga'a title and not extinguish it, and it must be based on the idea of "sharing," of a true accommodation between the people of the Nass valley and the rest of Canada.[17]

With these views in mind, the Nisga'a put forward the following "land claims goals":

To bring the Nisga'a people, lands, resources and cultural heritage into the Canadian confederation.

To define the relationship between the Nisga'a Nation, Canada, and B.C.

To provide the basis for the survival of the Nisga'a as an economically self-reliant and sustainable distinct society within Canada.

To establish certainty concerning Nisga'a lands and resources.

To preserve and enhance Nisga'a self-determination, cultural survival and well being for generations to come.

To obtain fair compensation.

To establish equitable fiscal relationships.

To guarantee these understandings through a lasting agreement entrenched in the Constitution of Canada.[18]

The Nisga'a have been at the negotiating table with the Government of Canada since 1976. For many years, the Province of British Columbia was only an observer. In March 1991 the province finally entered into these negotiations. A tripartite framework agreement between the Nisga'a, the federal government, and the province was signed at that time. This agreement establishes a two-year period as the target for reaching an agreement-in-principle that would be the basis for the final settlement. It also identifies several subjects for negotiation, including lands, renewable and non-renewable resources, environmental issues, cultural artifacts and heritage, economic development, Nisga'a government, compensation, and taxation.

The *Nisga'a Comprehensive Land Claims Framework Agreement* touches upon several additional matters that will continue to arise as long as the land question remains an active one in the province. One of these concerns is who will be allowed to take part in negotiations. The framework agreement makes it clear that "the only parties" to the final agreement will be the Nisga'a Tribal Council (NTC), Canada, and British Columbia, unless these parties agree otherwise.[19] Third parties will be represented at the negotiating table only in an indirect manner. This is a stance which all First Nations strongly endorse. The federal and provincial governments hold to it also. It is a position that troubles many non-aboriginal stakeholders, particularly those who fear for their economic future.

A second matter relates to the course of natural-resource development while negotiations are taking place. The framework agreement calls upon the parties who are involved to "use their best efforts" to establish "interim protection measures" that will "balance and protect the interests of the Nisga'a and other resource and land users pending a final land claim agreement."[20] This will be no easy matter.

Another item of interest in the framework agreement has to do with the way in which it treats—or does not treat—Nisga'a governing authority. Significantly, the agreement establishes that "any interim protection measures will be negotiated within the framework of existing legislation and appropriations of Canada and British Columbia."[21] This position is at one and the same time a protective measure for those third parties who have received "existing . . . appropriations" of natural resources and a clear assertion of the primacy of Canadian and British Columbian law over Nisga'a law and authority.

In fact, the Nisga'a framework agreement makes it clear that many self-government issues will not be treated in the final, constitutionally protected agreement, but rather in a separate, if related, subagreement that will be given the force of law through federal and provincial legislation. As a result, important elements of Nisga'a self-government will not be entrenched in the constitution. This requirement reflects current federal policy and practice, and is based on a stance that is sharply divergent from that of most British Columbia First Nations, who believe that it is fundamentally impossible and unacceptable to separate the land and self-government questions.

To date, the Nisga'a have been the only aboriginal people in British Columbia who have been able to reach the negotiating table, even though many First Nations in Canada over the last ten or more years have had comprehensive claims accepted by the federal government. Meanwhile, aboriginal peoples have had to stand by and watch their natural resources be threatened and exploited, as the pace of development has accelerated and extended into parts of the province that were previously untouched by large resource extractors. With no other recourse, an increasing number of First Nations have, reluctantly, appealed to the courts.

In 1984 MacMillan Bloedel, a large lumber company, obtained a tree-farm licence from the Province of British Columbia that gave it the right to log crown land on Meares Island. This island is part of the comprehensive claim of the Nuu-chah-nulth to the west coast of Vancouver Island, its adjacent islands, and surrounding waters. With little expectation that their claim would receive any active attention before the face of Meares Island was changed irreparably by clear-cut logging practices, the Nuu-chah-nulth actively and directly protested MacMillan Bloedel's plans.

Two of the Nuu-chah-nulth bands went to the Supreme Court of British Columbia shortly after the company received the licence. In their court action, the Clayoquot and Ahousat bands contended that Nuu-chah-nulth title had never been extinguished, that any provincial law infringing on that title had no legal force, and that the government had no right to give the company any authorization to log.[22]

The Nuu-chah-nulth bands were awarded an injunction by the Provincial Court of Appeal. This injunction stopped MacMillan Bloedel from cutting timber until the Nuu-chah-nulth's land rights were decided.

The judgment established a precedent, at least for the time being, for future cases of a similar nature involving other parts of the province. The Nuu-chah-nulth initiative contributed to an emerging pattern, on the part of aboriginal peoples, of engaging in direct action as a way of forcing judicial rulings that might slow the pace of development while their claims remained unresolved.

The Nuu-chah-nulth position on the land question highlights several fundamental issues with regard to the concept of aboriginal title and the nature of land-claims settlements. While the Nuu-chah-nulth assert title to Meares Island and the rest of their traditional land and sea territories, they are careful to note that they ultimately do not accept the concept of "aboriginal title." Rather, they put forward the idea of "Hereditary Chiefs' Title."[23]

As defined in British and international law, aboriginal title refers to the use and occupancy of the land. "Our ownership goes far deeper," Nuu-chah-nulth leader George Watts contends.[24] Nuu-chah-nulth title is passed along by generations of hereditary chiefs, he explains. Moreover, it involves a holistic political, economic, environmental, and cultural relationship with the land, the sea, and all they contain. This is a view of aboriginal title that is shared, in one form or another, by many British Columbia First Nations.

The Nuu-chah-nulth also challenge the idea of land-claims *settlements*. "I think we've got to get away from the word settlement because it has a finality to it," Watts argues. "We're not looking for something final."[25] Instead, the Nuu-chah-nulth chairman sees the need for an "agreement for co-existence" between aboriginal and non-aboriginal people. Until such an agreement comes about, Watts asserts, the Nuu-chah-nulth will continue to take as much power as they can under existing governmental arrangements and they will press their case in a variety of forums, including the courts. Such a multifaceted strategy is becoming characteristic of many First Nations in the province, as direct action complements judicial appeals and administrative initiatives reinforce jurisdictional assertions of governing authority.

The Meares Island case was joined with two other important aboriginal title and rights cases in the British Columbia Supreme Court, including one brought by the hereditary chiefs of the Gitksan and Wet'suwet'en peoples. In fact, the Nuu-chah-nulth action was temporarily put aside while the evidence in the Gitksan and Wet'suwet'en case—known as *Delgamuukw* v. *The Province of British Columbia and the Attorney General of Canada*—could be heard and weighed. Meares was brought up on a relatively specific, if extremely important, point of law. In this instance, the Nuu-chah-nulth asserted that their title had not been extinguished and the crown therefore had no legal basis for allowing their land and resources to be developed. They did so with reference to a specific area where they believed that they could prove a high degree of traditional use.

By ways of contrast, the Gitksan and Wet'suwet'en judicial action, initiated in 1984, was brought on a broad front. These peoples asked the courts to confirm their complete ownership and inherent jurisdiction over approximately 22 000 square miles of their traditional territories. In addition, the Gitksan and Wet'suwet'en asked the courts to confirm their assertion that their hereditary chiefs are the paramount authority in these territories. "It is our belief," the hereditary chiefs contended, "that the Province of British Columbia has no legitimate right to assert its jurisdiction over lands that have not been surrendered and are thus not under its control."[26]

"Recognize our Sovereignty, recognize our rights, so that we may fully recognize yours." The sentiments behind these words from the *Gitksan–Carrier Declaration* of 1977 have continued to characterize the position of these people on the land question to this day. (The term "Carrier" was formerly used to refer to the Wet'suwet'en.) Not comfortable with an approach that is piecemeal and attempts gradually to assert limited, if important, aspects of aboriginal entitlements through judicial judgments, the Gitksan and Wet'suwet'en hereditary chiefs asked the courts to give their political and economic system full and substantial recognition.

Much like the Nuu-chah-nulth, the Gitksan and Wet'suwet'en call for a widening of the accepted definition of aboriginal title. To date, the courts have gradually been moving, with some significant exceptions, to define aboriginal title as an interest to bear on the underlying title and sovereignty of the crown. From this perspective, aboriginal title is a limited, if extremely important, legal entitlement.

Although there was some confusion about the exact nature of their claim during their three-year hearing, the Gitksan and Wet'suwet'en have consistently asserted that they have a strong aboriginal title and jurisdiction. If the courts were to confirm this assertion, the aboriginal land question would, for once and for all, become the overriding political and economic issue in British Columbia since there then would be a legal recognition of two systems of law and two sovereignties (and all that that entails). The aboriginal land question would finally be presented in its truest and most essential form.

In March 1991 Chief Justice Allan McEachern, in a controversial and widely disputed judgment, dismissed the claims of the Gitksan and Wet'suwet'en hereditary chiefs. Aboriginal rights and title, he ruled, were extinguished by the colony of British Columbia before Confederation. Moreover, McEachern asserted that the key constitutional instrument that is most often cited as the source of the recognition of aboriginal title in Canadian law, the Royal Proclamation of 1763, does not apply in British Columbia.

In essence, McEachern argued that the crown is the sole and supreme sovereign and the bastion of civilization in the province. In no uncertain terms, McEachern made it clear that, as far as he is concerned, aboriginal peoples led very primitive lives before Europeans gave them the chance to expand their horizons. With specific reference to the Gitksan and Wet'suwet'en, he maintained, there is no doubt "that aboriginal life in the territory was, at best, 'nasty, brutish and short.'"[27] Aboriginal people did not loose their right to govern themselves, the chief justice's arguments indicated, for they had never really needed traditional political institutions. Their problems were so simple that they could rely on their survival instincts and informal customs.

At the end of his decision, Chief Justice McEachern felt compelled to add some general comments about the aboriginal land question in British Columbia. "This increasingly cacophonous dialogue about legal rights and social wrongs," he complained, "has created a positional attitude with many exaggerated allegations and arguments, and a serious lack of reality."[28] The simple fact, he contended, is that Indians have remained dependent for too long. The answers to their problems will not be found in the context of legal rights or land claims, he suggested. Their problems remain "social and economic ones" that should be confronted through political dialogue with the federal and provincial governments.[29]

Aboriginal peoples have been trying to initiate such a dialogue for over one hundred years. It was the failure of both the federal government and, particularly, the provincial government to respond to their grievances that led to court actions such as those of the Gitksan-Wet'suwet'en and the Nuu-chah-nulth. For this and other reasons, aboriginal peoples across the province were quick to join with the Gitksan and Wet'suwet'en in condemning the McEachern judgment.

"In a turn of retrogressive legal thinking," Don Ryan, a speaker for the Gitksan and Wet'suwet'en chiefs, commented, "this judge has attempted to push back justice for native people in Canada at least 20 years."[30] Ryan termed the McEachern judgment a "travesty, based upon the economic imperatives of a province driven by exploitation of people and resources."[31] He also suggested that British Columbia would experience considerable unrest, protest, and direct political action if the government were to attempt to use "this small, silly judgement to inform policy."[32] An appeal could be expected, Ryan noted, and, a short time later, an appeal was made.

The Gitksan and Wet'suwet'en and other First Nations were not the only ones to object to Chief Justice McEachern's judgment. *Globe and Mail* columnist Jeffrey Simpson noted that McEachern had tried to "kick the props" from under every legal argument ever advanced to support aboriginal rights. Simpson suggested that this effort could well backfire. "By relying on colonial precedents," the columnist contended, "Chief Justice McEachern left himself and the courts open to charges of a colonial mentality." The decision, Simpson predicted, would enhance the "profound sense of victimization by white society" felt by many aboriginal people in Canada. Far from calming an already difficult situation, the McEachern judgment, he feared, had made matters more "explosive."[33]

Interestingly, the response of the Nisga'a to the McEachern judgment was more measured than that of many aboriginal groups, if still supportive of the Gitksan and Wet'suwet'en. The McEachern decision, Joe Gosnell, the chair of the Nisga'a Tribal Council, maintained, had thrown "a wrench into the works" as far as the matter of aboriginal title was concerned.[34] Nevertheless, the Nisga'a were still hopeful for a positive outcome to their negotiations with the province and Canada. "We're looking at a win-win situation," Gosnell declared. He asserted that the Nisga'a were "totally different" from the Gitksan and Wet'suwet'en. "They would like to exercise absolute control over their territory," Gosnell contended. By way of contrast, Gosnell suggested, the Nisga'a are willing to share their land and resources.[35]

The Nisga'a attempt to draw a distinction between their aspirations and those of the Gitksan and Wet'suwet'en, as far as the resolution of the land question is concerned, may well be a harbinger of things to come in British Columbia. More and more First Nations will move to the negotiating table in the coming years and, as they do so, they will develop more specific views on what they want—and can obtain—from land-claims agreements. These views may also well become much more diverse. There is already evidence that this is happening. The Sechelt band provides a good, if rather pronounced, example.

The Sechelt submitted a comprehensive claim to Ottawa in 1984. It was rejected in 1988, because the federal government believed that the band had not provided sufficient documentation regarding the current extent of traditional land and resource use.[36] A year later, on the third anniversary of the Sechelt's federally and provincially sanctioned self-government arrangement, the Sechelt issued *A Practical Proposal for Resolving the Indian Land Claim in British Columbia as It Affects the Sechelt Indian Band*. With this proposal, the Sechelt departed in two important ways from most other First Nations in the province.

Reflecting the fact that its reserve land base is much more valuable than that of most British Columbia bands, the Sechelt assert that they will not seek any additional lands as part of a settlement. Instead, they request monetary compensation of $54 million, based upon their assessment of the dollar value of various settlements in other parts of Canada to date. This is a considerable departure from the stance of most British Columbia First Nations, who see land-claims agreements as a way to confirm clear and certain ownership over significant portions of their traditional land base.

A second feature of the Sechelt proposal is even more distinctive. The band asserts that a real settlement with Canada and the Province of British Columbia would "involve the relinquishment of title to all our aboriginal territory except for the Band lands that we already own in fee simple."[37] No other group of aboriginal people in the province have indicated that they would even consider extinguishment of their title as part of a settlement package.

Eventually, a proposal such as the Sechelt's may be appealing to, at most, a handful of First Nations in British Columbia. All but a few would have a difficult time with the idea that settlements should be primarily monetary and that they should lead to extinguishment. In fact, many insist that they will stay away from the negotiating table until the province and the Government of Canada recognize aboriginal title and full self-government as the basis upon which negotiations can take place.

This, for example, has long been the position of the Union of British Columbia Indian Chiefs, an organization that represents a good number of bands and tribal councils. The union has drawn up a *Comprehensive Framework Treaty* that it hopes will serve as a blueprint for a just accommodation on the land question. The first principle articulated in this document speaks clearly to the union's position: "Canada shall enter into treaties with First Nations based on the fundamental principle that aboriginal title and rights are inalienable and shall not be extinguished through treaty."[38]

There are quite significant differences between First Nations such as the Nisga'a, the Nuu-chah-nulth, the Gitksan-Wet'suwet'en, and the Sechelt and organizations such as the Union of British Columbia Indian Chiefs on their stances regarding the processes and preferred outcomes of deliberations on the land question. These differences may grow over time, but they should not obscure an important reality. After more than one hundred years of protest and assertion of their rights, aboriginal people in British Columbia have shown a remarkable consistency and unity in their perspectives.

The First Nations of British Columbia have continued to assert independent aboriginal title to their traditional lands. They have seldom strayed from their conviction that they must fully govern themselves, while maintaining their language and culture. They seek self-sufficiency and they are ready to share their land and resources with other British Columbians, on the basis of a just accommodation, mutual recognition, and full respect. Such consistency and steadfastness are, indeed, a challenge for the governments of Canada and British Columbia—and, perhaps, a basis for a new understanding between the native and non-native peoples of that province.

A New Beginning?

The federal government has not placed a very high priority on the resolution of the aboriginal land question in British Columbia. For many years, it has been able to hide behind the intransigence of the provincial government. Yet in recent times, the province finally began, in a measured way, to respond to the challenges represented by the land question, and this more active stance may well force the federal government to become more concerned with the matter.

A ministry of native affairs was created by British Columbia in 1988, and in 1989 the Premier's Council on Native Affairs was established. The purpose of this council was to meet with tribal councils and aboriginal organizations across the province and to make recommendations on provincial policies affecting aboriginal peoples. In July 1990 the council submitted its interim recommendations to Cabinet. Citing the province's jurisdiction over the natural resources and lands that might form the basis for various settlements, the council concluded that it is vital "that the Government of British Columbia be an active participant at the negotiating table."[39]

In the next few months, the Province of British Columbia agreed to join the Government of Canada and aboriginal peoples in negotiations. A claims registry and a negotiations unit were established in the Ministry of Native Affairs, and British Columbia joined with Canada and the Nisga'a to negotiate the framework agreement for their negotiations. In addition, the province appointed two representatives to sit on a joint task force on native land claims, with officials of the federal government and three First Nations representatives, to determine the scope, organization, and process of negotiations.

In early 1991 the province took further steps to flesh out a more active position on the land question. Asserting that it was "sincere in its commitment to resolve Native land claims, as quickly as possible, in a way that serves the interests of all British Columbians," the provincial government announced seven "Guiding Principles" it would follow in the settlement process:

Settlements should be fair, consistent, affordable, final and binding.

Settlements should respect the rights and interests of all British Columbians, including property ownership and legal rights emanating from contracts, leases, tenures and other legal arrangements.

Settlements should support Native aspirations to be part of the economic mainstream of the province.

Settlements should incorporate the principles of fiscal fairness, whereby all British Columbians have access to reasonably comparable levels of government services on the basis of reasonably comparable levels of taxation.

Settlements should provide Native people the same rights, privileges and obligations as apply to other British Columbians.

Settlements involving natural resources should include a framework for natural resource conservation and management.

Settlements must respect Natives' rights to live according to their unique culture and heritage.[40]

At this time, a third-party advisory committee on native land claims was also established. This committee consists of approximately twenty-five individuals, including management and labour representatives, particularly in resource-based industries, as well as representatives of local government and outdoor and environmental interests. Subject to the confidentiality of negotiations, it was charged with four tasks:

> to consider the general issues involved in the resolution of land claims and identify third party interests;
>
> to provide information and advice on different approaches;
>
> to analyse the impact of various options on individuals, employment opportunities, business investment and the economic well-being of the province as a whole; and
>
> to consider proposed settlements and provide advice on their ramifications.[41]

When the Delgamuukw decision was announced in March 1991, many observers thought that the province might feel it was "off the hook," that, with Chief Justice McEachern's judgment, the land question had become a dead issue for the provincial and federal governments. This was not to be the case, as Jack Weisgerber, then minister of native affairs, acknowledged in an announcement a few days after the judgment was released.

Chief Justice McEachern had suggested that "it is for elected officials, not judges, to establish priorities for the amelioration of the disadvantaged members of society."[42] In response, Weisgerber reaffirmed the policies the provincial government had developed in recent months, and importantly, its continued desire to participate in negotiations. The minister also expressed his hope that the province could move quickly and decisively to create a new partnership with aboriginal peoples. Shortly afterward, the province announced, for the first time, that it was willing "to share in the costs of negotiated settlements."[43]

Taken together, these initiatives would appear to indicate that in 1990 and 1991 the Province of British Columbia made a major change in its policies and forged a new beginning regarding the aboriginal land question. To understand this development, it is necessary to place it in context. The province's change of position took place only after years of intense pressure on it to do so. Judicial decisions, direct action on the part of First Nations, frustration and impatience on the part of third parties, and general public opinion all pushed the province to alter its traditional position and take a more active stance.

Another source of pressure on the province was the Official Opposition, the New Democractic Party. Sensing that the Social Credit government was out of touch with British Columbians on the matter, the New Democrats issued a new and aggressive policy statement in the spring of 1990, entitled *Towards a Just and Honourable Settlement: Indian Land Claims in British Columbia.* The "Indian Land Question," the New Democrats argued, is a critical political economic and moral issue "that could no longer be ignored."[44] The party committed itself to:

1. recognition of aboriginal title and aboriginal people's inherent right to self-government;

2. provincial participation in modern-day treaty negotiations to achieve a just and honourable settlement of the land question;

3. [consultations with] third-party interests in negotiated treaties on the land question;

4. sustainable economic development initiatives in both aboriginal and non-aboriginal communities resulting from settlement of the land question;

5. renewal of constitutional processes aimed at entrenching aboriginal people's inherent right to self-government in the Constitution of Canada.[45]

At a time when there was a general sense in many quarters that the province should move to the negotiating table, the Opposition had seemed to outflank the Social Credit government. Indeed, its recognition of aboriginal title and the inherent right to self-government was welcomed, with a bit of skepticism, by many First Nations, and its call for negotiations and just settlements was appealing to many third-party interests as well as the general public.

The Social Credit government's decision to move to the negotiating table and many of its subsequent actions in 1990 and 1991 enabled it to regain the political offensive on the aboriginal land question. Once it did so, it could portray itself as a responsive government ready to confront the issues involved. At the same time, it could also present itself as a tough bargainer, since it had not conceded, as the New Democrats had, that aboriginal title exists. In contrast to the New Democrats, the government and its supporters were quick to point out, a Social Credit government would not start negotiations "by giving the province away."[46]

From this perspective, it might be suggested that the province had not so much changed its stance on the aboriginal land question in 1990 and 1991 as it had up-dated and, to an extent, politicized it. To a significant degree, the government's measures could be seen as a way in which it could maintain a good deal of its historic position of protecting British Columbians from unreasonable and unfounded claims on the part of aboriginal peoples, while urging the federal government to take the major responsibility for any obligations that might arise. So, for example, the provincial government was careful to note that it had "agreed to join the federal government and Native people at the negotiating table to assist the federal government in fulfilling its responsibility for settling the claims."[47]

In October 1991, a New Democratic government was elected in British Columbia. In December, the new government recognized the political legitimacy of aboriginal title and the inherent right to self-government. Nevertheless, as 1992 began, it continued to defend the Delgamuukw judgment in the courts. There is still great pessimism in aboriginal communities about the possibilities of just settlements. It could be the case, many believe, that the political parties in the province are simply poised to make the land question just one more political issue upon which elections can be fought and opinion polls managed.

Despite the McEachern judgment, it might be thought that the courts may hold some answers for those who seek a resolution to this question, but as leaders such as Don Ryan note, there is a general perception that "the courts have always been notoriously hostile toward us." In the future, Ryan predicts, aboriginal peoples will get more involved in "direct political action" as they form stronger alliances between themselves and engage in acts of civil disobedience.[48]

The aboriginal land question is one that will not go away, for it is at the heart and soul of the province. How British Columbians respond to the challenges this matter entails will frame their future. In the end, there are only two roads that can be taken in Canada's western-most province. There can be continued uncertainty and frustration and a perpetual crisis of legitimacy, a crisis that will deprive the province of the very identity and vitality required to fulfill its vast potential. Or there can be a recognition of aboriginal peoples and their rights, including their title to the land, and on the basis of this recognition, a just accommodation of all interests. There are no other alternatives.

Documents

A. Nisga'a Declaration

The Nisga'a People is a distinct and unique society within the many faceted cultural mosaic that is Canada. The issue is whether the Nisga'a element within this mosaic will be allowed to face the "difficulties" and will be allowed to become full participants contributing in a positive way to the well being of the Nass Valley in particular and the country in general. The positive aspect of this participation, we feel, must be through self-determination, self-determination that is dependent on the shared and mutual responsibility of governments and Nisga'a People.

If Nisga'a Society and Canadian Society of which it is part, is to be truly free, we as a distinct people and as citizens, must be allowed to face the difficulties and find the answers, answers that can only be found by determining our own social, economic and political participation in Canadian life. Governments, both Federal and Provincial, must be persuaded that Nisga'a self-determination is the path that will lead to a fuller and richer life for Nisga'a People and all Canadians.

We, as Nisga'as, are living in a world where dynamic initiatives must be taken to achieve self-determination especially with respect to the natural resources of the Nass Valley, in order to control our own process of development within the larger Canadian Society and to make decisions that affect our lives and the lives of our children. We realize that our struggle for self-determination will be a difficult one, but we refuse to believe that it is in vain, if governments and the Nisga'a People agree to their mutual responsibility for that growth and development. Nisga'a self-determination of resource development within the Nass Valley is the economic base that will allow for self-determination of the other aspects of modern 20th Century Society that makes up this Canada of ours.

In 1969, NTC [Nisga'a Tribal Council] agreed in principle with the "statement of the Government of Canada on Indian Policy," in the face of strong opposition from other Native Peoples across the nation. That agreed principle was incorporated in the policy statement: "true equality presupposes that the Indian people have the right to full and equal participation in the cultural, social, economic and political life of Canada." Such an agreement in principle, however, does not necessarily mean the acceptance of the steps to implement as suggested by the 1969 Policy Statement. Co-existent with the NTC Agreement on the stated principle is also the NTC agreement with the Hawthorne Report, that "Indians should be regarded as Citizens-Plus; in addition to the normal rights and duties of citizenship, Indians possess certain rights as charter members of the Canadian Community."

Undergirding the whole of the above, is the demand that, as the inhabitants since time immemorial of the Nass Valley (the boundaries of which are stipulated in the case, "Calder et al vs the Attorney General of B.C.") all plans for resource extraction and "development" must cease until aboriginal title is accepted by the Provincial Government. Also, we, the Nisga'a People, believe that both the Government of B.C. and the Government of Canada must be prepared to negotiate with the Nisga'as on the basis that we, as Nisga'as, are inseparable from our land; that it cannot be bought or sold in exchange for "extinguishing of title."

Conclusion

What we seek is the right to survive as a People and a Culture. This, we believe, can only be accomplished through free, open-minded and just negotiations with the provincial and federal authorities, negotiations that are based on the understanding that self-determination is the "answer" that government seeks to the "difficulties" as they apply to the Nisga'a People.

B.   Gitksan-Carrier Declaration

Since time immemorial, we, the Gitksan and Carrier People of Kitwanga, Kitseguecla, Gitanmaax, Sikadoak, Kispiox, Hagwilget and Moricetown, have exercised Sovereignty over our land. We have used and conserved the resources of our land with care and respect. We have governed ourselves. We have governed the land, the waters, the fish, and the animals. This is written on our totem poles. It is recounted in our songs and dances. It is present in our language and in our spiritual beliefs. Our Sovereignty is our Culture.

Our Aboriginal Rights and Title to this Land have never been extinguished by treaty or by any agreement with the Crown. Gitksan and Carrier Sovereignty continue within these tribal areas.

We have suffered many injustices. In the past, the development schemes of public and private enterprise have seriously altered Indian life and culture. These developments have not included, in any meaningful way, our hopes, aspirations and needs.

The future must be different. The way of life of our people must be recognized, protected and fostered by the Governments of Canada and the Laws of Canada. Only then will we be able to participate fully in Canadian society.

We, the Gitksan and Carrier People, will continue to exercise our Sovereignty in the areas of Education, Social and Economic Development, Land Use and Conservation, Local and Regional Government.

We have waited one hundred years. We have been patient. Through serious negotiation, the basis for a meaningful and dignified relationship between the Gitksan and Carrier People and the Governments of Canada and of British Columbia will be determined. These negotiations require mutual and positive participation by the Federal Government and the Provincial Government.

Today, the Governments of Canada and British Columbia undertake a bold new journey to negotiate with the Gitksan and Carrier People. During this journey, we will fulfill the hopes and aspirations of our ancestors and the needs of future generations.

Let us begin negotiations.

Recognize our Sovereignty, recognize our rights, so that we may fully recognize yours.

C. Reasons for Judgment of Chief Justice Allan McEachern in Delgamuukw v. The Province of British Columbia and the Attorney General of Canada

Summary of Findings and Conclusions

1.   The last Great Ice Age, which lasted many thousands of years, covered nearly all of British Columbia. It ended about 10,000 years ago.

2.   The origins of the Gitksan and Wet'suwet'en and other aboriginal peoples of the north-west part of the province are unknown. It is generally believed they migrated here from Asia.

3.   There is archaeological evidence of human habitation in the territory as long as 3,000 to 6,000 years ago. This is limited to village sites both at the coast at Prince Rupert harbour and at a few locations alongside the Skeena and Bulkley Rivers. The evidence does not establish who those early inhabitants (or visitors) were.

4.   The plaintiffs are 35 Gitksan and 13 Wet'suwet'en hereditary chiefs who have brought this action alleging that from time immemorial they and their ancestors have occupied and possessed approximately 22,000 square miles in north-west British Columbia ("the territory"), and that they or the Indian people they represent are entitled, as against the province of British Columbia, to a legal judgment declaring:

  (a) that they own the territory;
  (b) that they are entitled to govern the territory by aboriginal laws which are paramount to the laws of British Columbia
  (c) alternatively, that they have unspecified aboriginal rights to use the territory;
  (d) damages for the loss of all lands and resources transferred to third parties or for resources removed from the territory since the establishment of the colony; and
  (e) costs.

5.   No relief is claimed by the plaintiffs in this action against Canada which was joined as a defendant for procedural reasons. The action against Canada is dismissed. In this Summary, "Crown" refers to the Crown in right of the Colony or Province of British Columbia except where the context indicates otherwise.

6.   The plaintiffs allege the territory is divided into 133 separate territories (98 Gitksan, and 35 Wet'suwet'en), and each of these separate territories is claimed by a hereditary chief for his House or its members. Some chiefs claim several territories, and some chiefs claim territories for other chiefs who are not plaintiffs.

7.   Map 1 on p. 6 of the judgment is a generalized map of the province showing the general location of the territory. Map 2 at p. 7 is a reduction of a detailed map of the territory. It shows the approximate external boundary of the territory. The individual territories claimed by the Gitksan and Wet'suwet'en chiefs are shown on maps 3 and 4, at pp. 8 and 9.

8.   Aboriginal interests arise (a) by occupation and use of specific lands for aboriginal purposes by a communal people in an organized society for an indefinite, long period prior to British sovereignty; or (b) under the *Royal Proclamation, 1763*.

9.   Aboriginal rights under (a) above arise by operation of law and do not depend upon statute, proclamation or sovereign recognition. Such rights existing at the date of sovereignty exist and continue at the Crown's "pleasure." Unless surrendered or extinguished, aboriginal rights constitute a burden upon the Crown's title to the soil.

10.   *The Royal Proclamation, 1763* has never applied to or had any force in the Colony or Province of British Columbia or to the Indians living here.

11.   Linguistics, genealogy, history, and other evidence establish that some of the ancestors of some of the plaintiffs or the peoples they represent have been present in the territory for an indefinite, long time before British sovereignty.

12.   These early ancestors lived mainly in or near several villages such as Gitanka'at, Gitwangak, Kitsegucla, Kispiox, Ksun, Old Kuldo, New Kuldo, Gitangasx and possibly at Gitenmaax (Hazelton) which are all on the Skeena River; at Kisgegas on the Babine River; and at Hagwilget and Moricetown on the Bulkley River. Each of these villages, six of which are now abandoned, were strategically located at canyons or river junctions where salmon, the mainstay of their diet, could most easily be taken. Further, these early ancestors also used some other parts of the territory surrounding and between their villages and rivers, and further away as circumstances required, for hunting and gathering the products of the lands and waters of the territory for subsistence and ceremonial purposes.

14.   Prior to the commencement of the fur trade these early aboriginals took some animals by snares, dead falls and other means, but there was no reason for them to travel far from their villages or rivers for this purpose, or to take more animals than were needed for their aboriginal subsistence.

15.   There may have been sparse incursions of European trade goods into the territory overland from the east or south, or from unknown seaborne sources (perhaps from Asia) before the arrival of Capt. Cook at Nootka on Vancouver Island in 1778. That date, however, or more particularly the start of the sea otter hunt on the north Pacific coast which started within the following 5 years, was the likely start of European influences in north-west North America.

16.   The fur trade in the territory began not earlier than the establishment of the first Hudson's Bay posts west of the Rockies (but east of the territory), by Simon Fraser in 1805–06, and more probably a few years after that.

17.   Trapping for the commercial fur trade was not an aboriginal practice. Apart from commercial trapping, there were no significant changes in aboriginal practices between first contact with European influences within a few years on either side of 1800 and the assertion of British sovereignty. The use of modern implements such as mechanical traps and guns since the time of contact does not change the nature of an aboriginal right.

18.   The law of nations and the common law recognize the sovereignty of European nations which established settlements in North America.

19.   Great Britain asserted sovereignty in the territory not earlier than 1803, and not later than either the *Oregon Boundary Treaty, 1846,* or the actual establishment of the Crown Colony of British Columbia in 1858. For the purposes of this case it does not matter precisely when sovereignty was first asserted.

20.   The title to the soil of the province became vested in the Imperial Crown (Great Britain) by operation of law at the time of sovereignty. The plaintiffs recognize this title, but argue that their claims constitute an interest which is a burden upon the title of the Crown.

21.   The purpose of sovereignty and of creating the Colony of British Columbia in 1858 was to settle the colony with British settlers and to develop it for the benefit of the Crown and its subjects.

22.   The aboriginal interests of the post-contact ancestors of the plaintiffs at the date of sovereignty were those exercised by their own more remote ancestors for an uncertain long time. Basically these were rights to live in their villages and to occupy adjacent lands for the purpose of gathering the products of the lands and waters for subsistence and ceremonial purposes.

23.   These aboriginal interests did not include ownership of or jurisdiction over the territory. Those claims of the plaintiffs in this action are dismissed.

24. But for the question of extinguishment, the plaintiff's aboriginal sustenance rights would have constituted a legally enforceable, continuing burden upon the title of the Crown.

25. Upon the establishment of the colony, the Crown, both locally and in London, enacted a number of laws providing: (a) that all the lands of the colony belonged to the Crown (which would be the Imperial Crown at that time); (b) that the laws of England applied in the Colony; (c) giving the Governor and later a Legislative Council authority to grant the lands of the colony to settlers; and (d) authorizing the Crown through the Governor to make laws and exercise legal jurisdiction over the colony including the territory.

26. The policy of the Colony of British Columbia was (a) to allot lands to the Indians for their exclusive use, called reserves, comprising their village sites, cultivated fields and immediately adjacent hunting grounds; (b) to encourage settlement by making land available for agriculture and other purposes; and (c) to permit Indians, along with all other citizens, to use the vacant Crown lands of the colony.

27. Part (a) of this policy did not usually work as well as intended. Reserves were mainly allotted in the territory in the 1890s and they were "adjusted" by a Royal Commission in 1912–14. Although reserves in the territory included most occupied villages, they were very small because it was thought secure access to strategic fishing sites was more important than acreage. The evidence does not fully explain why the Indians of the territory did not receive strategic sites and acreage except that the Indians often failed or declined to participate in the allotment process.

28. It is the law that aboriginal rights exist at the "pleasure of the Crown," and they may be extinguished whenever the intention of the Crown to do so is clear and plain.

29. The pre-Confederation colonial enactments construed in their historic setting exhibit a clear and plain intention to extinguish aboriginal interests in order to give an unburdened title to settlers, and the Crown did extinguish such rights to all the lands of the colony. The plaintiffs' claims for aboriginal rights are accordingly dismissed.

30. At the same time, the Crown promised the Indians of the colony, which applies also to the territory, that they (along with all other residents), but subject to the general law, could continue to use the unoccupied or vacant Crown land of the colony for purposes equivalent to aboriginal rights until such lands were required for an adverse purpose. Further, this promise extends to any alienated lands which are returned to the status of vacant Crown lands. Thus, lands leased or licensed for logging, for example, become usable again by Indians and others when such operations are completed.

31. The unilateral extinguishment of aboriginal interests accompanied by the Crown's promise and the general obligation of the Crown to care for its aboriginal peoples created a legally enforceable fiduciary, or trust-like duty or obligation upon the Crown to ensure there will be no arbitrary interference with aboriginal sustenance practices in the territory.

32. When the colony joined the Canadian Confederation in 1871 the charge of Indians and Indian lands was assumed by the Dominion (Canada); all colonial lands, subject to existing "interests," accrued to the province; and the province agreed to furnish whatever land was required for reserves. In 1924 Canada acknowledged that British Columbia had satisfied its obligations with respect to furnishing lands for Indian reserves.

33. The promise made and obligation assumed by the Crown in colonial times, while not an "Interest" to which Crown lands are subject, can only be discharged by the province and continues to the present time as a duty owed by the Crown subject to the terms mentioned above.

34. Since Confederation the province has had: (a) title to the soil of the province; (b) the right to dispose of Crown lands unburdened by aboriginal title; and (c) the right, within its jurisdiction under s. 92 of the Constitution, to govern the province. All titles, leases, licenses, permits and other dispositions emanating from the Imperial Crown during the colonial period or from the Crown in right of the province since Confederation are valid in so far as aboriginal interests are concerned. The province has a continuing fiduciary duty to permit Indians to use vacant Crown land for aboriginal purposes. The honour of the Crown imposes an obligation of fair dealing in this respect upon the province which is enforceable by law.

35. The plaintiffs, on behalf of the Gitksan and Wet'suwet'en people are accordingly entitled to a Declaration confirming their legal right to use vacant Crown land for aboriginal purposes subject to the general law of the province.

36. The orderly development of the territory including the settlement and development of non-reserve lands and the harvesting of resources does not ordinarily offend against the honour of the Crown. This is because the province has many other duties and obligations additional to those owed to Indians and because (a) the territory is so vast; (b) game and other resources are reasonably plentiful; and (c) most Indians in the territory are only marginally dependent upon sustenance activities.

37. The right of Indians to use unoccupied, vacant Crown land is not an exclusive right and it is subject to the general law of the province. The Crown has always allowed non-Indians also to use vacant Crown lands.

38. For the reasons stated in the Reasons for Judgement, it is not advisable to specify the precise rules that would govern the relationship between the Indians and the Crown. Instead, that question should be left to the law relating to fiduciary duties which provides ample legal remedies.

39. Part 15 of this judgment describes the circumstances which the province and the Indians should take into consideration in deciding whether any proposed Crown action may constitute a breach of its fiduciary duty to Indians. Generally speaking, the operative word is "reconciliation" rather than "rights" or "justification."

40. As the Crown has all along had the right to settle and develop the territory and to grant titles and tenures in the territory unburdened by aboriginal interests, the plaintiffs' claim for damages is dismissed.

41. If I have erred on the question of extinguishment, and the plaintiffs aboriginal interests or any of them are not extinguished, the evidence does not establish the validity of individual territories claimed by Gitksan and Wet'suwet'en Chiefs. Instead, therefore, the claim for aboriginal rights in such circumstances would be allowed not for chiefs or Houses or members of Houses, but rather for the communal benefit of all the Gitksan and Wet'suwet'en peoples except the Gitksan peoples of the Kitwankool Chiefs who did not join in this action.

42. These aboriginal rights, if any, would attach not to the whole territory but only to the parts that were used by the plaintiffs' ancestors at the time of sovereignty. The parts so used by each of the plaintiff peoples are defined in Part 16, and they are shown on Map 5 at p. 281.

43. The Counter Claim of the province, which was brought for procedural reasons, is dismissed.

44. Because of the importance of the matter, the divided success the parties have achieved, and other reasons mentioned in the judgment, no order is made for costs.

45. The specific judgment of the Court is detailed in Part 21.

46. In Part 22 I have made some comments about Indian matters.

Some Comments

Having spent nearly four years considering these important questions I hope I may be forgiven for adding these brief comments.

I have already said that I do not expect my judgment to be the last word on this case. I expect it to be appealed and I do not presume to suggest what course the parties should follow from this point forward.

Assuming that discussions between both governments and the Indians will continue, I respectfully offer the following for their consideration.

The parties have concentrated for too long on legal and constitutional questions such as ownership, sovereignty, and "rights," which are fascinating legal concepts. Important as these questions are, answers to legal questions will not solve the underlying social and economic problems which have disadvantaged Indian peoples from the earliest times.

Indians have had many opportunities to join mainstream Canadian economic and social life. Some Indians do not wish to join, but many cannot. They are sometimes criticized for remaining Indian, and some of them in turn have become highly critical of the non-Indian community.

This increasingly cacophonous dialogue about legal rights and social wrongs has created a positional attitude with many exaggerated allegations and arguments, and a serious lack of reality. Surely it must be obvious that there have been failings on both sides. The Indians have remained dependent for too long. Even a national annual payment of billions of dollars on Indian problems, which undoubtedly ameliorates some hardship, will not likely break this debilitating cycle of dependence.

It is my conclusion, reached upon a consideration of the evidence which is not conveniently available to many, that the difficulties facing the Indian populations of the territory, and probably throughout Canada, will not be solved in the context of legal rights. Legal proceedings have been useful in raising awareness levels about a serious national problem. New initiatives, which may extend for years or generations, and directed at reducing and eliminating the social and economic disadvantages of Indians are now required. It must always be remembered, however, that it is for elected officials, not judges, to establish priorities for the amelioration of disadvantaged members of society.

Some Indians say they cannot live under the paternalism and regulation of the *Indian Act*, but neither can many of them live without the benefits it provides. Some Indians object to the imposed Band structure created by the *Act* but it would be foolish to discard it until something acceptable to a majority of the Indians has been fashioned to take its place.

Clearly a new arrangement is required which should be discussed between both levels of government with the Indians other than in the context of land claims. The first priority should be for the two communities to find out what they expect of each other. In a successful, ongoing relationship, there must be performance on both sides.

This, however, should not be considered an endorsement for "self government" because details are required before any informed opinion may be given. Too often, catchy phrases gain quick recognition, momentum and even acceptance without a proper understanding of the real meaning or consequences of these sometimes superficial concepts. Also, different arrangements might be appropriate for different areas and the desired result may sometimes best be attained in stages.

Compared with many Indian Bands in the province, the Gitksan and Wet'suwet'en peoples have already achieved a relatively high level of social organization. They have a number of promising leaders, a sense of purpose and a likely ability to move away from dependence if they get the additional assistance they require. I cannot, of course, speak with confidence about other Indian peoples because I have not studied them. I am impressed that the Gitksan and Wet'suwet'en are ready for an intelligent new arrangement with both levels of government.

I am not persuaded that the answers to the problems facing the Indians will be found in the reserve system which has created fishing footholds, and ethnic enclaves. Some of these reserves in the territory are so minuscule, or abandoned, that they are of little or no use or value. On the other hand, it is obvious that some village reserves should have been larger but there is no profit in trying to assign blame on this. The solution to problems facing Indians will not be solved by another attempt to adjust reserves because that system has been tried and it has failed, and there are other ways to correct that historical failure.

It must be recognized, however, that most of the reserves in the territory are not economic units and it is not likely that they can be made so without serious disruption to the entire area which would not be in the best interest of anyone, including the Indians. Eventually, the Indians must decide how best they can combine the advantages the reserves afford them with the opportunities they have to share and participate in the larger economy, but it is obvious they must make their way off the reserves. Whether they chose to continue living on the reserves is for them to decide. Care must always be taken to ensure that the good things of communal life are not sacrificed just on economic grounds. As Mr. Sproat predicted in 1876, it may still be necessary to "... persevere, if need be, through a succession of failures."

In any new arrangement, some failures must be expected but we should at least be able to identify them. The worst thing that has happened to our Indian people was our joint inability to react to failure and to make adjustments when things were not going well. As social improvement can only be measured in generations, the answer to these social questions, ultimately, will be found in the good health and education of young Indian people, and the removal of the conditions that have made poverty and dependence upon public funding their normal way of life.

There must, of course, be an accommodation on land use which is an ongoing matter on which it will not be appropriate for me to offer any comment except to say again that the difficulties of adapting to changing circumstances, not limited land use, is the principal cause of Indian misfortune.

Lastly, I wish to emphasize that while much remains to be done, a reasonable accommodation is not impossible. After the last appeal, however, the remaining problems will not be legal ones. Rather they will remain, as they have always been, social and economic ones.

D. First Nations Congress: Fundamental Principles, 1991

1. We have an inalienable right to exist as distinct peoples.

2. Our participation in this and any subsequent discussions does not constitute abandonment of each First Nation's understanding of Aboriginal Title and Treaty Rights.

3. Our mandate is to advance discussions with Governments in order to position First Nations to conduct their own direct negotiations with the Government of Canada and the Government of British Columbia.

4. We are *not* proposing a process which promotes a blanket resolution but rather, a General Framework which would outline the scope of negotiations, the time frames, funding arrangements and the implementation of such interim measures as may be required.

5. We support and endorse negotiation currently underway in particular, those of the Nisga'a Nation. This is not an acceptance of any settlement model to be imposed on any other Tribal group or Nation.

6. We hereby reaffirm our conviction that all First Nations have the right to be represented by whomever they choose. First Nations' political institutions must be recognized, respected, and incorporated into the Process at the desire of those First Nations.

7. Third party interests are represented by the Federal and Provincial governments.

8. The CONTENT of any negotiations will include, among other things:
   a. Land and Water
   b. Compensation
   c. Self-government
   d. Access to natural resources

9. Final resolutions shall constitute land claims agreements within the meaning of s. 25 and s. 35 of the *Constitution Act, 1982.*

Notes

[1] Paul Tennant, *Aboriginal People and Politics* (Vancouver: University of British Columbia Press 1990), 3.

[2] Robin Fisher, *Contact and Conflict: Indian-European Relations in British Columbia, 1774–1890* (Vancouver: University of British Columbia Press 1977), 68.

[3] Ibid., 176.

[4] Shuswap Nation Tribal Council, *The Shuswap: "One People with One Mind, One Heart and One Spirit"* (Kamloops, B.C. 1988), 33–4.

[5] Tennant, *Aboriginal People and Politics*, 112–13.

[6] For a fuller discussion, see Frank Cassidy and Norman Dale, *After Native Claims? The Implications of Comprehensive Claims Settlements in British Columbia* (Victoria: Institute for Research on Public Policy 1988).

[7] Douglas Sanders, "The Aboriginal Title Question in British Columbia" (Prepared for Continuing Legal Education, Vancouver), 5.

[8] Premier's Council on Native Affairs, *Final Report* (Victoria: Government of British Columbia 1991), 4.

[9] Frank Cassidy, with Maureen Cassidy, Darcy Dobell, and James McDavid, *Third Party Interests and Comprehensive Claims Settlements in British Columbia* (Victoria: Institute for Research on Public Policy 1990), 16.

[10] Ibid., 116.

[11] Peter O'Neill, "Land Claims Imperil Jobs, Study Finds," *Vancouver Sun*, 20 October 1990, A1.

[12] Frank Cassidy, ed., *Reaching Just Settlements* (Victoria: Institute for Research on Public Policy 1991), xiv.

[13] Ibid., 147.

[14] Ibid., xiv.

[15] Nisga'a Tribal Council, *Forests for People: A Nisga'a Solution* (New Aiyansh, B.C., n.d.).

[16] Nisga'a Tribal Council, *The Nisga'a Position: Some of Your Questions with Nisga'a Answers* (New Aiyansh, B.C. 1983), n.p.

[17] Minesque (Roderick A. Robinson, Sr.), "Exploring the Objectives of Land Claims Settlements," *Legal Services Society Schools Program Newsletter*, April 1987, 13.

[18] Nisga'a Tribal Council, "Nisga'a Land Claims Goals" (New Aiyansh, B.C., n.d.).

[19] Nisga'a Tribal Council and Her Majesty the Queen in Right of Canada, as Represented by the Minister of Indian Affairs and Northern Development, *Nisga'a Comprehensive Land Claims Framework Agreement* (New Aiyansh, B.C. 1991), 3.

[20] Ibid.

[21] Ibid.

[22] Bob Soderlund and Charlotte Cote, "*Ha-Shilth-Sa* Interview: George Watts and Simon Lucas on Meares Island," *Ha-Shilth-Sa*, April 1986, 17.

[23] Ibid., 2.

[24] Ibid.

[25] Ibid., 3.

[26] Gisday Wa and Delgamuukw, *The Spirit in the Land* (Gabriola, B.C.: Reflections 1989), 1.

[27] Supreme Court of British Columbia, *Delgamuukw* v. *The Province of British Columbia and the Attorney General of Canada* (Smithers, B.C. 1991), 3.

[28] Ibid., 299.

[29] Ibid., 301.

[30] Don Ryan, "A Travesty of Justice" (Smithers, Wet'suwet'en Territory), 1.

[31] Ibid., 2.

[32] Ibid.

[33] Jeffery Simpson, "The Fallout Will Be Far Reaching from the BC Ruling on Aboriginal Rights," *Globe and Mail*, 12 March 1991, 14.

[34] "Claims Are Not the Same: Nisga'a Goals Differ from the Gitksan-Wet'suwet'en," *Interior News*, 24 April 1991, A1.

[35] Ibid.

[36] W. Graham Allen, "The Sechelt Land Claim" (Vancouver: Continuing Legal Education 1990), 1.

[37] Sechelt Indian Band Council, *A Practical Proposal for Resolving the Indian Land Claims in British Columbia As It Affects the Sechelt Indian Band* (Sechelt, B.C. 1989), 18.

[38] Union of British Columbia Chiefs, *Comprehensive Framework Treaty*, draft (Vancouver 1991), 7.

[39] Ministry of Native Affairs, Province of British Columbia, *Indian Land Claims in British Columbia* (Victoria, B.C. 1990), 12.

[40] Province of British Columbia, *Land Claims Settlements: Guiding Principles* (Victoria, B.C. 1991).

[41] Ministry of Native Affairs, Province of British Columbia, "Third Party Advisory Committee on Native Land Claims: Terms of Reference" (Victoria, B.C. 1991), 1.

[42] *Delgamuukw* v. *The Province of British Columbia*, 299.

[43] Ministry of Native Affairs, Province of British Columbia, "News Release: Province Will Pay 'Fair Share' of Land Claims" (Victoria 1991). See also Jack Weisgerber (Minister of Indian Affairs), "Ministerial Statement Regarding Gitksan-Wet'suwet'en Decision" (Victoria: Ministry of Native Affairs 1991).

[44] British Columbia New Democrats, *Towards a Just and Honourable Settlement: Indian Land Claims in British Columbia* (Vancouver 1990), 1.

[45] Ibid.

[46] Eddie Barlett and Tim Gallagher, "Harcourt's Gift to Zalm," *British Columbia Report*, 27 August 1990, 9.

[47] Ministry of Indian Affairs, *Indian Land Claims in British Columbia*, 2.

[48] "Low Hope from Claims Decisions," *Interior News*, 6 February 1991, 11.

Aboriginal Land Claims in the Prairie Provinces[1]

Thomas Flanagan

From the official point of view, Indians have surrendered all land in the three Prairie provinces of Manitoba, Saskatchewan, and Alberta in treaties that extinguished their aboriginal title. There can thus be "specific claims" based on the interpretation of treaties, but there should not be any "comprehensive claims" based on assertion of aboriginal title. This chapter will briefly recount the history of land surrender in the Prairie provinces and then study in some detail the Lubicon Lake dispute, which is the most prominent example of an attempt by Indians to shatter the official framework and assert the continuing existence of aboriginal title in this part of Canada.

In 1670 King Charles II of England gave the governors of the Hudson's Bay Company (HBC) ownership of all lands drained by rivers flowing into Hudson Bay. In keeping with the common understanding of seventeenth-century international law, according to which European powers could claim both sovereignty—the right to rule—and ownership of land in the New World, the company's charter made no mention of any rights to the land by the native inhabitants. Canadian title to the three Prairie provinces stems from this grant.

Although there were many inconsistencies, British imperial practice, at least from the Royal Proclamation of 1763 onward, was generally to negotiate land-surrender agreements with native peoples before allowing white settlement on a large scale. The only significant settlement in western Canada under the HBC regime was undertaken in 1812 in the Red River valley under the auspices of Thomas Douglas, Earl of Selkirk. In 1817 Selkirk signed an agreement with the chiefs of four local Indian bands by which they surrendered their claim to a two-mile strip on each side of the Red and Assiniboine rivers.[2] Although this treaty served as the basis of all HBC land grants in the Red River colony, it was later criticized on the grounds that Selkirk had dealt with Indians who were recent arrivals in the area and consequently had no aboriginal title to dispose of. This criticism is of no contemporary importance because all lands in Canada ceded by the Selkirk treaty were ceded again after Confederation in Treaty 1.

Two hundred years after Charles II granted the HBC charter, the company sold its rights to the Dominion of Canada. An aboriginal title to land was recognized in all documents connected with the transaction. The imperial Order in Council of 23 June 1870, which made the transfer effective, stated in part: "Any claims of Indians to compensation for lands required for purposes of settlement shall be disposed of by the Canadian Government in communication with the Imperial Government; and the Company shall be relieved of all responsibility in respect of them."[3]

Canadian authorities, anticipating the building of railways and immigration to the west, were eager to begin treaty-making. So too were at least some Indians, who petitioned Ottawa to act because they wanted concessions before settlement.[4] Treaties were not thrust willy-nilly upon the Indians of the Canadian plains. Their leaders knew that their old way of life, based on hunting and gathering, was coming to an end, and they hoped that treaties would help them make the transition to an agricultural existence. The results were the "Numbered Treaties," by which the three Prairie provinces, as well as much of northern Ontario and the Northwest Territories, were ceded.[5]

Treaties 1 through 7 opened up the prairies and parkland for agricultural settlement. The Treaty 6 area was slightly enlarged in 1889; otherwise, there were no new treaties until 1899, when a new cycle began, paving the way for exploitation of the natural resources of the north.

Although there were important differences among the treaty agreements, the similarities were also striking. In each case, the Government of Canada, by Order in Council, established a commission to negotiate the treaty, which was afterwards also approved by Order in Council. The Indians received cash gratuities and sometimes other presents for signing; annual payments in perpetuity; the promise of educational and agricultural assistance; the right to hunt and fish on crown land until such land was required for other purposes; and land reserves to be owned by the crown in trust for the Indians. Under Treaties 1 and 2, the reserves were calculated according to a formula of 160 aces per family of five. In subsequent treaties, that amount was increased to 640 acres, and Treaties 8 and 10 also allowed land ownership in severalty.

Before they went into the field, the treaty commissioners received precise instructions about the terms to be offered, and they could deviate only slightly from those terms. This made the negotiations rather one-sided. At first, Indians demanded large reserves on the American model, but the Canadian authorities were unyielding. They told the Indians, as A.G. Archibald said in the Treaty 1 negotiations, "White people will come here and cultivate [the land] under any circumstances. No power on earth can prevent it."[6] Indians got the same advice from the missionaries, Mounted Police, and Metis interpreters who accompanied the treaty commissions. Also, in several of the treaties, there was a series of meetings at different locations at which signings took place, but the terms were set at the first meeting. Thus Indian bands that were met later in the process had little say in the final result. Some Indian leaders refused to accept agreements in such circumstances; for example, Big Bear did not adhere to Treaty 6 until 1882. Indeed, a few bands deliberately stayed out of treaty until the mid-twentieth century, preferring to fend for themselves in the remote wilderness of the Rockies' eastern slopes, but these were rare exceptions.[7] The large majority of bands took the proferred terms, even if reluctantly.

Although the main outlines of the treaties were set in advance by Ottawa, Indian negotiators did succeed in getting some terms changed or added, such as the well-known "medicine chest" provision of Treaty 6: "That a medicine chest shall be kept at the house of each Indian Agent for the use and benefit of the Indians, at the discretion of such Agent."[8] In trying to persuade Indians to sign, the treaty commissioners also sometimes made verbal promises that have had varying degrees of effect in later implementation. The most famous case is the "outside promises" of clothing, buggies, livestock, and agricultural implements made in connection with Treaties 1 and 2, which were approved by Order in Council in 1875 and became part of the treaty agreements.[9] Much modern research on treaty-making consists of gathering evidence about such oral promises as well as about the role that Indians played in the negotiations. This is a useful complement to traditional historiography, based as it was on official reports of the treaty commissions and other statements of white participants.

Each treaty contains an explicit statement about the extinguishment of Indian title, such as these words from Treaty 1: "The Chippewa and Swampy Cree Tribes of Indians and all other Indians inhabiting the district hereinafter described and defined do hereby cede, release, surrender and yield up to Her Majesty the Queen and successors forever all the lands included within the following limits, that is to say. . . . "[10] Then follows a precise geographical description of the lands ceded to the crown.

Taken together, the Numbered Treaties describe every acre of land in Manitoba, Saskatchewan, and Alberta (as well as adjacent parts of Ontario, British Columbia, the Yukon, and the Northwest Territories). There can be no doubt that Canadian officials, when entering into treaties, intended to extinguish Indian title to all land in the Prairie provinces and wrote the treaties to have that effect.

The legal theory underlying the Numbered Treaties was articulated by the Judicial Committee of the Privy Council in 1889 when it decided the St Catherine's Milling case.[11] The committee held that Indian title to land was "a personal and usufructuary right, dependent upon the good will of the sovereign." Indian occupancy of land did not amount to ownership in the sense of a freehold estate that could be bought and sold under British property law. Indian title was a "usufruct," that is, a right to gather the produce of the land but not ownership of the land itself. Indians could enjoy this usufructuary right as long as the sovereign then held the *plenum dominium*—full and complete ownership of the land—and could dispose of it like any landlord with a clear title. Needless to say, the sovereign authority in this schema was the British crown and its political advisers, not Indian peoples.

Usufruct is a Roman law concept that is exotic in the common-law system. Another way to explain this view of aboriginal rights would be to draw a comparison with the familiar notion of a caveat, or burden on a land title. Someone who owns a home in Canada usually has a title with several caveats on it, such as the rights of utility companies to run service lines across the lot. Or a lender may register a caveat against a debtor's property, meaning that the debt goes with the property and the new owner becomes responsible for it. This was approximately the official view of aboriginal title in nineteenth-century Canada. The Canadian government recognized that it had bought Rupert's Land with a burden—the Indian right of occupancy—on the title, and that burden would have to be extinguished before Canada would enjoy a clear title. Treaties were a mechanism for extinguishing the Indian title in return for various forms of compensation. Although the form of an international agreement was employed, the substance of the agreement was a real-estate transaction.

There are now about 170 recognized Indian bands in the three Prairie provinces. The federal crown holds in trust for them about 350 pieces of reserve land, for a total of approximately 1.5 million hectares, or 3/4 of 1 per cent of the area of Manitoba, Saskatchewan, and Alberta.[12] Many of these bands are engaged in ongoing disputes with the federal government about the size and precise boundaries of their reserves. These claims have many different bases: that the reserves were too small in the first place because the band was undercounted at the time of treaty, that the reserves as originally promised were never provided, or that the government later reduced their size without adequate compensation.

Different as these claims are from one another, they are all "specific claims" in the sense that they assume the validity of the treaties but argue that they have not been properly fulfilled in some respect.

Can there be any contemporary comprehensive claims or aboriginal-rights disputes in the three Prairie provinces? The official answer of both the federal and provincial governments is "no," that the treaties have extinguished Indian title and cannot be reopened, that there can be treaty-entitlement claims but no aboriginal-rights claims. This view lies behind section 35 of the Constitution Act of 1982, inserted at the insistence of Premier Peter Lougheed of Alberta, which states that the constitution protects only "existing" aboriginal rights. For Indians, however, the matter is not so cut and dried.

First there is the problem of the Indian understanding of treaties. It is uncertain whether Indians in the last century understood the government's view of treaties. In particular, it is questionable whether Indians understood the official theory of extinguishment. The words of the treaties were plain enough, but since hardly any Indians could read, they were dependent upon oral explanations. One historian who has carefully considered the evidence concludes that we remain ignorant of exactly what Indians thought at the time:

> Unfortunately, we are dependent on inference from inadequate evidence for much of the Indian viewpoint. It appears that government and Indians began from different assumptions, and that there was little attempt on the part of the government either to understand the Indian viewpoint or to convey its own to the Indian people. Under these circumstances, it is hardly surprising that Indian interpretations of the treaties do not conform to those of the government, or that there are some variations in the viewpoints of Indian people themselves on the meaning of their treaties.[13]

In the mid-1970s, the Indian Association of Alberta sponsored an extensive oral-history program of interviews with Indian elders in the Treaty 6, 7, and 8 areas. Interviewers asked the elders how they understood the content of the treaties. Some of the Treaty 8 elders had actually witnessed the treaty-making as children in 1899, but elders in other areas had to rely entirely on oral tradition in answering such questions. The interviews elicited a wide variety of statements that contradict the wording of the treaties, such as this one: "Not one animal was given to the white man, not one piece of timber was given to the white man, not even the grass. That was not discussed in the agreement. Not one stone was discussed in the negotiations. Our forefathers always maintained that this country was ours, including the mountains. They were positive that they never gave up the land and the mountains. There was no agreement made. This includes the animals."[14]

Such evidence is highly problematic from an historical point of view. Historians prefer the evidence of written documents precisely because oral traditions and childhood memories are subject to great changes over time. Moreover, these statements about the treaties were gathered in a political context that may have affected the elders' memories. Nonetheless, it is possible that Indians of the Prairie provinces will be able to use evidence of this type to advance their cause.

The Dene of the Mackenzie valley provide an example of what can be achieved along this line. In spite of signing Treaty 8 in 1899 and Treaty 11 in 1921, they have persuaded the federal government to negotiate a new comprehensive agreement (most of the Dene rank and file have thus far refused to ratify the new agreement because it still speaks of extinguishment of aboriginal title).[15] Although federal officials will not openly admit that Treaties 8 and 11 are invalid, the Dene have effectively repudiated them by insisting that the clauses extinguishing their land title do not apply.[16] The political cause of the Dene was powerfully aided by René Fumoleau's book *As Long as This Land Shall Last*, which highlighted the differences between the official and Indian understanding of the treaties: "Whatever the Government intended to do, cession of land, extinguishing of title or monetary settlement of aboriginal rights, was not explained to the chiefs who signed the Treaty. The Indians accepted the Treaty without understanding all of its terms and implications."[17]

The situation in the Northwest Territories is unique in that most reserves under Treaties 8 and 11 were never allocated there, so the federal government can disguise a new agreement as a way of modernizing, not repudiating, the earlier treaties. But the analogy with the Prairie provinces remains strong. Treaty 8 after all, also applies to northern Alberta and Saskatchewan. If it can be repudiated in the territories, why not in the provinces?

Lubicon Lake, the main contemporary aboriginal-rights dispute in the Prairies, involves a different issue: that of Indian bands allegedly overlooked at the time the treaties were signed. Although the Lubicon Lake dispute has attracted attention around the world, it is oddly difficult for readers to obtain accurate information about it. There is virtually no published scholarship on the subject, and the journalistic accounts are highly partisan.[18]

Lubicon Lake lies in a vast wilderness of woods and water north of Lesser Slave Lake between the Peace and Athabasca rivers. When the Treaty 8 commissions passed through northern Alberta in 1899 and 1900, there were no trails in the region to accommodate a large party of white men and their supplies. They had to travel by water, making a circle around the area now claimed by the Lubicon Lake band and stopping at fur-trading posts and missions that the Indians were accustomed to visit. Although the government realized that as many as 500 Indians had not taken treaty, it decided that the Indian title could be considered extinguished and that it was not necessary to send out further treaty parties. The Treaty 8 inspectors were authorized to add individuals to treaty lists when they made their annual rounds, and many Indians came into Treaty 8 in this way.[19]

Over the years, numerous Indians added their names to the band list at Whitefish Lake, about forty miles southeast of Lubicon Lake. In 1933, fourteen men petitioned the government to create a separate reserve for them at Lubicon Lake, pleading that Whitefish Lake was too far away and they did not wish to live there. In 1940 the Indian Affairs Branch gave the Lubicons permission to elect their own chief, but it was too late for them to obtain a reserve directly from the federal government. The Alberta Natural Resources Act of 1930 had transferred public lands from the jurisdiction of the crown federal to the crown provincial, so the federal government, after validating the claim, would have to request land from Alberta to establish a reserve.[20]

An Indian agent visited Lubicon Lake in 1940 with a federal surveyor and selected an approximate location for the reserve at the west end of the lake.[21] The surveyor general could not afford to do the survey in 1941 because the Second World War had reduced his budget;[22] but in 1942 the Indian Affairs Branch requested the Province of Alberta to designate twenty-five square miles west of Lubicon Lake as a probable Indian reserve.[23] After the war ended, the surveyor general turned to the task of surveying the proposed reserves in northern Alberta. Lubicon Lake was last on a list to be done in the summer of 1946, but the surveyor, who went first to Hay Lake in the far north, did not get to Lubicon Lake.[24] For reasons unknown, the survey at Lubicon Lake was not carried out the following year and was apparently "forgotten."[25]

In 1950 the Lubicon Indians again asked for their reserve,[26] touching off several years of confusion. Indian Affairs officials were uncertain whether a reserve had ever been definitely promised and whether Lubicon Lake was the best place for it.[27] Local officials were instructed to ask the Lubicons if they really wanted a reserve at Lubicon Lake or if they might prefer some other location. These consultations proved unsatisfactory because the Lubicons were still actively trapping and hunting. Only a handful might show up for any particular meeting, and opinion about the location of the reserve varied, depending on who was present.[28]

The Province of Alberta, which had been carrying a provisional reserve on its books, now began to exert pressure for a final decision[29] and issued an ultimatum on 22 October 1953: if the federal government did not commit itself within thirty days, the province would take the reserve off its books and open the area to oil exploration.[30] Indian Affairs, being advised by its local officials that Lubicon Lake was an unsuitable location and that some other solution could eventually be found,[31] made no effort to block Alberta's action, and the hypothetical Lubicon reserve disappeared.

The Lubicons continued to live for another two decades as they always had—hunting, fishing, and trapping on crown land that was not otherwise used—until the province began an all-weather road from Grande Prairie to Little Buffalo in 1971. Rising world oil prices pointed to the development of northern Alberta's oil sands, and Premier Lougheed officially announced on 18 September 1973 that the Syncrude project would go ahead.[32]

In the 1970s, provincial and national associations of native people, with young and well-educated leaders, were rapidly gaining political influence. On 27 October 1975, one such organization, the Indian Association of Alberta (IAA), of which Harold Cardinal was president, intervened on behalf of the Lubicons. The IAA borrowed strategy from the Dene of the Northwest Territories and tried to register a caveat to about 25 000 square miles lying north of Lesser Slave Lake between the Peace and Athabasca rivers. This was on behalf of the "isolated communities"—half a dozen groups of Indians in the area—that claimed to be entitled to reserves under Treaty 8.[33] By attempting to register a caveat, the isolated communities were asserting an unextinguished aboriginal title to a large part of northern Alberta. Like the Dene, they were propounding the novel legal doctrine that Treaty 8 had not extinguished their aboriginal title even though the text purported to do so. As a matter of political strategy, they were trying to block Syncrude and other northern oil projects and thereby wring concessions from the provincial government.[34]

When the Supreme Court of Canada rejected the Dene caveat in 1976, it noted that one could probably register a similar caveat in Alberta because of the wording of the province's Land Titles Act.[35] Fearing that it might lose the impending court battle, the government of Alberta had the legislature revise the Land Titles Act.[36] The province declared that there were no unextinguished aboriginal rights in Alberta, only "unfulfilled land entitlements,"[37] and the attorney general challenged Indian groups to go to court if they thought that they could prove the existence of unextinguished aboriginal title.[38]

The isolated-communities coalition fell apart, and the Lubicon band emerged as a political actor in its own right. After Bernard Ominayak was elected chief in 1978,[39] he entrusted the Lubicons' legal strategy to a Montreal lawyer, James O'Reilly, who had been instrumental in bringing about the James Bay Agreement. In early 1980 Billy Diamond, chief of the James Bay Cree, flew in to meet Ominayak. Offering to guarantee a bank loan of $400 000 for the Lubicons plus another $300 000 if necessary, he told Ominayak to hire O'Reilly.[40]

The political-legal strategy that had worked for the James Bay Cree in the 1970s—claiming unextinguished aboriginal title, seeking an injunction to hold up natural-resource development, entering into negotiations to achieve a settlement—seemed like a model for the Lubicon Cree in the 1980s. But there was a key difference between the two situations. Before 1975 there had been no land surrenders of any kind in northern

Quebec, so the native claim to possess unextinguished aboriginal title had *prima facie* validity. By contrast, because Treaty 8 purported to extinguish the Indian title to all of northern Alberta, the Lubicons would have to make out the far more doubtful proposition that the absence of an adhesion by what may or may not have been a Lubicon band in 1899–1900 created an unceded region in the middle of the treaty area, like a hole in the middle of a doughnut.

Though it is only a single claim, the Lubicons' avowal of unextinguished aboriginal title is a fundamental challenge to the Numbered Treaties as a whole. According to the terms of these treaties, Indian bands did not cede specific parcels of land on which they were accustomed to live; they ceded "all their rights, titles and privileges whatsoever" to the large tract of land described in the treaty. When a band made an "adhesion" to the treaty after the original signing, its chief signed a document accepting the terms of the treaty, including the surrender of land rights in the area described in the treaty; the adhesion document did not describe a specific piece of land claimed by the adhering band.

Three exceptions prove this rule. In adhesions to Treaties 6 (1899), 5 (1908), and 9 (1929), Indians did sign adhesions surrendering title to additional lands precisely because these treaties were being extended beyond their original boundaries. To coin a distinction, these three cases were examples of "external adhesion," in which Indians were understood to retain their aboriginal title until signing a document bringing new lands within the treaty. All other adhesions, including all cases relevant to Treaty 8, belonged to the category of "internal adhesion," in which the aboriginal title of all Indians living within the defined treaty area was understood to be extinguished by the treaty. The Lubicon case is one of internal adhesion because their ancestral home is located entirely within the area described by Treaty 8, so for the government to admit the continued existence of their aboriginal title would undercut a century of administrative consistency. From the government's viewpoint, the Lubicon case is no different from the dozens of group adhesions to the Numbered Treaties that have taken place over the last century. The Lubicons have a right to their own reserve within the treaty framework, but the government will not recognize an assertion of aboriginal title to land that it views as already ceded.

O'Reilly's first action was in the Federal Court of Canada on 25 April 1980, against Canada, Alberta, and a number of oil companies. He asked for a declaratory judgment affirming the Lubicon's land rights, without requesting a specific remedy such as damages or an injunction. But the court held in November that the jurisdiction given to it by the Federal Court Act extended only to suits against the crown in right of Canada.[41] An appeal was quickly dismissed by the Federal Court of Appeal.[42]

These initial efforts did bring some result, however. The minister of Indian affairs accepted the Lubicon claim for negotiation as a treaty entitlement,[43] and in January 1982 there was a federal-provincial meeting to consider the issue.[44] But to negotiate for a reserve within Treaty 8 would undercut the Lubicons' position that they still possessed aboriginal title because they had never adhered to Treaty 8. O'Reilly, therefore, turned to the Alberta Court of Queen's Bench. On 19 February 1982 he filed a statement of claim requesting an injunction against resource development. He asked for complete cessation of activity in a "reserve area" of 900 square miles around Lubicon Lake, and a reduced level of activity in a surrounding area of 8500 square miles called the "hunting and trapping territory." The theory behind the claim was that unrestricted resource development posed imminent danger to the Lubicons' land rights, which were said to be of three types: (1) aboriginal title that still existed because the Lubicons had never formally adhered to Treaty 8; (2) "in the alternative," as lawyers like to say when they espouse contradictory theories simultaneously, the reserve that had been granted but never implemented by government officials; (3) the Indians' right to hunt, fish, and trap on unoccupied crown land protected by the Alberta Natural Resources Act, 1930.[45]

Justice Forsyth declined to grant the injunction. On 17 November 1983 he held that "damages would be an adequate remedy to the applicants in the event they were ultimately successful in establishing any of their positions advanced."[46] The Lubicons would first have to prove that their aboriginal title still existed, then seek damages if they could show that they had suffered loss. Justice Forsyth did not believe that interference with "their traditional way of life" threatened them with immediate "irreparable injury."[47] On 11 January 1985 the Alberta Court of Appeal upheld the lower court's decision. Without judging the merit of the Lubicons' theory about their aboriginal rights, the court held that there was ample time to try the claim and assess damages, if any. In March 1985 the Supreme Court of Canada refused leave to appeal. Two weeks later, after the British Columbia Court of Appeal granted an injunction against logging on Meares Island in circumstances that bore some similarity to the Lubicon case, O'Reilly again sought leave to appeal but was refused a second time.[48]

This defeat marked the end of the Lubicons' attempt to use the courts to achieve their objectives. Their supporters say that "it had become obvious they could in all likelihood never get justice through this route,"[49] whereas skeptics think that they realized the weakness of their aboriginal-rights claim and had never seriously intended to litigate it. The band did unsuccessfully seek an injunction in the Federal Court of Canada to compel the Department of Indian Affairs to pay its legal fees (more than $2 000 000),[50] but this was a sideshow. The Lubicon would now rely increasingly on tactics of political guerrilla warfare.

During *Ominayak v. Norcen* they had already turned to the churches, and the result was a letter from the World Council of Churches to Prime Minister Pierre Trudeau accusing the Alberta government of genocide.[51] The Alberta government referred the letter to the provincial ombudsman, who reported in August 1984 that he had found "no factual basis" for charges of genocide.[52] Bernard Ominayak then released a sixty-one-page statement attacking the ombudsman's report.[53] It was indoor-outdoor political theatre, with NDP members of the Alberta legislature and the House of Commons recycling the news stories created by ecclesiastical denunciations of the government.

The political situation changed markedly with the election of a Progressive Conservative majority in parliament in September 1984. The new minister of Indian affairs, David Crombie, was an accomplished practitioner of ethnic politics. He met personally with Ominayak in November and agreed to appoint a federal fact-finder to examine the Lubicons' case.[54] In January 1985 he announced that the investigator would be E. Davie Fulton, one-time federal minister of justice and member of the Supreme Court of British Columbia.

Starting in April, Fulton spent a great deal of time with the Lubicons and ended up virtually as their advocate. On his recommendation, the federal government made an *ex gratia* payment of $1.5 million to the band on 8 January 1986;[55] much of this was used to repay the money borrowed for legal expenses. On 7 February 1986 Fulton submitted a long "Discussion Paper" that isolated contentious issues and highlighted points of common ground among the province, the federal government, and the Lubicons, and suggested concessions by all parties.[56]

Perhaps spooked by the prospect of a Fulton report relatively favourable to the Lubicons, the province offered in December 1985 to make an immediate transfer of twenty-five square miles to the band if they would drop all litigation (although their attempt to gain an injunction had been defeated, their main suit was still theoretically alive).[57] But the Lubicons dismissed this offer out of hand because a reserve of twenty-five square miles corresponded to their band size in 1940—127 members—and they had grown much larger in the meantime and wanted a correspondingly larger reserve. To an outsider, a quantitative issue such as the size of the band seems like an ideal subject for negotiation and compromise, but for the Lubicons it was a matter of principle. Their theory of aboriginal rights asserted that they were not yet bound by Treaty 8 because they had never adhered to it. To accept any external definition of their size would undercut their claim to continued possession of aboriginal title.

The federal government was not happy with Fulton's report, and Crombie moved on to another portfolio.[58] The prime minister then appointed a new negotiator, Roger Tassé, a retired deputy minister of justice and a main architect of the Canadian Charter of Rights and

Freedoms. Bilateral discussions between Tassé and the Lubicons began on 16 June 1986, but the Lubicons broke off the talks on 8 July when the federal government disputed the band size claimed by the Lubicons and denied their theory of continuing aboriginal title.[59]

With the failure of negotiations, the Lubicons began to put more emphasis on their attempts to influence public opinion. They had filed a complaint before the United Nations Human Rights Committee in 1984[60] and also spoke of disrupting the 1988 Calgary Winter Olympics, particularly by asking museums around the world not to participate in the Glenbow Museum's Indian exhibition, "The Spirit Sings." In August 1986 Ominayak, his political adviser Fred Lennarson, and some Lubicon elders went on a tour of seven European countries to generate support for the boycott.[61]

Such actions continued unabated during 1986 and 1987. The boycott had some success as a number of museums declined to loan artifacts to "The Spirit Sings," but it did not prevent the Glenbow from mounting the exhibit. Lubicon supporters also picketed the cross-country Olympic torch relay sponsored by Petro-Canada.[62] Again, they got media attention but did not seriously interfere with the relay nor with Petro-Canada's publicity bonanza.

Although not immediately successful, these efforts did indirectly lead to results. In October 1987 the federal government appointed a new negotiator, Calgary lawyer Brian Malone.[63] A meeting involving two Cabinet ministers, Bill McKnight and Joe Clark, was set up in Ottawa for 21 January 1988 in an attempt to get movement before the Winter Olympics opened in February. But the meeting got nowhere, and the minister of Indian affairs, Bill McKnight, gave the Lubicons an ultimatum: return to the table within eight days or the federal government would take further steps toward a legal resolution.[64]

On 3 February 1988 McKnight wrote to Jim Horsman, the Alberta attorney general and minister of federal and intergovernmental affairs, to request that Alberta provide land for a reserve according to what became known as the "McKnight formula," and he made scarcely veiled threats to sue the province if it did not quickly comply. The McKnight formula would have produced a reserve larger than Alberta had previously been willing to grant but smaller than the Lubicons were demanding.

Around this time, the provincial Cabinet decided that Premier Don Getty should approach Bernard Ominayak personally and try to work something out.[65] The two men met for the first time on 4 March 1988.[66] They got on well personally, and Getty became almost a champion of the Lubicons in the spring of 1988. He tried to get the federal government to accept a proposal for arbitration in which the Lubicons would name Davie Fulton, the two governments would agree on another choice, and the two arbitrators would settle on a neutral chairman.[67] But the federal government would not accept the proposal, perhaps because the Lubicons did not want the arbitration to be binding.[68]

McKnight then made good on his threat to litigate. On 17 May 1988 federal lawyers filed a statement of claim in the Calgary district of the Alberta Court of Queen's Bench demanding that the province make land available for a reserve according to the McKnight formula.[69] Alberta and the Lubicon band were joined as defendants in a strange reversal of the litigation of the early 1980s.

It quickly became evident that the Lubicons would do everything possible to avoid testing their claim in court. In early June, Bernard Ominayak began to say openly that the Lubicons were ready to "assert jurisdiction," that is, to assume governmental control over their traditional territory in validation of their claim that they had never relinquished their aboriginal title.[70] On 21 September Ominayak announced that his band would assert jurisdiction on 15 October if an agreement was not reached; this would mean a blockade of roads onto oil-producing lands.[71] On 6 October O'Reilly read a statement in court that the Lubicons were asserting jurisdiction and would not participate in any further judicial proceedings.[72]

Events now moved quickly in elaborate choreography. Although the province declared that it would enforce the law, the Lubicons set up their blockade on 15 October. The province secured an injunction against it on 19 October, and early on the morning of 20 October heavily armed RCMP officers took down the blockade and arrested twenty-seven people.[73] Getty and Ominayak, who had certainly been in contact behind the scenes, then met on 22 October in the little town of Grimshaw. The same day, Getty agreed to sell the federal government seventy-nine square miles with mineral rights, and another sixteen square miles without mineral rights, for a reserve.[74] The total of ninety-five square miles conformed to the Lubicons' own count of their membership.

But no settlement was possible without the agreement of the federal government. Negotiations began well when Ottawa accepted the ninety-five-square-mile reserve but broke down on 24 January 1989. The biggest single issue was compensation. Maintaining that they had a "comprehensive" claim based on aboriginal rights, the Lubicons demanded compensation from the federal government for failure to extinguish their aboriginal title in 1899. The amount owed—$167 million according to one calculation—would compensate the Lubicons for various federal benefits that they had allegedly not received since 1899 because they had no reserve. The Lubicons were willing to negotiate the amount of compensation but not the principle that something had to be paid. The federal government, on the other hand, viewed this as only a "specific" claim based on treaty entitlement. It recognized the Lubicons' right to a reserve, and it was willing to pay to set one up—$45 million, according to its calculations. But it refused to pay a general amount for extinguishment of aboriginal title, because in its view aboriginal title had been extinguished all over northern Alberta with the signing of Treaty 8. The federal government could not accede to the Lubicons' claim for compensation without undercutting the validity of the treaties, on which it had always insisted. If it deviated from this principle in the Lubicon case, it might be forced to regard many other current and potential claims across Canada as "comprehensive" (aboriginal title) rather than "specific" (treaty entitlement) claims.[75]

Since the breakdown of negotiations, the Lubicons have persisted in their refusal to compromise. They have also continued to "assert jurisdiction" by delivering an ultimatum to oil companies: obtain permits from us or shut down your operations.[76] On 1 December 1989 Petro-Canada and Norcen shut in twenty wells rather than make an issue of it.[77] Although such tactics have not yet had any political success, the Lubicons are also trying to keep the Daishowa pulp mill from cutting any trees in their "hunting and trapping territory," which is a large part of the forest-management area granted to Daishowa by the province.[78] In November 1990 there was an attack upon a logging subcontractor's camp, after which thirteen Lubicon band members were charged with arson.[79]

Meanwhile, the solidarity of the Lubicons has begun to disintegrate. Only days after the failure of negotiations, Brian Malone was contacted by Lubicon band members, some of whom favoured forming another band and negotiating a separate settlement. Ominayak called a snap band election for 31 May to dispel rumours of opposition to his leadership. He was re-elected chief by a unanimous show of hands,[80] but this could not stop the defectors. On 28 August 1989 the Department of Indian Affairs recognized a new Woodland band of about 350 members, including 117 names previously on the Lubicons' own list. About thirty of these had been expelled by the Lubicons; the rest seem to have left voluntarily.[81] The new band is an amalgamation of Lubicon dissenters with Indians from nearby isolated communities, such as Cadotte Lake, that had not previously been recognized as bands.

The Woodland leaders immediately began to negotiate a specific claim for a reserve at Cadotte Lake, resulting in an agreement in principle on 26 March 1990. Its terms resemble the final offer that the Lubicons rejected.[82] Meanwhile, the federal position is that it will extend similar treatment to any other bands in the isolated-communities area that want to enter negotiations.[83] If this policy is successful, it will leave the Lubicons isolated and may lead to further defections from their ranks.

The Lubicon Lake dispute has been so bitter and protracted because it pits two different views of Indian land rights against each other. Canada and Alberta refuse to recognize any aboriginal claim because they insist that Treaty 8 has extinguished aboriginal title. The Lubicons do not deny that treaties can extinguish aboriginal title; but they say that, because their ancestors did not sign the treaty, they still possess unextinguished aboriginal title. Canada will find it difficult ever to concede this point because there are other groups of Indians in the Prairie provinces, and indeed in other regions of the country, who claim that they also have never adhered to the local treaty. There is no problem in giving the Lubicons, as well as other groups in their situation, a treaty entitlement; but to recognize the continuing existence of unextinguished aboriginal title would threaten to upset the entire treaty system.

The Lubicon dispute is an instructive example of the importance of principle in human affairs. Canada admits the Lubicons' right to a reserve, and Alberta is ready to provide the land. If it were not for the difference in views of aboriginal title, the dispute could be settled in a few months of negotiation, as has occurred with other specific claims in northern Alberta in the 1980s. But there will be a deadlock as long as the Lubicons assert the existence of a continuing aboriginal title.

Documents

A. Extract from Letter of A.G. Archibald Relating to Treaty 1[84]

A.G. Archibald, the first lieutenant governor of Manitoba, was present when Treaty 1 was negotiated at Lower Fort Garry. These passages from a letter to Ottawa, written while negotiations were under way, illustrate the clash between the official and Indian perspectives on land. The Indians obviously thought of themselves as original proprietors able to retain most of Manitoba, whereas the government representatives just as obviously thought of Canada as the true owner, setting aside small tracts for the Indians.

. . . the Indians seem to have false idea of the meaning of a reserve. They have been led to suppose that large tracts of ground were to be set aside for them as hunting grounds, including timber lands, of which they might sell the wood as if they were proprietors of the soil.

I wished to correct this idea at the outset. . . .

In defining the limits of their reserves, so far as we could see, they wished to have two-thirds of the Province. We heard them out, and then told them it was quite clear that they had entirely misunderstood the meaning and intention of reserves. . . . We told them that whether they wished it or not, immigrants would come in and fill up the country; that every year from this one twice as many in number as their whole people there assembled would pour into the Province, and in a little while would spread all over it, and that now was the time for them to come to an arrangement that would secure homes and annuities for themselves and their children.

We told them that what we proposed to allow them was an extent of one hundred and sixty acres for each family of five, or in that proportion; that they might have their land where they chose, not interfering with existing occupants; that we should allow an annuity of twelve dollars for every family of five, or in that proportion per head. We requested them to think over those propositions till Monday morning.

If they thought it better to have no treaty at all, they might do without one, but they must make up their minds; if there was to be a treaty, it must be on a basis like that offered.

That under some such arrangements, the Indians in the east were living happy and contented, enjoying themselves, drawing their annuities, and satisfied with their position.

The observations seemed to command the acquiescence of the majority, and on Monday morning we hope to meet them in a better frame for the discussion and settlement of the treaty.

B. Treaty 8[85]

Treaty 8 was negotiated at Lesser Slave Lake, 20–21 June 1899. Other bands accepted the same terms in a series of a dozen adhesions over the years 1899–1900 (and one in 1910). The text is included here as the foundation of the Lubicon dispute as well as an example of the Numbered Treaties. While each of the Numbered Treaties has distinctive minor features, they are very similar as a group. Perhaps the chief distinctive feature of Treaty 8 is its allowance of land in severalty (that is, individual ownership), instead of collective reserves, for those Indians who wished it. This was intended to be an adaptation to the mode of life of the Indians of the boreal forest, who did not live in such well-defined bands as the plains Indians. In practice, however, the severalty provision has not been greatly used.

Articles of a Treaty made and concluded at the several dates mentioned therein, in the year of Our Lord one thousand eight hundred and ninety-nine, between Her Most Gracious Majesty the Queen of Great Britain and Ireland, by Her Commissioners the Honourable David Laird, of Winnipeg, Manitoba, Indian Commissioner for the said Province and the Northwest Territories; James Andrew Joseph McKenna, of Ottawa, Ontario, Esquire, and the Honourable James Hamilton Ross, of Regina, in the Northwest Territories, of the one part; and the Cree, Beaver,

Chipewyan and other Indians, inhabitants of the territory within the limits hereinafter defined and described, by their Chiefs and Headmen, hereunto subscribed, of the other part:—

WHEREAS, the Indians inhabiting the territory hereinafter defined have, pursuant to notice given by the Honourable Superintendent General of Indian Affairs in the year 1898, been convened to meet a Commission representing Her Majesty's Government of the Dominion of Canada at certain places in the said territory in this present year 1899, to deliberate upon certain matters of interest to Her Most Gracious Majesty, of the one part, and the said Indians of the other.

AND WHEREAS, the said Indians have been notified and informed by Her Majesty's said Commission that it is Her desire to open for settlement, immigration, trade, travel, mining, lumbering, and such other purposes as to Her Majesty may seem meet, a tract of country bounded and described as hereinafter mentioned, and to obtain the consent thereto of Her Indian subjects inhabiting the said tract, and to make a treaty, and arrange with them, so that there may be peace and good will between them and Her Majesty's other subjects, and that Her Indian people may know and be assured of what allowances they are to count upon and receive from Her Majesty's bounty and benevolence.

AND WHEREAS, the Indians of the said tract, duly convened in council at the respective points named hereunder, and being requested by Her Majesty's Commissioners to name certain Chiefs and Headmen who should be authorized on their behalf to conduct such negotiations and sign any treaty to be founded thereon, and to become responsible to Her Majesty for the faithful performance by their respective bands of such obligations as shall be assumed by them, the said Indians have therefore acknowledged for that purpose the several Chiefs and Headmen who have subscribed hereto.

AND WHEREAS, the said Commissioners have proceeded to negotiate a treaty with the Cree, Beaver, Chipewyan, and other Indians, inhabiting the district hereinafter defined and described, and the same has been agreed upon and concluded by the respective bands at the dates mentioned hereunder, the said Indians DO HEREBY CEDE, RELEASE, SURRENDER AND YIELD UP to the Government of the Dominion of Canada, for Her Majesty the Queen and Her successors for ever, all their rights, titles, and privileges whatsoever, to the lands included within the following limits, that is to say:—

Commencing at the source of the main branch of the Red Deer River in Alberta, thence due west to the central range of the Rocky Mountains, thence northwesterly along the said range to the point where it intersects the 60th parallel of north latitude, thence east along said parallel to the point where it intersects Hay River, thence northeasterly down said river to the south shore of Great Slave lake, thence along the said shore northeasterly (and including such rights to the islands in said lakes as the

Indians mentioned in the treaty may possess), and thence easterly and northeasterly along the south shores of Christie's Bay and McLeod's Bay to old Fort Reliance near the mouth of Lockhart's river, thence southeasterly in a straight line to and including Black Lake, thence southwesterly up the stream from Cree lake, thence including said lake southwesterly along the height of land between the Athabasca and Churchill Rivers to where it intersects the northern boundary of Treaty Six, and along the said boundary easterly, northerly and southwesterly, to the place of commencement.

AND ALSO the said Indian rights, titles and privileges whatsoever to all other lands wherever situated in the Northwest Territories, British Columbia, or in any other portion of the Dominion of Canada.

TO HAVE AND TO HOLD the same to Her Majesty the Queen and Her successors for ever.

And Her Majesty the Queen HEREBY AGREES with the said Indians that they shall have right to pursue their usual vocations of hunting, trapping and fishing throughout the tract surrendered as heretofore described, subject to such regulations as may from time to time be made by the Government of the country, acting under the authority of Her Majesty, and saving and excepting such tracts as may be required or taken up from time to time for settlement, mining, lumbering, trading or other purposes.

And Her Majesty the Queen hereby agrees and undertakes to lay asides for such bands as desire reserves, the same not to exceed in all one square mile for each family of five for such number of families as may elect to reside on reserves, or in that proportion for larger or smaller families; and for such families or individual Indians as may prefer to live apart from band reserves, Her Majesty undertakes to provide land in severalty to the extent of 160 acres to each Indian, the land to be conveyed with a proviso as to non-alienation without the consent of the Governor General in Council of Canada, the selection of such reserves, and lands in severalty, to be made in the manner following, namely, the Superintendent General of Indian Affairs shall depute and send a suitable person to determine and set apart such reserves and lands, after consulting with the Indians concerned as to the locality which may be found suitable and open for selection.

Provided, however, that Her Majesty reserves the right to deal with any settlers within the bounds of any lands reserved for any band as She may see fit; and also that the aforesaid reserves of land, or any interest therein, may be sold or otherwise disposed of by Her Majesty's Government for the use and benefit of the said Indians entitled thereto, with their consent had and obtained.

It is further agreed between Her Majesty and Her said Indian subjects that such portions of the reserves and lands above indicated as may at any time be required for public works, buildings, railways, or roads of whatsoever nature may be appropriated for that purpose by Her Majesty's Government of the Dominion of Canada, due compensation being made to the Indians for the value of any improvements thereon, and an equivalent in land, money or other consideration for the area of the reserve so appropriated.

And with a view to show the satisfaction of Her Majesty with the behaviour and good conduct of Her Indians, and in extinguishment of all their past claims, She hereby, through Her Commissioners, agrees to make each Chief a present of thirty-two dollars in cash, to each Headman twenty-two dollars and to every other Indian of whatever age, of the families represented at the time and place of payment, twelve dollars.

Her Majesty also agrees that next year, and annually afterwards for ever, She will cause to be paid to the said Indians in cash, at suitable places and dates, of which the said Indians shall be duly notified, to each Chief twenty-five dollars, each Headman, not to exceed four to a large Band and two to a small Band, fifteen dollars, and to every other Indian, of whatever age, five dollars, the same, unless there be some exceptional reason, to be paid only to heads of families for those belonging thereto.

FURTHER, Her Majesty agrees that each Chief, after signing the treaty, shall receive a silver medal and a suitable flag, and next year, and every third year thereafter, each Chief and Headman shall receive a suitable suit of clothing.

FURTHER, Her Majesty agrees to pay the salaries of such teachers to instruct the children of said Indians as to Her Majesty's Government of Canada may seem advisable.

FURTHER, Her Majesty agrees to supply each Chief of a Band that selects a reserve, for the use of that Band, ten axes, five hand-saws, five augers, one grindstone, and the necessary files and whetstones.

FURTHER, Her Majesty agrees that each that elects to take a reserve and cultivate the soil, shall, as soon as convenient after such reserve is set aside and settled upon, and the Band has signified its choice and is prepared to break up the soil, receive two hoes, one spade, one scythe and two hay forks for every family so settled, and for every three families one plough and one harrow, and to the Chief, for the use of his Band, two horses or a yoke of oxen, and for each Band potatoes, barely, oats and wheat (if such seed be suited to the locality of the reserve), to plant the land actually broken up, and provisions for one month in the spring for several years while planting such seeds; and to every family one cow, and every Chief one bull, and one mowing-machine and one reaper for the use of his Band when it is ready for them; for such families as prefer to raise stock instead of cultivating the soil, every family of five persons, two cows, and every Chief two bulls and two mowing-machines when ready for their use, and a like proportion for smaller or larger families. The aforesaid articles, machines and cattle to be given one for all for the encouragement of agriculture and stock raising; and for such Bands as prefer to continue hunting and fishing, as much ammunition and twine for making nets annually as will amount in value to one dollar per head of the families so engaged in hunting and fishing.

And the undersigned Cree, Beaver, Chipewyan and other Indian Chiefs and Headmen, on their own behalf and on behalf of all the Indians whom they represent, DO HEREBY SOLEMNLY PROMISE and engage to strictly observe this Treaty, and also to conduct and behave themselves as good and loyal subjects of Her Majesty the Queen.

THEY PROMISE AND ENGAGE that they will, in all respects, obey and abide by the law; that they will maintain peace between each other, and between themselves and other tribes of Indians, and between themselves and others of Her Majesty's subjects, whether Indians, half-breeds or whites, this year inhabiting and hereafter to inhabit any part of the said ceded territory; and that they will not molest the person or property of any inhabitant of such ceded tract, or of any other distinct or country, or interfere with or trouble any person passing or travelling through the said tract or any part thereof, and that they will assist the officers of Her Majesty in bringing to justice and punishment any Indian offending against the stipulations of this Treaty or infringing the law in force in the country so ceded.

IN WITNESS THEREOF Her Majesty's said Commissioners and the Cree Chief and Headmen of Lesser Slave Lake and the adjacent territory, HAVE HEREUNTO SET THEIR HANDS at Lesser Slave Lake on the twenty-first day of June, in the year herein first above written.

Signed by the parties hereto, in the presence of the undersigned witnesses, the same having been first explained to the Indians by Albert Tate and Samuel Cunningham, Interpreters. *Here follow the signatures of the Chiefs and Headmen, Treaty Commissioners, and Witnesses.*

C.   Adhesion to Treaty 8[86]

Because of the huge distances involved, it was impossible to gather all the Indians together at one time and place to negotiate Treaty 8. Thus, after the first meeting there was a series of adhesions in which various bands accepted the terms negotiated at Lesser Slave Lake. The following is the text of the last adhesion, signed at Fort Nelson, British Columbia, on 15 August 1910. Although this adhesion offers a close historical parallel to the Lubicon situation, it does not support the Lubicons' contention that they still hold unextinguished aboriginal title to a particular tract of land within the Treaty 8 area.

The Slaves and Sicanees Indians of Fort Nelson, in the Province of British Columbia, having met Her Majesty's Commissioner, Henry

Anthony Conroy at Fort Nelson on this fifteenth day of August, in this present year 1910, and having had explained to them the terms of the treaty unto which the Chief and Headmen of the Indians of Lesser Slave Lake and adjacent country set their hands on the twenty-first day of June, in the year 1899, do join in the cession made by the said treaty, and agree to adhere to the terms thereof, in consideration of the undertakings made therein.

In witness whereof, His Majesty's said Commissioner, and the following the said Sicanees Indians, have hereunto set their hands, at Fort Nelson, on the fifteenth day of August in the year herein first above written.

Signed by the parties thereto in the presence of the undersigned witnesses, after the same had been read and explained by Joseph Villeneuve Interpreter. [*Here follow the signatures.*]

D. Extract from Federation of Saskatchewan Indians, Indian Treaty Rights Handbook[87]

This excerpt shows how contemporary Indians espouse a view of treaties much different from the official interpretation of them as land surrenders. The Indian view sees treaties as international agreements between sovereign nations. While this text does not explicitly deny that the Numbered Treaties brought about the extinguishment of aboriginal title to land, it takes an expansive view of the land rights remaining to Indians. It would be instructive for the student to compare this text to the wording of Treaty 8 to see how far this view departs from the wording.

Introduction

Between 1817 and 1929 the Indian/Dene nations conducted negotiations with the British government (or with Canada in the right of the Crown) resulting in the signing of more than twenty major international treaties.

Through this treaty process the Indian nations agreed to cede certain lands for use and settlement in return for specific guarantees.

These guarantees are our TREATY RIGHTS. The treaties gave Canada use and benefit of land for political, social, economic and spiritual development. The treaties *reserved* lands and resources for continued Indian use and existence as nations. The treaties also guaranteed specific social and economic rights [to] and Indian nations to ensure continuation of strong Indian government.

The Indian leadership, during treaty negotiations, guaranteed:

(1) all powers of Indian nationhood

(2) Indian jurisdiction

(3) the right to be born, and live, an Indian

(4) socio-economic rights.

To Indian/Dene Government and Nationhood, "Nations make Treaties, Treaties do not make Nations"

The treaties clearly establish the sovereign to sovereign relationships between Indian Nations and Canada in the following way:

I. *Indian Sovereignty*   The sovereign power of the Indian nations is that fundamental authority of any state to which none other is superior or equal.

Indian governments entered into treaty exercising all the powers of nationhood including the powers necessary for self-government and the powers necessary to maintain political, social and economic stability. In the treaty negotiations these powers are recognized and their continuance guaranteed.

Nations remain sovereign as long as a functioning government exists. A nation's sovereignty is no less real because one or more nations refuse to recognize its existence.

During the treaty negotiations, the Crown came to the Indian nations and at all times conducted itself in recognition of the powers and symbols of Indian nations. . . .

For a treaty to be binding, the parties must have legal capacity to enter into such an agreement. Only sovereign nations have such a capacity.

The Spirit and Intent of Treaty to Indian Lands, Water and Resources

The establishment of reserved Indian land under treaty is clear.

Reserve Land—is land that was reserved by the Indians as sovereign territory.

It is important to recognize this fact—reserves were not granted to the Indian nations, they are land not ceded under treaty.

In addition to specific Indian reserved land, Indian jurisdiction is maintained over a range of other lands. Some of these extraterritorial land rights include:

Hunting and Trapping Areas

Fishing Stations

Gathering Areas

Hay Meadows

Burial Grounds and Sacred Lands

Traditional Meeting Grounds

Timber Berths
Anything not specifically ceded by the Indian nations by the articles of
treaty remain under Indian jurisdiction.

Treaty established a sovereign to sovereign relationship. There was no
consent reached with regard to a variety of natural resources which
therefore remain under Indian jurisdiction subject to additional negotia-
tion and agreement. These include:
Water
Minerals
Forests
Game
Air Space

E. Extract from Appellants' Factum in the case of Ominayak v. Norcen[88]

The case of Ominayak v. Norcen *arose in 1982 when the Lubicon Lake band
asked the Alberta Court of Queen's Bench to grant an injunction against further
resource development in their claim territory. When the band lost at that level, it
appealed to the Alberta Court of Appeal. A "factum" is the written argument filed
by counsel in appellate proceedings. This extract summarizes the legal theory
underlying the Lubicon claim.*

21. Appellants allege and argue three principal and *alternative* categories of rights upon which their statement of claim and the present proceedings for interim injunction are based; a) aboriginal rights, b) treaty
rights, c) rights under the Alberta Natural Resources Transfer
Agreement *(Constitution Act, 1930)*.

22. In the first place, they claim aboriginal rights over the entire
Hunting/Trapping Territory. Appellants allege and argue that:

    a) These aboriginal rights are existing aboriginal rights within the
meaning of Section 35 of the *Constitution Act, 1982*.

    b) These aboriginal rights entail the exclusive use and enjoyment
of all the lands in the Hunting/Trapping Territory as well as the
natural resources thereof including the minerals and the wildlife.

    c) These aboriginal rights can be invoked by all of Appellants or
any one of Appellants indivisibly but they are collective rights.

    d) Aboriginal rights include aboriginal or Indian land title, which
title can have a number of different sources, such as historical occupancy (from time immemorial, or occupancy at the time of assumption of British sovereignty or even occupancy at the time of treaty),
the *Royal Proclamation, 1763*, and recognition by the Crown.

e) Aboriginal rights also *include*, as an element thereof, hunting and trapping rights.

f) Moreover, in the present proceedings, Appellants allege and argue that Treaty No. 8 did not extinguish their aboriginal rights since, *inter alia*, neither they nor their ancestors were ever a party to it or adhered to it, nor were their aboriginal rights or those of their ancestors otherwise surrendered or extinguished.

23. The second principal category of rights invoked by Appellants is that of treaty rights.

a) If Appellants no longer have aboriginal rights in and to the Hunting/Trapping Territory, then it is because Treaty No. 8 extinguished these aboriginal rights.

b) Thus, as an alternative, Appellants allege and argue that they at least have existing treaty rights pursuant to Treaty No. 8. . . . *[The rest of the section develops the Lubicons' contention that they already possess the twenty-five-square-mile reserve promised to them around 1940, even though it was never surveyed.]*

24. The third general category of rights invoked is the right of hunting, fishing and trapping for food over the entire Hunting/Trapping Territory based on the Alberta Natural Resources Transfer Agreement. . . .

25. The three categories of rights claimed relate to an interest in or to land or in or to the natural resources thereof (including the wildlife) and comprise, at a minimum, hunting and trapping rights. In respect of their content, they can be further distilled as follows:

a) Aboriginal Rights. They involve the exclusive right to the full use, occupation and benefit of the Hunting/Trapping Territory and all lands therein. They include:

i)   the exclusive enjoyment, possession and use of the land and the resources and access thereto;

ii)   the right to the wildlife and the right to hunt and trap the wildlife;

iii)   the right to carry on and maintain a traditional Indian way of life based on hunting, fishing and trapping;

iv)   the right to the use and benefit of the minerals. . . .

Notes

[1] I use the term "aboriginal title" to refer to land rights. I do not attempt to deal here with other aboriginal rights, such as self-government, that may not have been extinguished by the treaties.

[2] The Selkirk treaty is reprinted in Archer Martin, *The Hudson's Bay Company's Land Tenures* (London: William Cloves & Sons 1898), 12–13.

[3] Peter A. Cumming and Neil H. Mickenberg, *Native Rights in Canada*, 2nd ed. (Toronto: General Publishing 1972), 148.

[4] J. R. Miller, *Skyscrapers Hide the Heavens: A History of Indian–White Relations in Canada* (Toronto: University of Toronto Press 1989), 161.

[5] All the Numbered Treaties are covered in the *Treaty Research Report* series published by Indian and Northern Affairs Canada, Treaties and Historical Research Centre, 1983–86.

[6] D. J. Hall, "'A Serene Atmosphere'? Treaty 1 Revisited," *The Canadian Journal of Native Studies* 4 (1984), 351.

[7] George H. Gooderham, "The Gypsy Indians and the Last Treaty," *Alberta History* 34 (1986), 15–19.

[8] Cumming and Mickenberg, *Native Rights in Canada*, 128.

[9] Alexander Morris, *The Treaties of Canada with the Indians of Manitoba and the North-West Territories* (Toronto: Belfords, Clarke & Co. 1880; Coles reprint, 1979), 126–7.

[10] Treaty 1, printed in W. E. Daugherty, *Treaty Research Report: Treaty One and Treaty Two* (Ottawa: Indian and Northern Affairs Canada, Treaties and Historical Research Centre 1983), 27.

[11] 14 App. Cas. 46. See Donald B. Smith, "Aboriginal Rights a Century Ago," *The Beaver* 67 (February/March 1987), 4–15.

[12] Indian and Northern Affairs Canada, *Schedule of Indian Bands, Reserves and Settlements* (Ottawa, 1 June 1987).

[13] John Leonard Taylor, "Canada's Northwest Indian Policy in the 1870s: Traditional Premises and Necessary Innovations," in Richard Price, ed., *The Spirit of the Alberta Indian Treaties* (Montreal: Institute for Research on Public Policy 1979), 44–5.

[14] Interview with Cree elder Lazarus Roan, 30 March 1974, in ibid., 116–17.

[15] *Comprehensive Land Claim Agreement in Principle Between Canada and the Dene Nation and the Metis Association of the Northwest Territories* (Ottawa: Department of Indian Affairs and Northern Development, September 1988).

[16] C. Gerald Sutton, "Aboriginal Rights," in Mel Watkins, ed., *Dene Nation: The Colony Within* (Toronto: University of Toronto Press 1977), 155; Thomas Berger, *Northern Frontier, Northern Homeland* (Ottawa: Supply and Services 1977), 167–8.

[17] René Fumoleau, *As Long as This Land Shall Last* (Toronto: McClelland and Stewart [1973]), 306.

[18] Boyce Richardson, "The Lubicon of Northern Alberta," in Boyce Richardson, ed., *Drumbeat: Anger and Renewal in Indian Country* (Toronto: Summerhill Press for the Assembly of First Nations 1989), 229–64; John Goddard, "Forked Tongues," *Saturday Night* (February 1988), 38–45; John Goddard, "Last Stand of the Lubicon," *Equinox* 21 (May/June 1985), 66–77. John Goddard, *The Last Stand of the Lubicon Cree* (Vancouver: Douglas & McIntyre 1991).

[19] Thomas Flanagan, "Some Factors Bearing on the Origins of the Lubicon Lake Dispute, 1899–1940," *Alberta* 2 (1990), 47–62.

[20] Memorandum of agreement, 14 December 1929, s. 10, enacted by the Alberta Natural Resources Act. S. C., 1930, c. 3.

[21] N.-P. L'Heureux to secretary, Indian Affairs Branch, 1 October 1940. This and following correspondence is found in Exhibit B attached to Affidavit 2 of Chief Bernard Ominayak, filed 23 September 1982, in *Ominayak* v. *Norcen*, contained in the papers of Judge N. D. McDermid, Glenbow-Alberta Institute, 6992, appeal book 3.

[22] T. R. L. MacInness to N.-P. L'Heureux, 9 September 1941, ibid.

[23] H. W. McGill to N. E. Tanner, 17 February 1942, ibid.

[24] C. D. Brown to R. A. Hoey, 29 October 1946, ibid.

[25] D. J. Allan to G. H. Gooderham, 15 March 1952, ibid.

[26] G. S. Lapp to G. H. Gooderham, 21 July 1950, ibid.

[27] D. J. Allan to G. H. Gooderham, 15 March 1952, ibid.

[28] Compare G. S. Lapp to G. H. Gooderham, 13 June 1952, ibid., with Lapp to Gooderham, 17 June 1953, ibid.

[29] T. W. Dalkin to D. J. Allan, 11 February 1952, ibid.

[30] T. W. Dalkin to G. H. Gooderham, 22 October 1953, ibid.

[31] G. S. Lapp to E. A. Robertson, 5 May 1954, ibid.

[32] Larry Pratt, *The Tar Sands: Syncrude and the Politics of Oil* (Edmonton: Hurtig 1976), 18.

[33] Lubicon Lake, Chipewyan Lake, Sandy Lake, Trout Lake, Peerless Lake, and Loon Lake.

[34] Richard Charles Daniel, *Indian Rights and Hinterland Resources: The Case of Northern Alberta* (University of Alberta: MA thesis in sociology 1977), 195–203.

[35] *Paulette* v. *R.*, [1977] 2 S.C.R. 628 at 638, 645.

[36] (Bill 29) The Land Titles Amendment Act, S. A., 1977, c. 27, s. 10, amending s. 141 of the Land Titles Act. Royal assent 18 May 1977.

[37] Bob Bogle, *Alberta Hansard*, 17 March 1978: 262.

[38] Jim Foster, *Alberta Hansard*, 6 April 1977: 672–3.

[39] Goddard, "Forked Tongues," 43.

[40] Roy MacGregor, *Chief: The Fearless Vision of Billy Diamond* (Markham, Ont.: Viking 1989) 257–8.

[41] *Lubicon Lake Band* v. *The Queen*, [1981] 2 F.C. 317.

[42] Decided 5 May 1981, 13 D.L.R. (4th) 159.

[43] *Alberta Hansard*, 12 May 1981, 953–4.

[44] Richardson, "The Lubicon of Northern Alberta," 242–3.

[45] The theory of the case is best summarized in the appellants' factum, GAI, McDermid Papers.

[46] *Ominayak* v. *Norcen*, 29 Alta. L.R. (2d) 152 (1984) at 157.

[47] Ibid., 157–8.

[48] Richardson, "The Lubicon of Northern Alberta," 246; [1985] 1 S.C.R. xi.

[49] Richardson, "The Lubicon of Northern Alberta," 246.

[50] *Ominayak* v. *Canada (Minister of Indian Affairs and Northern Development)*, [1987] 3 F. C. 174.

[51] *Alberta Hansard*, 20 March 1984: 233–5.

[52] *Alberta Hansard*, 13 November 1984: 1494–5.

[53] *Alberta Multi-Media Society of Alberta* (a weekly Indian newspaper; hereafter cited as *AMMSA*), 14 September 1984: 3.

[54] *AMMSA*, 30 November 1984: 3.

[55] United Nations Human Rights Committee, decision of 26 March 1990, CCPR/C/38/D/167/1984: 8; hereafter cited as UNHRC.

[56] E. David Fulton, "Lubicon Lake Indian Band—Inquiry: Discussion Paper," 7 February 1986, photocopy.

[57] *AMMSA*, 13 December 1985: 1, 3.

[58] Richardson, "The Lubicon of Northern Alberta," 252.

[59] *Windspeaker* (successor to *AMMSA*), 12 December 1986: 3, 5; Richardson, "The Lubicon of Northern Alberta," 253.

[60] UNHRC, 1.

[61] *Windspeaker*, 12 December 1986: 3, 5.

[62] *Windspeaker*, 20 November 1987, 3.

[63] Richardson, "The Lubicon of Northern Alberta," 254.

[64] Ibid., 256; *Windspeaker*, 22 January 1988: 2; House of Commons Debates, 21 January 1988: 12151–3.

[65] Interview with Dave Russell.

[66] *Windspeaker*, 11 March 1988: 1.

[67] Don Getty, *Alberta Hansard*, 6 May 1988: 876–7.

[68] Bill McKnight, House of Commons *Debates*, 18 May 1988: 15577–8.

[69] *A. G. Canada* v. *A. G. Alberta and the Lubicon Lake Band*, Alberta Court of Queen's Bench, no. 8801–07584.

[70] *Windspeaker*, 3 June 1988: 3.

[71] Richardson, "The Lubicon of Northern Alberta," 258.

[72] *Windspeaker*, 7 October 1988: 1.

[73] Richardson, "The Lubicon of Northern Alberta," 260; *Windspeaker*, 21 October 1988: 1.

[74] *Windspeaker*, 26 October 1988; Richardson, "The Lubicon of Northern Alberta," 261.

[75] *Calgary Herald*, 7–8 February 1989: A5.

[76] *Windspeaker*, 3 November 1989: 1.

[77] *Windspeaker*, 1 December 1989.

[78] *Alberta Report*, 24 September 1990: 21–2.

[79] *Alberta Report*, 28 January 1991, 10–11.

[80] *Windspeaker*, 2 June 1989: 1.

[81] *Windspeaker*, 28 July 1989: 1–2; 15 October 1990: 1, 3; UNHRC, 20–1, 25.

[82] Canada, press release, 26 March 1990.

[83] Interview with Brian Malone, 4 July 1990.

[84] A. G. Archibald, lieutenant governor of Manitoba, to Joseph Howe, secretary of state for the provinces, 29 July 1871, in Alexander Morris, *The Treaties of Canada with the Indians*, 33–5.

[85] Dennis F. K. Madill, *Treaty Research Report: Treaty Eight* (Ottawa: Treaties and Historical Research Centre, Indian and Northern Affairs Canada), 127–30.

[86] Ibid., 144–5.

[87] Delia Opekokew, *The First Nations: Indian Government and the Canadian Confederation* (Saskatoon: Federation of Saskatchewan Indians 1980), 80–6.

[88] GAI, Neil D. McDermid Papers, 6992, appeal book 3.

Aboriginal Land Claims in Ontario*

David T. McNab

Aboriginal people have asserted their title and rights to their territories and lands in Ontario for hundreds of years. This historical fact has not been supplanted or markedly changed either through events covering two hundred years of British imperial trusteeship, or, later, through Canadian assimilationist policy as expressed in the Indian Act and other legislation and regulations. In terms of their sheer diversity, if nothing else, aboriginal peoples' land claims can be seen as a microcosm of the total Canadian experience. Treaties cover large geographical areas but certainly not all lands. They do not cover the beds and the waters of the Great Lakes and connecting waterways, to name but one significant example. Some treaties do not include all aboriginal people who live in a specific treaty area. There are unfulfilled treaty entitlements and there are unsold surrendered Indian reserve lands. The challenge is immense for both the crown and the aboriginal people to seek settlements. It will be difficult and the price, in many ways, will be high.

Modern land claims in Ontario, while they have a long, honoured past and a basis in aboriginal oral traditions for centuries, are generally

---

* Any views or opinions expressed in this paper are solely those of the author and do not represent, nor are they intended to represent, any view, statement, policy, or position on any land claim, or related issue, of the Government of Ontario.

perceived by governments to be relatively recent phenomena rather than a direct continuation of the treaty-making process in the province. For the most part, it is true, the modern land-claims movement dates from the late 1960s and early 1970s in Canada. From the perspective of aboriginal people, however, many of the issues have been around for as long as two hundred years and are now firmly embedded in their own rich oral tradition—their history—as real grievances that affect their control over their lives. Their future social and economic condition hinges on the degree and extent of the power that they are able to exercise over their traditional self-governing institutions, customs, laws, and territory. Aboriginal people across Canada have never been conquered. Instead they have negotiated arrangements with the crown through a lengthy and dynamic treaty-making process in the context of British imperial policy. One commentator has aptly described that policy as one of "perpetual compromises between principle and immediate exigency." The history of land claims in Canada is no different.

The treaty-making process not only has continuity but it also is characterized by substantive concerns over lands and natural resources and by cross-cultural conflicts. There are real differences and cultural incongruities, much like a cultural traffic intersection in which cars can and do collide. This incongruence is multidimensional; it is not well understood and is a result of the relationship of two very different traditions—aboriginal and European—both of which are predicated on highly diverse tribal origins and still exist today. The European tradition is based largely on institutional relationships and promises, while the aboriginal one rests on personal, family consensus and commitments. These differences are often rationalized and justified after the fact and thus are usually explained away.

This is not helpful, especially when the two traditions collide in land-claims negotiations. There, the cultural chasm is frequently shown in a lack of respect and concern for the land by Europeans, or, in the Canadian context, by their colonial fragments—the newcomers. Put another way, in aboriginal-governance discussions, Europeans think of self-government in terms of local, municipal institutions whereas aboriginal people think in terms of self-determination and sovereignty over territory. The result is more often stalemate than understanding and agreement. Yet, at the same time, attempts at negotiating land claims and aboriginal-governance issues are being made.

This paper will attempt to describe the character and extent of land claims in Ontario as well as outline some general principles that are based on the experience of land-claims negotiations since 1970. It will draw some tentative conclusions about modern land claims and similar issues in the Ontario context.

The Ontario experience with respect to land claims has not been much different from that of the rest of Canada; in fact, from the perspective of the historian, it can be seen as an amalgam of the Canadian experience. Where Ontario is distinctive, however, is in the extent and age of its treaties with native peoples. The roots of the province's treaties stretch back at least to the time of the Royal Proclamation of 1763, if not before. There are more than thirty major treaties in Ontario that cover most, but not all, of the land mass of Ontario. Ontario treaties include ones that predate the land treaties of the late eighteenth century, signed after 1763. These, as well as the later land treaties, established a nation-to-nation relationship between aboriginal people and the crown that was based on peace and friendship. This relationship is sometimes dormant, sometimes alive.

Such is the context in which modern land claims must be understood if misunderstandings and conflict are to be avoided.

Background

Ontario is a large province covering an area of 412 582 square miles of land and water. Almost 87 per cent of this land and water has not been alienated from the crown. In northern Ontario, well over 90 per cent is still crown property; in southern Ontario, a smaller but more populous land base stretching along the Great Lakes and the connecting waterways, the figure is closer to 50 per cent. About 3 per cent is federal government land, much of which is categorized as Indian reserve land. This does not include large areas covered by land claims.

Apart from the more than fifty land claims that cover a large part of the province, there are more than 130 First Nations or bands living on almost two hundred reserves that together comprise about two million acres of land. The Ontario aboriginal population amounts to over 100 000 persons.

The extent of the modern land-claims challenge is therefore extremely large in scope as well as in its complexity. The treaty-making process has been varied and dynamic in Ontario, covering a time span of over two hundred years from Sir William Johnson to the current minister of Indian affairs and northern development, Tom Siddon. Some areas are included within the treaties; others are not. Some aboriginal people in Ontario participated in treaties; others did not. Most treaties have been circumscribed, if not completely circumvented, by federal and provincial legislation. Aboriginal and treaty rights have been denied or rendered valueless by settlement of the frontier and by legislation, regulations, enforcement of existing laws, or, as in the case of Temagami, adverse court judgments. Perhaps it is time to take an empathetic, more generous and understanding approach to modern land claims and their settlement. In doing so, we may learn more about ourselves and about aboriginal people.

Some estimates of the number of land claims in Canada, over the more than thirty major treaty areas, have been as high as five hundred. Modern settlements in Ontario have been, compared to those in northern Canada, in the low to medium range of about $100 000 to about $8–10 million. The largest settlement offer made in Ontario to date dealt with the Temagami land claim, and was not accepted; it amounted to $30 million and involved a mix of land, money, and other considerations. There have been only a handful of settlements, all of which have been bilateral rather than trilateral. Clearly the obstacles to these multi-dimensional negotiations are many and complex.

The First Nations and Ontario have recently concluded a bilateral agreement for about 90 000 acres of unsold surrendered Indian reserve lands, thereby renewing and completing a treaty concluded at Manitowaning on Manitoulin Island in 1862. This agreement was preceded by almost three years of intensive negotiation and the final settlement was signed early in December 1990 in Toronto. Ontario has also in the past few years signed two natural-resource-development agreements with respect to mining and is currently negotiating a third, more comprehensive, agreement. In 1989 Ontario signed the first environmental-mitigation agreement as well as the first framework agreement in the history of southern Canada; the latter, involving the native people on Walpole Island in Lake St Clair, addresses issues of territoriality and jurisdiction with respect to lands and natural resources. The following year, in April 1990, to avoid a third summer of blockades of the Red Squirrel Road extension in the Lake Temagami area, Ontario signed a memorandum of understanding with the Teme-Augama Anishnabai to develop a stewardship council to protect old-growth pine and to begin negotiations on a treaty of co-existence.

There was even more activity following the election of the New Democratic Party in the fall of 1990. A second land-claim settlement was signed with the Batchewana First Nation for lands at Batchewana Bay which are part of the original Batchewana Indian reserve at Sault Ste Marie. In addition, interim agreements have been signed on hunting and fishing with the Algonquins of Golden Lake. A framework agreement has been signed to negotiate land and a land base for some of the communities north of Lake Superior. Early in 1992 a memorandum of agreement may be signed to begin negotiations to provide a land base for the Caldwell First Nation, which has been landless since the early nineteenth century.

Participation in land claims in Canada and Ontario provides great opportunities to learn about and understand the history and oral traditions of a dynamic and ongoing treaty-making process that is more than two hundred years old. It can also illuminate the reasons for the lack of economic development in native communities, where conditions are often similar to or worse than those in the Third World, and for the rise of native resistance movements. In this regard we need to understand the reasons for the survival and vitality of the culture, traditions, and economy of aboriginal people in spite of the administrative "partition of Ontario" through the government perception and treatment of the land as a frontier rather than as a homeland.

Some Definitions and Problems

The most striking thing about native land claims is the lack of congruence between aboriginal concepts of land and the practice embodied in the process of resolving issues inherent in land claims or land issues. Part of the debate over the past twenty years about land claims in Ontario centres on definition and the key policy questions involving the federal government's categories of land claims. In short, definitions are few; yet the meanings are, unfortunately, many.

The senior (federal) government has a published land-claims policy that divides claims into two basic categories—comprehensive and specific. Briefly, specific claims are basically unfulfilled treaty entitlements that are legally outstanding to the First Nations by Canada. Comprehensive claims are those that cover a large geographic area in which no treaty or other agreement has been signed with the First Nation(s). In the Ontario context, the federal government denies this category entirely. The Ontario government has no published or otherwise stated policy and avoids any categories. Instead Ontario reviews and responds to claims based on the criteria of legal obligations and fairness in an historical context. The process works: about thirty claims were in negotiation over the past decade and only two have been rejected. Even these two are currently being reviewed because the law has changed. The aboriginal people, the claimants, refer to their oral traditions and to the fact or facts of their land claims, avoiding categories to get at the substance of the issues. Given this lack of congruence, it is not surprising that there is much misunderstanding as negotiations proceed at any stage of a claim. Many fruitless hours are spent talking through concepts rather than addressing the issues, merits, and principles of land claims.

What are the merits of land claims and what is their substance or meaning and long-term significance? Land claims are about aboriginal governance and all that means—power and control over one's destiny and the means to achieve that power and control. From a narrow perspective, land claims are statements or assertions of rights or interests in land(s) that are presented to government. More broadly, they are explicit statements of the First Nations' timeless and seamless world view, particularly as it concerns their ancient grievances, present wrongs, and future relationship to lands and natural resources and society as a whole.

This is not a linear view, but rather a holistic one. For example, distinctions in and about time melt away as the universal fact takes precedence over the specific event. Thus statements such as "this is our land" or "you stole our land" take precedence over ones such as "the crown promised that," "the treaty document states that," "this land was used for," "this land was not surveyed in," or "this land was not patented." The general statements capture the timeless, dynamic quality of land claims and their linkage to the power of aboriginal governance. Without a land base that is not fragmented and resources that are not partly or entirely alienated, people have little or no control over their community and its development and self-determination is not possible.

The linkages between land claims and aboriginal governance are real. They epitomize the following components. There is a clear understanding of the past and the spirit and intent of the treaties. There needs to be a process to re-establish a coherent land and natural-resource base where that has been eroded or lacking because of the non-fulfillment and dislocation of aboriginal and treaty rights. Traditional governmental structures and organizations must be recognized and affirmed to have the power to control the present destiny of aboriginal people. Capital and labour are required to plan and build aboriginal communities in the future. In this relationship, present land claims are transforming forms of the past into a dynamic new future.

The fundamental point of divergence between the crown and aboriginal people in Ontario is the European idea, which was inherited by colonial regimes in North America, that the crown holds land for aboriginal people. This was conceived by British imperial policy to protect aboriginal people from, in the words of the Royal Proclamation of 1763, "great frauds and abuses." Although it may have been the intention of the crown to protect aboriginal people and their lands, the concept was predicated as well on the notion of the "commons"—meaning that crown lands were held for all the crown's subjects. Thus, the crown's honour and intentions were effectively split and, in practice, control was exercised by the crown in its "honourable" dealings with all of its subjects over the "commons."

Over time the crown's control was interpreted, as it is today, to mean that land could be severed from the "commons" or from treaty areas or from Indian lands, or Indian reserve lands. In other words, the effect of the crown's policy for aboriginal people was that their land and natural resources were alienated. The vision of an Indian territory affirmed in the Royal Proclamation of 1763 was soon forgotten as the crown turned its attention to the practical task of signing treaties with native people. It remains, however, fundamental to the native campaign for the settlement of land claims and the achievement of self-government.

Diversity of Land Claims
in Ontario

There is a remarkable diversity in Ontario's native land claims because of the variety of treaties and the different crown commitments in them. And there are more than land claims. There are claims to aboriginal rights involving traditional activities of fishing, hunting, trapping, harvesting of wild rice, and gathering. There are treaty entitlements for the same natural-resource activities made both in the treaty documents as well as in oral or "outside" promises. There are treaty entitlements to what were probably seen by the Indian people as relative exotica, such as agricultural implements and oxen. There were promises to Metis as well as status or "registered" Indian people. There were promises of salaries for chiefs and suits of clothing to promote the status of those Indians who were seen as collaborators by non-native authorities and as diplomats, spokesmen, or merely cross-cultural messengers by native people themselves.

Aboriginal claims to land were predicated on the Indian concept of the "Indian territory" and a sharing of the land as understood by the elders in the original treaties. Treaty claims include unfulfilled treaty-land entitlements. Some of these are still outstanding today. The reasons for these claims are many and include administrative changes made after a treaty document was signed that altered the boundaries of a reserve. They also include claims to compensation for the building of roads, the appropriation of shorelines, lakes, and rivers, and the flooding of Indian reserve lands. There are claims for mineral and water rights, as well as larger claims to aboriginal title on the basis either that no treaty was signed or that the specific aboriginal people for whatever reason did not participate in a treaty. The latter category involves land areas covering from 4000 to 25 000 square miles.

The historical record and the oral tradition of aboriginal people both show that the crown made commitments to aboriginal people and there are past injustices with respect to lands and natural resources which have not yet been redressed by the crown. Aboriginal people entered into treaties on the basis of sharing lands and natural resources with the European "newcomers." This is reflected in the treaties as well as in the context of the negotiations and matters related to the treaty or other promises of the crown after the treaties were signed. In keeping with the spirit and intent in which the treaties were signed, native views must be respected and understood today and in the future if there is to be an accommodation between the two peoples. Legal obligations to aboriginal people arising out of land claims should be kept. Alternative procedures for the resolution of land claims and treaty matters under dispute should be developed. Criteria for the resolution of land claims must include cross-cultural perspectives and standards based on the universal concept of "fairness" rather than on an ethnocentric and culture-bound legal system of whatever ilk. Agreement among the different levels of government—Canada, Ontario, First Nations—on the various claims, issues, and approaches to the negotiations should be devised in a mutual way and not imposed by any one of the parties. If possible, land claims should be reviewed and negotiated in a tripartite forum. Research and interpretation of research should be done jointly to overcome initial mistrust and cultural misunderstanding at later stages. To break deadlock in the review process or in the negotiations, various forms of mediation such as fact-finders, facilitators, non-binding mediation—for example, a tribunal such as the Maori Court in New Zealand—can be used. Negotiations should be low profile and should not be conducted through the media; there should be a continual, conscious building of trust and respect through the sharing ideas and information; a process for identifying issues and resolving them at each stage of the negotiations should be developed; the negotiations should recognize the complexity of the issues and develop tolerance for different positions; interim arrangements to protect the negotiations, as well as framework agreements to serve both as touchstones and as benchmarks to measure progress or the lack thereof, should be devised; third-party interests should be kept informed, and along with the wider population, should be involved in discussions of the public-policy dimension of land claims; and finally, the permanence of the negotiation arrangements and the certainty of agreements should be guaranteed. To be successful in negotiations, the parties must recognize that they are embarking on a means of changing the power-sharing relationship between aboriginal people and the crown in the context of aboriginal self-determination and governance.

Current State of Aboriginal Title and Land Claims

The primary case of aboriginal title in the Ontario setting has been the assertion by the Teme-Augama Anishnabai that they hold aboriginal title to about four thousand square miles of territory, identified by them as N'Daki Menan, their tribal motherland, and is located in the northeastern part of Ontario in and around the Lake Temagami area. This is a classic example of aboriginal resistance, unchanging in time. The Supreme Court of Canada, in its decision of August 1991, found against the Teme-Augama Anishnabai. Superficially, it may be concluded on the basis of this ruling that similar assertions may not succeed and should be dismissed out of hand.

This approach would be short-sighted and, moreover, damaging to the new accord between Ontario and the First Nations embodied in the recent bilateral *Statement of Political Relationship.* A key assumption behind this statement is that aboriginal title is a fact; the treaties are dynamic and alive and the aboriginal people of Ontario have the inherent right to govern themselves. With the establishment of these ideas in the policy and legislation of the Ontario government (and perhaps within the next few years, in the Canadian constitution), it is anticipated that the close cultural relationship between aboriginal people and their homelands will be renewed. There will be a shift in the way in which non-aboriginal people, their governments, and their courts will view aboriginal title and the claims of aboriginal people to their territories. So the Temagami case is not yet resolved even though the Supreme Court of Canada has rendered its decision. In a sense there has been a fresh beginning.

The Temagami case rests on the argument of the Teme-Augama Anishnabai that they occupied the lands in question prior to 1763. This has been acknowledged both by the Supreme Court and, at least by implication, by Ontario through a bilateral memorandum of understanding signed in April 1990. The Ontario memorandum recognizes the need for a "treaty of co-existence" between the Teme-Augama Anishnabai and Ontario. Sadly, the federal government did not recognize the aboriginal title and the rights of the Temagami people in the litigation. Thus far it has not participated in any negotiations despite the federal constitutional and fiduciary responsibilities for "Indians, and lands reserved for the Indians" specified in the Constitution Act, 1867.

Aboriginal title was, as a deliberate policy measure, confirmed by the British government through the Royal Proclamation of 1763. The proclamation also established a mechanism as well as a formal process by which Indian lands, including those of the Teme-Augama Anishnabai, could be shared with the crown under the terms of formal agreements between native people and the crown's representatives. The implication is that aboriginal title remained intact. Through the late eighteenth and, one might well add, into the mid-nineteenth century, the Teme-Augama Anishnabai, situated as they were inland from well-travelled non-aboriginal routes along the Great Lakes and connecting waterways, were relatively isolated from Euro-Canadians and their activities. Except for trapping and some logging that began in the 1860s, their homeland remained untouched until early in the twentieth century.

From the late 1830s, the Teme-Augama Anishnabai had come to Manitoulin Island to obtain presents from the crown. However, being few in number, they were not well known or understood by the government. Accordingly, although recognized as a separate group, the Teme-Augama Anishnabai were not considered to be important enough to contact and invite to the meetings of September 1850 that led to the making of the Robinson-Huron Treaty. Moreover, no member of the Teme-Augama Anishnabai, including their "principal or headman" at the time, Peter Nabonagonai, ever signed the treaty or a formal adhesion to such a document. Nevertheless, four days after the conclusion of the treaty, representatives of the Teme-Augama Anishnabai were recorded by government as receiving their initial payment under the treaty, and they continued to receive their annuities for five years thereafter.

It is unknown, either from the written documentation or oral tradition, whether the Teme-Augama Anishnabai believed that they were collecting treaty annuities or whether they saw such payments as nothing more than presents. The giving of presents by the crown was also an act of policy by the British government that was discontinued only in 1858. From the mid-1850s to the late 1870s there is a lacuna of information on relations between the crown and the Teme-Augama Anishnabai, and the natives seem to have been forgotten or overlooked by government officials, likely a sign of what little information the government had about them or their territory prior to the 1880s. In 1877 the Temagami Indians informed their Indian agent that they had not signed a treaty and wished to make arrangements to receive a reserve.

In spite of efforts by the local Indian agent, the treaty-making process in the 1870s and beyond was once again fundamentally flawed. After acceding to the desire of the Temagami Indians for a treaty and lands for a reserve, the federal government unilaterally decided to enrol the Teme-Augami Anishnabai into the Robinson Huron Treaty annuities process from 1883 and to promise their representatives lands at the south end of Lake Temagami in excess of 100 square miles. But at the same time government officials did not provide, mainly because of an absence of records, the back-annuity payments from the period 1856–82. In addition, before making its promise of a reserve, the government did not consult with Ontario officials to determine whether provincial lands for such a reserve were available. And, steadfastly and intractably, the provincial government until the 1980s refused to grant the land because it was getting royalties from logging companies for cutting the valuable red- and white-pine trees in the area. Thus the major goals of the Teme-Augami Anishnabai—a treaty and reserve land—remained unachieved.

Gradually from the 1880s the Teme-Augama Anishnabai were driven off their ancestral lands by governments and non-native private interests, the latter headed by logging companies and the tourism industry. In the middle of the Great Depression of the 1930s the Temagami Indians were forced by Ontario government officials either to buy their own land on Bear Island in Lake Temagami or to face eviction for "squatting" on crown lands without payment of rent. This situation continued until the Teme-Augami Anishnabai took matters into their own hands in 1973 and filed cautions under the Ontario Land Titles Act for approximately 4000 square miles of their lands in the Temagami area. This action has effectively frozen non-native economic development within the land-claim area since that time. Court action was begun in the District Court of Nipissing in 1978 as the Ontario government decided to sue the Teme-

Augama Anishnabai for their own lands, a move reminiscent of its actions in the 1880s and the 1930s. Now that the Supreme Court of Canada has ruled in favour of Ontario, this legal tactic may be used again, notwithstanding the 1990 memorandum of agreement and the current land-claim negotiations.

After the trial court ruled in December 1984 against the Teme-Augama Anishnabai, Ontario, on 30 September 1986, made an offer of settlement; as noted earlier, this offer consisted of a combination of land, cash, and other considerations, the entire package being valued at up to $30 million. One of the conditions placed on the offer by the province, however, was that the court action be suspended for one year so that negotiations could take place. This condition proved to be a major stumbling block to the proposed negotiations and the offer was declined by the Teme-Augama Anishnabai early in 1987. Another obstacle to the negotiations was the role of the federal government, which had been involved in talks with the Temagami Indians under the mediation of the Indian Commission of Ontario in 1981–82. The federal government had supported the claim of the Teme-Augama Anishnabai for over one hundred years and then, near the end of the 1984 trial, had taken an opposite view. Although the federal minister was informed of Ontario's offer of settlement before it was presented in 1986, it is unclear, perhaps even doubtful, whether the federal government would have participated and accepted its equal share of the $30-million offer on the basis of the missing annuity payments between 1856 and 1883 plus interest since 1883. The federal government took the position that the problem here was the treaty entitlement of land and land was a provincial, not a federal, responsibility. The same was true for the Ontario offer of settlement made in February 1989 after the Ontario Appeal Court decided that the Teme-Augama Anishnabai were entitled to one hundred square miles of land at the south end of Lake Temagami, which was an enrichment of the 1986 offer. The Teme-Augama Indians rejected this offer as well. Since April 1990, with the signing of the memorandum of understanding, the Wendaban Stewardship Authority has been established and the treaty of co-existence negotiations have begun. The latter are, to date, still in progress notwithstanding the August 1991 Supreme Court of Canada ruling.

Whether these negotiations can continue is a difficult question given the Supreme Court ruling and the current controversy over the land claims centring on Algonquin Provincial Park that has been put forward by the Algonquin of Golden Lake. It is hard to be optimistic. Moreover, there still remains a deep division between Ontario and the Teme-Augama Anishnabai over the matter of aboriginal title. Ontario continues to hold to the position it advanced before the Supreme Court of Canada, namely that the issue is not one of aboriginal title but rather of treaty-land entitlement. For the Temagami Indians, the province's view and theirs cannot be reconciled. This is a classic case of aboriginal people mounting a resistance campaign that has been hard fought, often tremendously bitter, and partly successful. The actions taken by the Teme-Augama Anishnabai to date have effectively blocked development and thus prevented N'Daki Menan from exploitation by non-aboriginal timber and mining interests.

This resistance movement will likely be seen by historians in the twenty-first century both as a major advance by aboriginal people in protecting the integrity of aboriginal lands, and as a breakthrough for the recognition of aboriginal title and the aboriginal understanding of the treaty-making process. It may be viewed similarly to the way in which we now view the Riel resistance movements of 1869–70 and 1885. In this scenario the denial of the Bear Island case may one day be seen as a failure of Euro-Canadian courts in addressing significant aboriginal issues, just as the Donald Marshall and the Manitoba Justice inquiries highlighted the injustices suffered by native people at the hands of the judicial and law-enforcement systems.

It is significant that, in Ontario, most land claims are subject to negotiation rather than litigation. Although this may soon change given the growing gap between the rhetoric of the federal government and the reality of what is necessary to be accomplished on a wide number of issues, only one claim has been in litigation thus far—a fact that may indicate the extreme forbearance of aboriginal people. It is also significant that the elders have chosen not to speak out on the Bear Island case despite the negative result. From this perspective, after more than one hundred and forty years the struggle for N'Daki Menan is not over. In the "land-claims business" there are too many beginnings and too few endings.

There are other aboriginal title claims in Ontario. Besides the Teme-Augama Anishnabai, there are at least three other First Nations in the area north of Lake Superior that were clearly not present at the treaty negotiations and did not sign the Robinson Superior Treaty of September 1850 or any other treaty with the crown. A negotiation process is now in place and negotiations are expected to begin soon with many of the native communities in the area. Another claim, already mentioned, is that of the Algonquins of Golden Lake.

There are also aboriginal-title issues regarding the beds and the waters of the Great Lakes that have been used extensively by the First Nations and that have never been the subject of the treaty-making process. One of the best examples is the assertion of the Walpole Island First Nation that their title and rights to their territory arise from the Royal Proclamation of 1763. The territory includes the bed and the waters of the southern portion of the St Clair River and Lake St Clair to the Canadian side of the international boundary, except for a few islands already surrendered and part of a channel for the St Lawrence Seaway built in the late 1950s. The Walpole Island territory has never been surrendered or subject to the treaty-making process. This includes the islands that have erroneously been perceived by governments to be the narrow boundaries of the Indian reserve known over the years as Walpole Island Indian Reserve #46. That reserve has never been surveyed or set apart by the crown as an Indian reserve. Thus the reserve is, in fact, coterminous (exceptions aside, noted above) with the territory immediately around it and is thus a pure manifestation of aboriginal title, much like the outstanding claims of the Wikwemikong First Nation to the eastern part of Manitoulin Island and the islands adjacent. Similar claims have been made to the bed and the waters of the other Great Lakes and the St Lawrence River and connecting waterways.

The Walpole Island First Nation, Canada, and Ontario signed a framework agreement on this matter on 19 January 1989 to begin negotiations. Three subagreements were negotiated and approved on interim arrangements and air-quality and water-quality monitoring on 30 October 1991, and it is expected that these will be signed soon. Although the story is not yet over, it has not, like so many others, been marred by sadness and tragedy. Rather, it has been characterized by resistance and survival.

With the signing of the framework agreement in 1989, the Walpole Island First Nation, Canada, and Ontario embarked on substantive negotiations to resolve matters with respect to the Walpole Island Indian territory. This is the first framework agreement on such specific matters to be signed in the history of southern Ontario, and it came after nine years of research, policy review, and negotiation. The framework agreement was jointly announced by the parties at a media conference at Walpole Island on Tuesday, 11 April 1989. The announcement was well received at the local and provincial levels. Other subjects listed in the agreement as items to be negotiated include the boundaries of the Walpole Island territory, ownership and management of subsurface resources, wildlife harvesting rights, wildlife management, water quality and environmental protection, navigation and shoreline erosion, and enforcement of applicable laws. Considering the complexity and scope of the subject matter before the parties, the negotiations will probably last several years. Chief Dan Miskokomon rightly stated on the signing of the framework agreement that "this is an act of great historic importance." He added: "The waters in dispute have been vital to us for thousands of years and we know that this territory has continued to remain under our jurisdiction. We believe that commencing these negotiations in a spirit of mutual respect is a positive way to seek a resolution to a number of very important issues in a peaceful, co-operative manner. I believe we have a genuine chance to advance our common concerns while expanding the opportunities for our people."

Negotiations have also started (June 1991) on the claim of the Algonquins of Golden Lake that they hold aboriginal title to their territory and homeland in the Ottawa valley. As with the Walpole Island claim, the complexity of the issues and the large geographic area included in the Golden Lake claim (one-third of the area, including Algonquin Provincial Park, is in Ontario and two-thirds in Quebec) mean that the negotiations will take many years to complete. The modern assertion of the claim was presented in 1977 and to date federal officials still have not joined the Ontario government at the negotiating table. From this, it can be seen that claims can be innately political creatures and are at bottom treated as such by governments. The reactions of governments run the gamut from outright denial by the Ontario Tories in the 1970s to acceptance by the New Democratic Party in the 1990s.

Each claim has its own very different history and its own special merits. So one hesitates to develop categories that always act as blinkers and perimeters on policy development; moreover, no sooner is a category developed than an exception to it is discovered. For example, after the summer events at Oka, the federal government, which had ruled against the claim on the basis of policy principles, began negotiating a settlement on other grounds to resolve the matter without further bloodshed. Thus the federal government's practice over the past fifteen years of developing policies on the basis of categories to evaluate claims is completely unnecessary. It is better to have no policy and a flexible, sensitive approach with clear criteria based on legal obligations and a concept of fairness in a cross-cultural context. It is always tempting to rationalize existing practice but in the end such arguments serve only to distort cultural reality and ignore the diversity of aboriginal people. And this is particularly true for Ontario's aboriginal history.

The federal government discovered the fallibility of the process of categorization about a decade ago when it said that there were only two categories of claims—specific and comprehensive—and developed a policy for each. The categories and then the policy suffered from their inherent contradictions and from the criticisms of aboriginal people, and gradually the entire edifice fell apart. Responding to the Kanesatake claim recently, the federal government has "invented" a new category of claim that is to be judged on the basis of something called "injustice," which could be applied to any claim, anywhere. In doing so, it is missing a major point about the history and the significance of all land claims. They are all ancient grievances beyond the boundaries of time in the context of oral traditions and thus are all characterized by some form of "injustice." This is not a criterion that can be used to evaluate land claims. In point of fact, there are only two questions that need be asked about the merits of land claims, but nonetheless they are profound: Was it legal? and according to whose justice system? And was it fair?

Notwithstanding the caveats referred to above, there are forms of and claims that can be outlined on the basis of the history of the aboriginal people. These can be stated simply as:

- No treaty or agreement signed with aboriginal people for their territory;
- Aboriginal people are not signatories to a treaty or other agreement;
- Unfulfilled treaty-land entitlements;
- Surrendered Indian-reserve-land issues;
- Compensation, or the lack thereof, for roads and highways or other rights of way through Indian reserve or treaty lands;
- Flooding of Indian reserve or treaty lands;
- Invalidity of a treaty or a land surrender or cession;
- Taking of treaty lands and rights without an agreement;
- Errors in the location of boundaries of Indian reserve lands;
- Maladministration of Indian lands and trust funds holding compensation for lands after the signing of a treaty or agreement.

Whatever the form or style of claim, aboriginal people have not, in my experience, advanced spurious or frivolous ones. To do so would discredit the meritorious claims and moreover would deny their own oral tradition, heritage, and culture. The claims all have merit in some way based on past injustice and current experience.

Over the past twenty years or so, no more then a small handful of land claims have resulted in settlement agreements. Only one, the Temagami case, has been through the expensive and inconclusive process of litigation, and in that instance the court indicated that the nations were owed something under the treaty and negotiations are taking place. There have been a few bilateral settlements between the First Nations and the federal government and one between the First Nations and Ontario. However, the federal government's settlements have been relatively small in scale—up to about $3 million. No others have broken through this fiscal policy barrier although one is getting closer, the Whitefish Island land claim at Sault Ste Marie. The Ontario government's settlement in December 1990 with the United Chiefs and Councils of Manitoulin was for land and cash compensation worth $9.3 million for about 90 000 acres. This settlement came after years of initial work and litigation as well as almost three years of active negotiations that initially included the federal government and in the end did not.

This is a living testament to the policies of the current federal government and to the fact that since 1986 Ontario has not been a priority area for the settlement of land claims. It accounts for the view that "nobody cares" about land claims, which was widely held before the full force of aboriginal resistance was felt in 1990. Instructively, the government's priorities are beginning to change. Land claims acquired a new currency after August 1990 and were, ironically, deemed to be legitimate. Whether this trend continues remains to be seen. However, there is no doubt that if it does it will be the result of continuing resistance by aboriginal people.

Non-Aboriginal Responses
to Land Claims

Although land claims have only recently achieved a greater prominence, such is not the case with private "third parties" that may have a direct or an indirect interest in the outcome of land-claim negotiations. Over the last two decades there has been a dichotomy between, on the one hand, the high public support shown in the opinion polls for land claims and aboriginal issues in general, and, on the other, the local reactions of certain private interests that may be couched in language that has racial overtones. They see aboriginal peoples' interests in a direct contradiction to their own, whether that is true or not, and sometimes work actively to undermine the negotiations. Public support of native people in opinion polls does not automatically translate into tangible results in negotiations. The best example occurred in the spring of 1991 in Ontario when the province announced that it would begin discussions with the Algonquins of Golden Lake on their land claim. Fortunately, despite ignorance and a lack of public education, the negotiations are continuing. This is a tribute to the perspicacity and tenacity of the representatives of the aboriginal people who had to wait fourteen years for the beginning of negotiations. For the most part, it has been the aboriginal people themselves who have taken on the challenge of informing and educating non-aboriginal people and third-party interests before, during, and after the negotiations. It is unlikely, for example, that a settlement of the Manitoulin Island claim would have been achieved without the primary role played by the United Chiefs and Councils of Manitoulin Island.

Generally third-party interests have three major concerns. These are usually expressed in the following statements. "We support aboriginal people but any negotiations to bring about change should begin elsewhere first we are not ready and we want to participate directly in the negotiations." This is the argument that "change is too painful now." The second is that all "Canadians are equal" and aboriginal people are no different. And even if they choose to be different, they are wrong—they should want to be like the rest of us. This is at best an assimilationist view. The third argument is a complete denial of our history and the place of natives in it: "Aboriginal people were conquered and the treaties made by the Government with them have little or no validity and they should not get any special rights of treatment." This is often framed in the blunt statement that aboriginal people should "pay like the rest of us." The reality is that aboriginal people have paid and paid and paid again over the centuries with the alienation of their land and labour.

None of these arguments can be sustained. Still, governments have done relatively little to respond to them or to inform and educate the public on these matters. This is a serious omission and it must change. In fact, third-party arguments are actively fostered, perhaps unwittingly, by governments in policy statements which indicate that third-party interests will not be affected by any settlement, thereby contributing to the illusion that no change to the social or economic status of aboriginal people is either possible or desirable. Unless there is a radical, active new approach to third-party interests, all the support in public-opinion polls will be for naught and many current land-claim negotiations will founder much like the aborted Ontario fishing negotiations in 1982 and in 1986–87.

Although public opinion continues to show a high degree of support for native demands, especially for a limited form of "self-government on a municipal model," this may reflect only a lack of understanding of aboriginal people themselves, their history, cultures, and aspirations. The aboriginal perception of "sovereignty" is not at all understood and is continually misrepresented in the constitutional discussions. It is easy to support a general idea that seems to have little or no meaning and is based on abstract notions of equality and rights. However, native peoples' land claims and their concept of the inherent right of self-government are very specific and are always part and parcel of their relationship with the land—and the land, to them, is immutable, coherent, and concrete in focus. There is therefore a fundamental and dangerous dichotomy growing between non-aboriginal support of native people and the fears and desires of third-party interests.

In Ontario this dichotomy recently manifested itself in the concern about Algonquin Provincial Park and the Algonquins of Golden Lake who have always hunted and fished and trapped in the park. There is something primeval about the debate that evokes what Professor Northrup Frye called the "garrison mentality." There has also been on the other side a growing frustration and bitterness among aboriginal people about the prospects of social and economic change in the future. This is compounded by what has been termed the profundity of despair wrought by community dislocation and aboriginal peoples' responses to that dislocation. When governments fail to respond to the demands of aboriginal people for the same quality of life enjoyed by their non-aboriginal neighbours, native despair deepens. This trend will likely be exacerbated by the continuing constitutional debate.

Prospects

It is not easy to resolve land claims that have been outstanding for more than two hundred years. For example, it took almost ten years, depending on one's involvement and perspective, to begin the Manitoulin Island negotiations in February 1988. Then it took almost three years of intensive negotiations, without much support or resources, to reach an agreement. The agreement was a tribute to the two aboriginal people who acted as negotiators for the United Chiefs and Councils of Manitoulin Island and the Ontario government, Albert (Hardy) Peltier and Mark Stevenson respectively. And this type of land-claim negotiation is relatively devoid of conflict compared to, say, the Temagami or Bear Island claim, which, fraught by fourteen years of litigation and community strife, has taken almost twenty years to reach the negotiating table. The prospects for fair and just settlements in the foreseeable future are immensely clouded by the negative racial attitudes of non-aboriginal people and by third-party interests. Both can only see themselves as "losers" and aboriginal people as "winners" in what they mistakenly see as a zero-sum game. It is not surprising that aboriginal people are realistic and expect very, very little to change in their communities for the better in the immediate future. At this point, it is not certain that "progress," especially material progress, has been achieved.

The renewal of the flawed treaty-making process has been enormously painful and slow. Perhaps this has been unavoidable. In Ontario, after the events at Oka in 1990, the process requires renewal in order to restore the peaceful relationship between natives and non-natives. With no effective federal government presence in the area of Ontario land claims—the priority is now the province of British Columbia—"business as usual" in this context means a "closed land-claims shop" at least in the foreseeable future. Given the major obstacles, it is likely that there will be a staggering increase in the costs of resolving land claims in Ontario outside negotiations, particularly through the expensive litigation route. There will be many more "Temagamis" soon. This will have a substantial negative impact on the upcoming constitutional discussions, as we have seen from the failure of "executive federalism" in the Meech Lake Accord debate of June 1990. Ontarians, both aboriginal and non-aboriginal, can no longer afford to delay coming to terms with native issues.

Retrospect

Land claims in Ontario are, in short, in a precarious balance between negotiation and litigation, subject to passive and active native-resistance movements and government policy and inaction. Whether they can continue in their present form is debatable. What is certain is that aboriginal people have many outstanding land grievances flowing from a more than two-hundred-year-old treaty-making process that is flawed and must be changed. Tenaciously, aboriginal people hold to their concept of aboriginal title and the rights flowing from it. This, they will never relinquish. To use the words of Chief Mawedopenais, a prominent spokesman in the Treaty 3 negotiations of 1873: "Our hands are poor but our heads are rich, and it is riches that we ask so that we may be able to support our families as long as the sun rises and the water runs." The native position is clear: they understand the significance of "their birthright, and lands" and expect that "promises" made by the crown will be kept forever.

Documents

A. Agreement with Walpole Island First Nation

Press Release, 11 April 1989

Representatives of Walpole Island First Nation, Canada and Ontario announced today the signing of a "Framework Agreement" to begin negotiations on issues of mutual concern regarding the location of the boundaries of the Walpole Island Indian Reserve #46.

This is the first "Framework Agreement", which addresses identified issues, to be signed by Canada, Ontario and a First Nation in the history of this Province.

Walpole Island First Nation is special. The First Nation has never signed a Treaty with the Crown for the Lake St. Clair–St. Clair River area. However, there have been surrenders of a few specific areas such as the Southeast Bend Cut-off Channel.

The area known as Walpole, and adjacent islands in Lake St. Clair and marshlands immediately south of the islands, have been administered as Indian Reserve land for over 150 years. However, the location of the boundaries of the Indian Reserve have never been surveyed or clearly defined.

The parties involved have different positions on the location of the boundaries of the Reserve.

The Walpole Island First Nation has stated for many years, that their Reserve includes most of the water, islands, marshlands and the land under the water in Lake St. Clair, the southern part of the St. Clair River and the Chenail Ecarte.

The Honourable Ian Scott, Minister Responsible for Native Affairs for Ontario, indicated that Ontario has taken the view that the area of the Reserve only includes the islands and the marshlands south of the islands. Canada agrees with the First Nation concerning part of its boundary while being uncertain as to the balance.

The objective of the proposed negotiations is to clarify and define with greater certainty the boundaries of Walpole Island Reserve #46.

Ontario, the First Nation and the Federal Government will also discuss other issues, including environmental planning and protection, air and water quality, navigation and shoreline erosion, policing, the enforcement of applicable laws and wildlife conservation.

Mr. Scott stated that one of the first items contemplated for these negotiations is environmental planning and protection.

By 1990, the parties hope to reach an agreement in principle on a plan to protect the environment in the Lake St. Clair area. It is expected the parties will, in part, focus on monitoring and improving air and water quality in the area.

Framework Agreements have been signed in other areas of Canada to facilitate negotiations intended to assist in the resolution of issues between Governments and aboriginal people. Such agreements are used to assist and guide the parties in their negotiations on matters which the parties agree are of mutual concern.

Chief Dan Miskokomon of the Walpole Island First Nation stated: "Signing this framework Agreement is an act of great historic importance to the Walpole Island First Nation and the negotiations to follow are one of our highest priorities. We must move forward quickly and effectively to reach practical agreements to protect our fragile environment before it is completely destroyed." Chief Miskokomon went on to say that, "The waters in dispute have been vital to us for thousands of years and we know that this territory has continued to remain under our jurisdiction. We believe that commencing these negotiations in the spirit of mutual respect is a positive way to seek a resolution to a number of very important issues in a peaceful, co-operative manner. I believe we have a genuine chance to advance our common concerns while expanding the opportunities for our people."

Framework Agreement, 19 January 1989

WHEREAS all three parties have participated in discussions for a number of years designed to resolve the boundaries of Walpole Island Indian Reserve No. 46.

WHEREAS all three parties agree that the territory marked in red on the map attached hereto as Schedule A has never been surrendered with the exception of the areas identified in Schedule B by the Walpole Island Band or subject to a treaty.

WHEREAS all three parties recognize the importance of the need to address certain critical issues described herein

AND WHEREAS all three parties are desirous of negotiating a satisfactory resolution to these matters

THE PARTIES HERETO make the following commitment

1.   The Parties hereby declare their commitment to enter into tripartite negotiations to resolve outstanding issues relating to the scope and exercise of their respective jurisdiction and powers in the territory marked in red on the map attached hereto and forming part of this agreement.

2.   The Parties agree that the tripartite discussions shall be without prejudice to their respective positions and shall include discussion of the location of the precise boundaries of Walpole Island Indian Reserve No. 46, and shall also include discussions concerning the following issues, among others, throughout the entire territory in question:

(a) ownership and management of sub-surface resources;
(b) wildlife harvesting rights;
(c) wildlife management;
(d) water quality and environmental protection;
(e) navigation and shoreline erosion; and
(f) enforcement of applicable laws.

3.   The Parties agree to do whatever is necessary to confirm the Reserve that may be agreed to as a "reserve" within the meaning of the Indian Act.

4.   The Parties agree to take whatever action is necessary to request necessary ratification of any agreement(s) reached through this process in a manner appropriate to each Party with the intention that such agreement(s) will be legally enforceable by any Party after all Parties have ratified such agreement(s).

5.   This Agreement and all commitments contained herein shall come into force on the date of its execution and shall continue in force unless terminated by one or more of the Parties after having given six (6) months notice in writing to the other Parties hereto.

6.   The Parties agree that this Agreement shall not preclude and shall be without prejudice to any other tripartite or bilateral discussions between the parties.

7.   The Parties agree that nothing in this Agreement shall be construed so as to effect, derogate from or abrogate aboriginal, treaty, constitutional or any other rights of the Walpole Island Band and its members or of Ontario or Canada.

8.   The Parties further agree that all reasonable effort will be made to negotiate and conclude agreement(s) that resolve the issues indicated in paragraph 2 above in a spirit of goodwill and good faith.

B. Teme-Augama Anishnabai Stewardship Agreement

Press Release, 23 April 1990

An historic agreement, the first of its kind in North America, was signed today by the Government of Ontario and the Teme-Augama Anishnabai (The Deep Water People). The agreement provides for joint stewardship of about 40,000 hectares in the Temagami forest.

Timber-cutting licences for the Temagami area were also issued today. No approvals have been granted for the areas to be included in the stewardship agreement—the district townships of Delhi, Acadia, Shelburne and Canton. This area includes 3,800 hectares of old red and white pine.

"This step represents the kind of partnership that we are seeking with all those who have an interest in the resources of the area," said Natural Resources Minister Lyn McLeod. "The stewardship council that we are establishing for these four townships will allow us to work together to determine the best way to manage those lands."

The council will include equal numbers of representatives appointed by the Teme-Augama Anishnabai and the provincial government. Future decisions about management of those four townships will be made by the council. The Teme-Augama Anishnabai will also review timber management plans for other areas of the forest.

"This is the first time in 113 years that the Teme-Augama Anishnabai is signing a document that begins the process toward our vision of co-existence and certainty for the future life of n'Daki-Menan," said Chief Gary Potts. "We applaud the courage the Ontario government has shown in taking this first step," he added.

"The creation of the stewardship council shows that the province's commitment to native self-government, including the co-operative management of natural resources, is real and not theoretical," said Ian Scott, Minister Responsible for Native Affairs. "Our guidelines for aboriginal self-government are another example of our commitment to this process."

The four townships include 1,805 hectares of forest that were identified in the interim timber management plans for harvest.

The approved licences account for 7,386 hectares identified for harvest and will provide a timber supply to nine mills.

"Recognizing that the agreement will have an impact on the operations of some mills in the area, the provincial government will meet with local businesses to address short-term and long-term wood supply needs," Mrs. McLeod said.

The Temagami/Timiskaming Coordinating Committee, a group consisting of representatives of several government ministries, will continue work to address current economic conditions in the Temagami area.

The Lake Temagami area, an hour's drive north of North Bay, is one of the province's most beautiful natural areas. The unique quality of the region's interconnecting lakes and rivers, mixed forests and rugged landforms have inspired a long tradition of wilderness appreciation.

The natural resources of Temagami have long supported tourism, industry and recreation. More than 3,000 people live and work in the Temagami area, and thousands more visit each year.

Memorandum of Understanding

WHEREAS Ontario and the Teme-Augama Anishnabai agree to work toward a Treaty of Co-Existence so that our peoples can live in harmony;

AND WHEREAS Stewardship of the land will form a Fundamental Basis of Co-Existence;

AND WHEREAS the Stewardship of the Teme-Augama Anishnabai Homeland is crucial to the future of all peoples of Ontario;

AND WHEREAS participation of the Teme-Augama Anishnabai is essential;

THEREFORE, INITIALLY, IT IS RESOLVED THAT for the four townships of Delhi, Acadia, Shelburne, and Canton:

    a) a Stewardship Council will be created;

    b) the Council will be made up as follows: 50% Council members appointed by the Teme-Augama Anishnabai and 50% appointed by Ontario, and a neutral chair agreed to by both Ontario and the Teme-Augama Anishnabai;

    c) no timber licences will be issued without the approval of the Stewardship Council;

    d) the parties agree to establish an evaluation process;

    e) the parties agree to jointly review the results of this evaluation to facilitate their consideration of the possibility of extending the concept of shared stewardship to n'Daki-Menan.

An interim bi-lateral process is agreed to. It involves:

    a) the Teme-Augama Anishnabai examining and consulting with the Ministry of Natural Resources on the Latchford and Temagami Crown Management Unit Plans;

    b) the Teme-Augama Anishnabai making recommendations as to how the plans should be modified;

    c) the Ministry of Natural Resources undertaking to modify the plans where feasible.

The Ministry of Natural Resources will provide the Teme-Augama Anishnabai with the timber management plans covering the balance of the Teme-Augama Anishnabai lands with a view to further consultation and modification possibilities for 1991 and beyond.

FURTHER IT IS RESOLVED THAT core funding for three years consistent with the above will be provided to the Teme-Augama Anishnabai to meet their monetary needs for the Stewardship Council, the bi-lateral process as stated herein, and the Treaty Negotiation process.

FINALLY, it is agreed that all three processes will proceed concurrently.

. . . .

C. Ontario and the First Nations: A New Relationship

Press Release, 6 August 1991

THUNDER BAY—Ontario and the Chiefs of First Nations in Ontario have ratified a new political relationship in which the province and First Nations will now deal on a government-to-government basis.

The Statement of Political Relationship was signed today by Premier Bob Rae and Gord Peters, Ontario Regional Chief of the Chiefs of Ontario as well as Bud Wildman, Ontario Minister Responsible for Native Affairs and 11 Chiefs representing regional First Nations organizations and independent First Nations.

The intent and wording of the document is the result of several months of negotiations between Ontario and the First Nations, represented by the Chiefs of Ontario. Now that the document is signed, Ontario and the First Nations will begin a process of consultation on ways in which the principles in the Statement of Political Relationship can be put into practice.

The Statement of Political Relationship recognizes that the First Nations in Ontario have an inherent right to be self-governing within the Canadian Constitution. The document is a commitment by Ontario that it will deal with the First Nations as governments and that it will work to make self-government a reality.

The Chiefs of First Nations' organizations and independent First Nations who signed the document were:

Ontario Regional Chief Gord Peters, Chiefs of Ontario; Grand Chief Joe Miskokomon, Union of Ontario Indians: Grand Chief Steve Fobister, Grand Council Treaty #3; Grand Chief Harry Doxtator, Association of Iroquois and Allied Indians; Grand Chief Bentley Cheechoo, Nishnawbe-Aski Nation; Grand Chief Mike Mitchell, Mohawks of Akwesasne First Nation; Chief William Montour, Six Nations of the Grand River First Nation; Chief Roy McDonald, Islington First Nation; Chief Howard Pamajewon, Shawanaga First Nation; Chief Gary Potts, Teme-Augama Anishnabai First Nation; Chief Robert Williams, Ojibways of Walpole Island First Nation; Chief George St. German, Chippewas of Rama First Nation; and Chief Doug Sinoway, Whitesand First Nation.

The signing took place on Mount McKay on the Fort William First Nation near Thunder Bay.

Statement of Political Relationship

WHEREAS the First Nations represented by the Chiefs-in-Assembly (hereinafter "the First Nations") exist in Ontario as distinct nations, with their governments, cultures, languages, traditions, customs and territories;

AND WHEREAS the Government of Ontario (hereinafter "Ontario") recognizes that its relationships with the First Nations are to be based on the aboriginal rights, including aboriginal title, and treaty rights of the First Nations recognized and affirmed in the *Constitution Act, 1982*, including those formally recognized in the Royal Proclamation of 1763, and in the treaties and agreements with the Crown;

AND WHEREAS Ontario's commitment to and participation in this Statement of Political Relationship is subject to the limits on provincial constitutional authority;

AND WHEREAS it is desirable to minimize conflicts between Ontario and the First Nations;

AND WHEREAS the First Nations and Ontario recognize the need for a mutual understanding of the government(s) to government relationships between them;

Now therefore the First Nations and Ontario agree as follows:

1.   The inherent right to self-government of the First Nations flows from the Creator and from the First Nations' original occupation of the land.

2.   Ontario recognizes that under the Constitution of Canada the First Nations have an inherent right to self-government within the Canadian constitutional framework and that the relationship between Ontario and the First Nations must be based upon a respect for this right.

3.   The First Nations and Ontario—involving the Government of Canada where appropriate—are committed to facilitate the further articulation, the exercise and the implementation of the inherent right to self-government within the Canadian constitutional framework, by respecting existing treaty relationships, and by using such means as the treaty-making process, constitutional and legislative reform and agreements acceptable to the First Nations and Ontario.

4.   Nothing in this Statement of Political Relationship shall be construed as determining Ontario's jurisdiction or as diminishing Canada's responsibilities towards First Nations.

5.   This Statement of Political Relationship expresses the political commitment of the First Nations and Ontario and is not intended to be a treaty or to create, redefine or prejudice rights or affect obligations of

the First Nations or Ontario, or the aboriginal and non-aboriginal peoples in Ontario.

References

Bear Island et al. v. *The Attorney General for the Province of Ontario. Reasons for Judgment*, 15 August 1991.

Bill 200, *An Act to Confirm a Certain Agreement between the Governments of Canada and Ontario*, chapter 26, 20 June 1989, *Statutes of Ontario* (Toronto 1989). [This is the first modern legislation on Indian lands and territories and is known as the Lands Agreement Legislation. It provides authority to negotiate surrendered Indian reserve-lands agreements. Similar legislation has been passed by the federal government.]

Bray, Matt, and Ashley Thompson, ed. *Temagami: A Debate on the Wilderness.* Toronto: Dundurn Press 1990, 147–51.

"First Nations and Governments of Canada, Ontario to Negotiate Land-related Matters." Press Release, Ontario Native Affairs Secretariat, 5 August 1991.

Gautreau, J. *Regina* v. *Ireland and Jamieson. Judgment*, cited in *Ontario Reports*, third series, vol. 1, 1991, 577–92. [This recent case involving hunting in southwestern Ontario affirms the land rights of the Iroquois Confederacy set out in a treaty signed in 1701 with the British crown. According to the judgment, Indian lands and their use of their lands and territories are not severable. Similarly, aboriginal land and treaty rights are effectively inseparable from land claims within Indian territory.]

"Governments Sign Agreement with Walpole Island First Nation." Press Release, Ontario Native Affairs Secretariat, 11 April 1989, including a copy of the framework agreement and appendices, 19 January 1989.

"Interim Enforcement Policy Statement to the Legislature by the Honourable Bud Wildman, Minister of Natural Resources, Minister Responsible for Native Affairs," 20 May 1991 (Ministry of Natural Resources). [This statement also included reference to the land claim of the Algonquins of Golden Lake and related interim agreements with respect to Algonquin Provincial Park.]

"Lac La Croix First Nation. Statement to the Legislature by the Honourable Bud Wildman," 3 June 1991 (Ministry of Natural Resources).

Minutes of the General Council of Indian Chiefs and Principal Men Held at Orillia, Lake Simcoe Narrows on Thursday, the 30th and Friday the 31st July, 1846 . . . (Montreal 1846).

Morris, Alexander. *The Treaties of Canada with the Indians.* Toronto 1880; Coles reprint 1971, 52–76.

"Ontario and First Nations Sign the Statement of Political Relationship." Press Release, Ontario Native Affairs Secretariat, 6 August 1991.

"Ontario and Manitoulin Island Chiefs Sign Historic Land Claim Settlement." Press Release, Ontario Native Affairs Secretariat, 5 December 1990.

"Ontario Offers Land to Enlarge Long Lake #58 Indian Reserve." Press Release, Ontario Native Affairs Secretariat, 2 November 1990.

"Province and Teme-Augama Anishnabai Sign Historic Stewardship Agreement." Press Release, Ontario Native Affairs Secretariat, 23 April 1990, including a copy of the memorandum of understanding, 23 April 1990.

Richardson, Boyce, ed. *Drumbeat: Anger and Renewal in Indian Country*. The Assembly of First Nations and Summerhill Press 1989, 11–20, 108–11.

Trainor, J. *Her Majesty the Queen* v. *Wayne Taylor and Douglas Williams. Reasons for Judgment*, 13 December 1979. [The crown's appeal of this judgment was rejected by the Ontario Court of Appeal and the Supreme Court of Canada denied the crown's leave to appeal in 1982. See also *Regina* v. *Ireland and Jamieson*.]

"Transcript of Remarks by Premier Bob Rae to the Assembly of First Nations Banquet," University of Toronto, Tuesday, October 2, 1990" (Ontario Native Affairs Secretariat).

Aboriginal Land Claims
in Quebec

Toby Morantz

$\mathbf{A}$rchaeological research has established that Indians occupied the southern regions of what is now Quebec by at least six thousand years ago and probably earlier.[1] In the central regions, glacier-free only some five thousand years ago, there are the remains of Indians hunters from about thirty-five hundred years before the present.[2] As for the farthest northern regions of Quebec, Nunavik, the pre-Dorset peoples first came south to that area about four thousand years ago.[3] With indisputable evidence such as this, it seems unnecessary to have to undergo long negotiations or court procedures to demonstrate that the first peoples of Quebec were the Indians and the Inuit. For the aboriginal people themselves, they must find it strange to have to prove that their ancestors were here prior to 1534, when Micmac and Iroquois greeted Cartier and his men on their sailing into the Baie des Chaleurs, or to 1608, the date of the establishment of Champlain's first permanent settlement. Nevertheless, as clear as the native claim is, the Canadian bureaucracy and judicial system have fabricated a complex context that obscures the historical record.

Present-day Quebec was carved out of territory that once belonged to the Inuit and ten Indian peoples, namely, the Micmac, Malecite, Montagnais, Huron, Abenaki, Atikamekw, Algonquin, Cree, Naskapi, and Mohawk. Of these, the Huron and Mohawk are Iroquoian-speaking peoples whose main pre-contact economic activity was maize horticulture; the others are Algonquian-speaking peoples who lived primarily by hunting and fishing. Quebec acquired hegemony over its expanse of land in several stages and under two different mother countries, and this in part explains why there developed a variety of legal arrangements that govern the conditions under which the land is held by the Inuit and Indians. Canadians of European origin view the question of land claims as a matter of land ownership, but the aboriginal peoples never thought of land only as real property *per se* but rather as geographical zones in which they could control their rights to certain activities, be they fishing, hunting, or commerce, without external restrictions. Thus, as one anthropologist has stated, land is viewed as a "unit of management."[4] Therefore, land disputes in Quebec involve not just native claims to ancestral territories but also rights to engage in specific activities. Often these predate the land disputes.

There were no land-cession treaties[5] in Quebec until recently. The land was gradually appropriated by settlers and then by the provincial government as timber, mining, and then hydroelectric interests forced it eventually to assert its control over all the lands deeded it by the federal government, a development that was completed only about thirty years ago (1962) when Quebec established a government ministry, the Direction générale du Nouveau Quebec, and began to take an active interest in the northern lands and their people. This was a dramatic turnaround from the 1930s when the Quebec-based Inuit became a political football between the two levels of government. Neither wished to take on the financial responsibility for the Inuit and Quebec appealed to the Supreme Court. The decision, handed down in 1939, stated that indeed "Eskimos are Indians" and therefore responsibility for them lay with the federal and not the provincial government.[6]

The Acquisition of Native Land

In the era of New France no treaties covering the area of modern Quebec were signed because the French believed that their rights to the territory had been gained through "discovery and conquest."[7] What they offered the native people they encountered was the opportunity to become "Francisised," that is, both French and Catholic. A 1627 charter for the Company of One Hundred Associates allowed Indians to become French citizens if they converted to Catholicism.[8] Practically speaking, however, the French government was never forced into making treaties with native people because the small number of French colonists rendered unnecessary the acquisition of large expanses of land. When New

France was ceded to England in 1763, it had a grand total of seventy thousand people compared to the two and a half million in the British-American colonies to the south.[9]

Yet France did recognize some form of aboriginal title. Article XL of the articles of capitulation in 1760 reads in part: "The Savages or Indian allies of his most Christian Majesty, shall be maintained in the Lands they inhabit; if they chose to remain there, they shall not be molested on any pretence whatsoever, for having carried arms, and served his most Christian Majesty; they shall have, as well as the French, liberty of religion, and shall keep their missionaries."[10] No matter how this is interpreted, it is a fact that the British conquerors of New France did recognize Indian title to the land. The Royal Proclamation of 1763, issued by King George III of England, was partly intended to establish a single Indian policy that would provide security for the British colonies. The proclamation set out how native land was to be acquired (by purchase) but at the same time reserved the natives' "hunting territories" for their use until such time as treaties were made. Accordingly, it served to "promote and clarify the *pre-existing and conceded* rights [emphasis mine] of Indian people rather than to "create" some "new" native right."[11] That these provisions applied to Quebec is made clear in the instructions sent to Governor James Murray of Quebec in 1763. These read: "Whereas We have, by our Proclamation dated the seventh day of October in the Third Year of Our Reign, strictly forbid, on the pain of Our Displeasure, all Our Subjects from making any Purchases or Settlements whatever, or taking Possession of any of the Lands reserved to the several Nations of Indians, with whom We are connected, and who live under Our Protection, without Our especial Leave for that Purpose . . . ."[12] Recognition of Indian rights to these lands was once again made plain in 1775 in instructions to Governor Guy Carleton following the Quebec Act of 1774.

Quebec's boundaries were altered several times in the politically turbulent eighteenth century, the last change occurring in 1791 when the Constitutional Act provided for the creation of the provinces of Upper and Lower Canada. However, the northern boundary, which undoubtedly was of little interest to anyone at that time because the vast territory beyond it was unsuitable for agriculture, remained the same. Not well defined, it seems to have run to the south of the height of land and excluded the Abitibi region.[13] Beyond was Rupert's Land, the domain of the Hudson's Bay Company, where the native inhabitants consisted of the Inuit, Cree, Montagnais, Naskapi, Atikamekw, and Algonquin.

The northern boundary did not become important until the mid-nineteenth century. Expansionist dreams of a country extending from the Atlantic to the Pacific and northward to the Arctic led to the purchase of Rupert's Land in 1870. Subsequently, the Province of Ontario began taking note of these distant lands and successfully sought support in the Privy Council to extend its boundaries northward. Following the success of Ontario, Quebec made similar demands.[14] Accordingly, over the next thirty or so years, the federal government gradually reduced the size of its northwest territorial holdings by transferring land to the provinces. Thus in 1898 Quebec received a transfer of land that extended northward to the Eastmain River. This was the homeland of the Montagnais, Atikamekw, Algonquin, Naskapi, and Cree. Although the 1898 legislation itself made no reference to Indian rights, these rights had been recognized by the 1870 agreement transferring Rupert's Land to the Dominion of Canada. The Order in Council implementing the transfer specifically stated that "any claims of Indians to compensation for lands required for purposes of settlement shall be disposed of by the Canadian Government in communication with the Imperial Government."[15] In the case of northern Quebec, however this provision remained a dead letter.

The final transfer of land by Canada to Quebec took place in 1912. The territory involved, bounded on the south by the Eastmain River, stretched east to the Labrador coast and north to Hudson and Ungava Bays—a vast territory inhabited by the Cree, Naskapi, Montagnais, and Inuit. Indian rights were clearly recognized in the Quebec Boundaries Extension Act of 1912, which set out the following provisions:

> (c) That the province of Quebec will recognize the rights of the Indian inhabitants in the territory above described to the same extent, and will obtain surrenders of such rights in the same manner, as the Government of Canada has heretofore recognized such rights and has obtained surrender thereof. . . .

> (e) That the trusteeship of the Indians in the said territory, and the management of any lands now or hereafter reserved for their use, shall remain in the Government of Canada subject to the control of Parliament.[16]

The last episode in the story of Quebec's evolving boundaries occurred in 1927. That year the province's present-day boundaries were established with the award to Newfoundland of a large inland chunk of Labrador (home to bands of Inuit, Montagnais, and Naskapi).

The foregoing discussion sets out the history of the gradual encroachment northwards of Canadian and Quebec jurisdiction over Indian and Inuit lands, none of which was covered by treaty or surrender. However, both levels of government or their predecessors did grant title over small allotments of land to some of the native peoples, as the following survey demonstrates.

Circumstances and Terms of
Early Land Agreements

The first parcel of land in Quebec that was set apart by the French crown for Indian use was at Sillery, now a suburb of Quebec City. It was granted in 1637 as a seigneury to Christian Indians under Jesuit supervision and was inhabited until the 1680s by converts drawn from a number of Indian nations, but mainly the Montagnais.[17] This model of land grant, in which the Indians were treated as proprietors, was repeated often in the seventeenth century. Over the years, however, much of the land has disappeared from Indian control and thus is the basis of present-day land claims by the descendants of the original grantees. Such transactions affect, today, the Hurons, Mohawks, Algonquins, and Abenakis. Two of the seigneuries will be discussed to illustrate the circumstances under which land was given and then taken away.

Kahnawake, located just to the southwest of Montreal, originated in 1680 as a seigneurial land grant (known as Sault St Louis) by the French king to the Society of Jesus. In 1762, however, General Gage, the military governor of Montreal, declared the seigneury a grant in possession of the Indians, and this decision was ratified in 1764 by Governor Murray.[18] Notwithstanding these pronouncements, the post-Confederation period has witnessed numerous surrenders of land at Kahnawake, all effected by Orders in Council. A few examples appear in Table 1.

This list, though by no means complete, shows the type of transactions and the often large expropriations that have occurred at Kahnawake. There were several smaller expropriations for the construction of the St Lawrence Seaway, eventually amounting to a total of more than 1000 acres. The compensation, by the Seaway Authority, originally had been set at $3000 but this was increased to $1.5 million in 1973 after bitter disputes over seventeen years and an attempt by the Mohawks to block the project by petitioning the United Nations to prevent Canada's "confiscation . . . by brutal force" of their land. Of the final compensation paid, about half of this sum was applied to the landscaping of the seaway canal.[19]

The original size of the seigneury of Sault St Louis, established in 1680, was 40 320 acres. Since Kahnawake today is only 12 478 acres in area, some 28 000 acres have disappeared from the original grant.[20] In fact, there is an ongoing land claim for much of this land, which covers six parishes. As well, ultimate jurisdiction over the lands at Kahnawake is at the heart of the confrontation between Mohawk traditionalists (the Longhouse) and Quebec and federal authorities over the Mohawk's self-declared right to sell tobacco without federal or provincial taxes and operate gambling ventures, such as bingo halls.

Table 1			
Date	**Documents**	**Remarks**	**Acres** (1 arpent= 1 1/4 acres)
6 April 1871	OC 777	Recommends that the Caugnhawaga Ship Canal Co. be allowed to purchase land for canal purposes.	
17 February 1888	OCPC 211	Authorizes sale of land to Atlantic and Northwestern Railway Co.	60 arpents
7 December 1895	OC 3454	Authorizes sale of land to South Western Railway Co., purchased later by St Lawrence and Adirondack Railway Co.	63 arpents
23 April 1897	LP 11698	Granting of railway right-of-way to New York Central Railway	53 arpents
8 June 1911	OCPC 1362	Power line right-of-way granted to Canadian Light and Power Co.	55 acres
6 June 1911	OCPC 1530	Granting of authority for CPR to purchase additional land.	18 acres
4 May 1933	PC 1362	Granting of right-of-way to Hydro-Quebec	55 acres
21 December 1940	OCPC 7527	For the purpose of widening the Malone-New York Highway	37 acres
2 June 1955	OCPC 1955–797	Consent to the expropriation of land in the seigneury of St Louis by the St Lawrence Seaway. Compensation of $3,000.	
16 September 1955	OCPC 1955–1416	Expropriation of lands for the St Lawrence Seaway	1,262 acres

SOURCE: Toby Ornstein, *The First Peoples in Quebec. A Reference Work on the History, Environment, Economic and Legal Position of the Indians and Inuit of Quebec*, 3 vols. (Montreal: Native North American Studies Institute 1973), 3:108–18.

A similar land grant made to the Abenaki Indians of Odanak in 1700 shows much the same kind of pressures on the land. In this area, too, the federal government ordered surrenders without any significant consultation beforehand with the resident owners. Only in the 1960s did government officials attribute land alienation to "band council resolutions" rather than to governmental Orders in Council. A government summary of the land transactions at Odanak concludes as follows:

> This reserve was created by a concession from Dame M. Hertel, widow of the seignior of Saint François, and Sieur A. Plagaish. The reserve originally was composed of lands which were part of the seigniories of Pierreville and St. François-du-Lac. Much of this land has since been surrendered. A large amount of land was surrendered in 1868 to Her Majesty the Queen. This land was to be sold and the interests from this were to be used for the benefit of the Indians. More surrenders were made in 1880 and 1893. The Government of Canada and the Department of Indian Affairs have since sold numerous tracts of land for a railway right-of-way and station, for a dock and for road purposes. Since 1944 leases and permits have been granted to different organizations and individuals. The Department of Indian Affairs Welfare Division holds a 25-year lease on part of Lot 1217. Shawinigan Water and Power Company has a 20-year lease for a transformer station and Valmore Rauillard has a 15-year lease which was renewed in 1969 for a second term.[21]

Besides seigneurial grants of land to Indians that created a total of six reserves, there are three other categories of reserves in Quebec. In 1851, as forestry, mining, and settlement of new frontier regions became of prime importance, an act passed by the legislature of the United Canadas permitted the use of not more than 230 000 acres in Lower Canada for the creation of Indian reserves. No doubt this was in response to the explosion of large numbers of Eurocanadian immigrants into what once were isolated regions; for instance, in the 1840s loggers began moving into the Saguenay–Lac St Jean region, with the result that the total number of non-Indian people increased from fewer than 1500 in 1844 to 5000 in 1851 and double that number again ten years later.[22] Eight reserves were created by virtue of the 1851 act, encompassing the central regions of Quebec and incorporating some of the Montagnais, several Atikamekw, and Algonquin bands, and one Micmac band. The land set aside for these reserves fell somewhat short of the legislated 230 000 acres, amounting to 170 012 acres.

Another act was promulgated in 1922 to solidify Indian reserve lands in regions newly acquired by Quebec. The Quebec Lands and Forests Act permitted the use of not more than 330 000 acres and led to the creation of another eight reserves. Interestingly, the total acreage turned over for Indian use was considerably less than that in 1851, a total of 13 930 acres. Whereas the largest reserve established in 1851 was Bersimis with 63 100 acres, in 1922 it was 5281 acres in size. Obviously the Quebec government was now acting more cautiously regarding Indian lands. An indication that other interests superseded Indian ones is a clause in the 1922 act stipulating that reserve land could not be granted on land that had already been conceded for timber cutting. Under both acts, the land was transferred from the Province of Quebec to the Government of Canada to be administered by the latter in trust for the Indian bands. The rights to these lands were deemed usufructuary and, once occupation ceased on the lands, they were to revert to the province.

A number of Indian communities do not occupy legally constituted reserves and their parcels of land are classified as settlements. Before the James Bay Agreement of 1975, almost all the Cree communities occupied settlements rather than reserves. Today there are only about four settlements—three Algonquin and one Montagnais on the lower north shore. In these cases, the land acknowledged as part of the settlement is small— about ten to fifteen acres. Such a settlement is the Algonquin one at Kipawa which, interestingly, in 1924 petitioned Indian Affairs to establish a hunting reserve measuring fifty square miles in order to offset the animal decline caused by the influx of white trappers, a request that was refused two months later by Duncan Scott, assistant deputy secretary of Indian Affairs.[23] The settlement at Kipawa today comprises a land allotment of fifteen acres.[24]

Research on land claims in Quebec has not been sufficiently detailed to provide precise figures on what percentage of land transactions carried out in the name of the Indians would be considered, today, fraudulent. A Quebec government publication on the native peoples of Quebec[25] refers to "considerable reductions" of the Huron village at Lorette and mentions a 1904 sale that is still being contested. Other evidence of land swindles is from the documentation on the Abenaki reserve at Durham. In a letter of 1937 to the Quebec deputy minister of mines and resources, an Indian Affairs official notes that the Abenakis in 1847 had leased their lands to white men for ninety-nine years. The leases, recognized in 1852 and again in 1860, stipulated that the superintendent of Indian affairs was to hold them and collect the money. Years later, this same official, R. Rogers Smith, indicated that "the Indians had been deprived of their lands and the rentals from these lands."[26] Furthermore, no records had been kept for whatever monies had been collected.

Although the historical records may not show all the cases where Indians were illegally deprived of their lands, the Indians certainly knew of them at the time. There are a few examples of petitions that various groups made to correct some of these wrongs, and these petitions refute the view that the Indians have been submissive in their dealings with Canadian authorities.

The earliest recorded (though not necessarily the earliest) land claim was made by the Mohawks of Kahnawake in 1762 when the Jesuits leased a fifteen-hectare strip of the seigneury to a French farmer. General Gage, as noted earlier, confirmed the Mohawks as the proprietors of this particular strip of land but the decision was reversed and the natives vigorously pursued their claim, even sending a delegation to England in 1830. A commission appointed to inquire into the affairs of Indians in Canada in 1845 reviewed the eighty years of evidence and ruled against the Mohawks.[27]

The Hurons of Loretteville also pursued a claim, beginning in 1791,[28] which involved a delegation of four Huron chiefs travelling to England in 1824 to petition King George IV. They argued that the lands of the old mission at Sillery should be turned over to them, citing the fact that their ancestors had settled there in the seventeenth century. Although the chiefs, ornately dressed, created an impressive sight at the royal court, the king simply referred them back to the colonial government, which refused their claim.[29] The Huron have been more successful in recent times. In May 1990 the Supreme Court of Canada recognized their fundamental right to observe traditional rites in what is today a provincial park (Jacques Cartier), even if that right entailed cutting trees, camping, and making fires. In this case, known as the Sioui case, the jurists also recognized the 1760 agreement between Governor Murray and the Huron as a treaty between two nations.[30]

In fact, wherever European settlement occurred, the Indians felt that their rights were ignored and they petitioned government for redress. The Micmac at Restigouche began doing so from the time New France fell to the British. Initially they complained that the Acadians were trespassing on their salmon-fishing areas, and after 1780, once the loyalists began arriving, the transgressions and petitions increased.[31]

The claim of the Kanesatake Indians at Oka is a longstanding, complex one stemming from the grant of the seigneury of Oka, on the Ottawa River, in 1717 by the king of France to the Sulpician priests who formed a mission that originally included Algonquins, Nipissings, and Iroquois. The British authorities subsequently enlarged and confirmed the grant but did not make clear whether the Sulpicians or the Indians were in possession of the land. With the opening of the seigneury to white settlement in 1784, the Oka Indians began a series of claims to confirm their rights.[32] At the heart of these claims was the argument that the Sulpicians never had the right to sell off tracts of this land. In doing so, the Mohawks claim, the Sulpicians ignored their obligations as a trustee of the land. A series of proposed settlements of the claims were never considered by the Mohawks to be a final solution and their grievances continue today.[33]

Access to resources, rather than the land itself, is another example of longstanding disputes between the Indians, Eurocanadians, and the government. In 1857, the Quebec government began leasing to white Canadians and Americans the privilege of fishing the salmon rivers located along the lower north shore of the St Lawrence. Control of this resource was assigned to the owners of the private fishing clubs, which, of course, barred the Montagnais from access to their age-old food staple.

Such legislation has turned, and continues to turn, Indians into "poachers." Petitions, over the years, have not worked. Only in recent times at Restigouche, on the Baie des Chaleur, have the Quebec Provincial Police refrained from raiding the Micmacs' fishing nets. This is, no doubt, owing to the 1985 Supreme Court of Canada decision in the Simon case, which granted Micmacs, under a 1752 Treaty of Peace and Friendship promulgated in Nova Scotia, the right to hunt and fish freely. The judgment even suggests that they may have the right to sell the products of their hunting and fishing.[34]

Respect for animals and a strict code governing the killing and use of them have long characterized the woodland Indians.[35] One can well imagine, then, the horror that Indians experienced when, in the late 1800s and well into the 1920s, white trappers simply moved onto their territories and stripped them clean of fur-bearers. The anthropologist Father John Cooper noted in his report to the Department of Indian Affairs in 1933 that the Indians of James Bay had become "demoralized" by the disappearance of game.[36] The demoralization would have increased each time a hunter came across evidence that the white trapper who had moved onto native lands was dynamiting the beaver lodges or using poisoned bait in traps.[37]

Indian Affairs records on land issues for James Bay begin only in 1896 but as early as 1898 the Abenaki of Becancour petitioned Prime Minister Wilfrid Laurier to stop the white trappers. These are their words: "We are troubled with a great number of Canadian hunters who have taken our best hunting grounds and moreover we are forbidden the right of killing beaver (and caribou during the month of March). The close season established by the law is alright as regards the Canadians as they have other means of subsistence. . . . Your game warden will agree with us that there are a hundred Canadians to ten Indians who are engaged in hunting."[38] The situation intensified over the years and everyone complained—the Indian agent, the missionary, the manager of the Hudson's Bay Company post, and especially the Indians. In a memo to the deputy superintendent of Indian affairs in 1926, the supervisor of Indian timber lands commented that "the average white trapper is not concerned with continuously trapping in one district. Having picked out a promising territory his main object is to clean it out during one season and to move to new grounds the following year."[39] The ruthless slaughter carried out by white trappers endangered the species, as did the new forestry and agriculture operations that reduced the natural habitat of the animals. In 1925 Dr E.B. Rioux warned that "very soon, all the Indians will be starving."[40] This did, in fact, happen some four years later when food and fur animal hunts failed and many died from starvation.[41]

Although at this time the Indians were not making claims to land specifically, they were claiming their rights to the resources on their lands, be they fish or meat. As the land is the "housing" for resources, these claims cannot be separated from land claims. For the Indians, they were—and are—one and the same.

Major Examples of Land Disputes and Processes

James Bay

As explained, there are no historic land treaties in Quebec, and government officials might well have liked this situation to remain unchanged in the twentieth century. A memo, dated 1903, to Clifford Sifton, the federal minister of the interior and superintendent general of Indian Affairs, sums up the government position that was in effect until the mid-1970s when the government was forced to change its policy. This early memo reads:

> As far as the Indians of Quebec are concerned, it is suggested that no treaty should be made with them or that any Quebec Indians living temporarily in Ontario should be included in the Ontario treaty, but we should endeavour to obtain an understanding from the Province of Quebec that as claims are made by the outlying tribes not included in those provided for by 14-15 Vic, Cap 106, whereby 231,000 acres were set aside for the Indians, the Province should be wiling to set apart at proper times, suitable reserves. The Indian title in the Province of Quebec has never been recognized or surrendered as in the Province of Ontario and, I presume, that it is not proposed to change the policy in that regard.[42]

Nine years later, a federal act extending the boundaries of Quebec stipulated that the province should obtain surrenders to the territory from the Indians in the same manner as the federal government had done elsewhere, that is, by treaties. If Indians in northern Quebec regretted in 1912, and thereafter, that they were shut out of the treaty-making process, this regret turned to anger in the spring of 1971 when Premier Robert Bourassa officially launched the James Bay Project. The land was not his!

The decision to build the James Bay hydroelectric project came as a surprise for the population at large and a shock to the Cree. With no public knowledge of the feasibility and environmental-impact studies that had been ordered but not yet completed, Bourassa seemingly pulled the project out of a hat. He announced it, along with the promise of 100 000 jobs, at a large Liberal Party rally in Quebec City, exclaiming that "James Bay is the key to the economic and social progress of

Quebec, the key to the political stability of Quebec, the key to the future of Quebec."[43] So undeveloped was the hydroelectric project at the time of this announcement that one year later its location was changed from the Nottaway–Broadback–Rupert river system to the La Grande River, some 1000 kilometres farther north.

At the time, the Cree numbered about six thousand people divided among eight bands. They had no political organization. There were no roads, few airports, no telephones, and half the population spent the winter months in the bush, hunting and trapping. Similarly, the Inuit who were to be affected on their southern lands also had none of this infrastructure (political, administrative, or physical). Yet within a year the Cree and Inuit filed proceedings for an interlocutory injunction to halt the project.[44]

The case was heard seven months later by Judge Albert Malouf. It lasted 71 days and involved 167 witnesses, three-quarters of whom were native. In November 1973 Judge Malouf granted the interlocutory injunction and ordered the construction work (ongoing since August 1972) halted. He did so on the grounds that the Cree and Inuit "have had since time immemorial and continue to exercise personal and usufructuary rights, including rights of hunting, fishing and trapping" over their territory. He also noted that these rights had never been extinguished.[45]

Within a week, the Quebec Court of Appeal suspended the injunction, using the "balance of inconvenience argument" rather than addressing the issue of aboriginal rights. It held that the interests of six thousand people should not take precedence over those of the six million Québécois, an argument that the lawyer for the defence, James O'Reilly, termed a case of "might makes right" or "the majority always rules."[46]

In December 1973 the Supreme Court heard the natives' petition to appeal. It did not find the Quebec Court of Appeal's decision judicially faulty, but two dissenting judges expressed the opinion that there were material issues involved which warranted a full hearing before their court. The Quebec government could not take the chance that the James Bay natives would make their way through all the layers of the justice system and end with their rights ultimately being recognized by the Supreme Court. Only eleven months earlier the Supreme Court had handed down its judgment in the Calder Case, in which the Nisga'a's unextinguished aboriginal rights were recognized by three of the judges but not recognized by another three. The seventh judge hearing the case rejected the claim on a technical issue.[47] Thus the possibility that the Cree and the Inuit could win forced the provincial government to begin negotiations in earnest.

The federal government was (and is) the trustee of Indian lands, the whole basis of the Indian Act. Yet, although asked to intervene on behalf of the Cree and Inuit of James Bay, the federal government chose not to do so, presumably for political reasons. In Quebec at the time, "separatism" sentiments were running quite high and the federal government did not wish to be seen as interfering in provincial affairs. According to Harvey Feit, an anthropologist and consultant to the Cree in the court case and subsequent negotiations, the federal government adopted a position of "alert neutrality." This position was a great disappointment to the Cree, who had until then considered the government of Canada as a "benevolent protector."[48] Instead of intervening, the Canadian government made substantial interest-free loans and grants to the Cree and Inuit.

Months and months of almost round-the-clock negotiations involving Cree and Inuit representatives, government officials, and a host of biological, social science, and legal experts resulted in the signing of an agreement-in-principle on 15 November 1974. One year later, the final agreement was signed by native leaders and government officials. It was ratified in the Cree communities one month later by a vote of 922 to 1, though this represented only 24 per cent of the population of approximately 6000. The Inuit ratified the agreement in February 1976 with 95 per cent in favour among the 65 per cent of the population (some 4000) that voted.[49] By this agreement, almost all the James Bay and northern Quebec territories were opened to development, something short of 375 000 square kilometres. For their part, the federal and provincial governments were obligated to upgrade local services to Canadian standards. The monetary compensation provided in the agreement was $150 million ($15 000 per capita), $75 million to be paid in installments on a 56/44 per cent split between Quebec and Canada and the remaining half by Hydro-Québec in the form of royalties.[50] At the federal and provincial levels, some twenty to thirty bills were enacted to give the agreement legislative force, the principle ones being Bill 32 in Quebec and Bill C-9 in Ottawa. The agreement came to be known as the "James Bay and Northern Quebec Agreement." As Feit points out, it was the first modern land-claims agreement that recognized aboriginal rights as well as the rights of native people to maintain and develop a subsistence economy.[51] The agreement has the status of a treaty and therefore its provisions are guaranteed by the constitution of Canada.

During the one-year period for discussion of the agreement-in-principle, intensive negotiations fine-tuned its provisions. At the same time there were important negotiations among natives themselves. Three Inuit communities (Povungnituk, Ivujivik, and Salluit) objected to the surrender of rights and opted not to sign. These communities have come to be known as "the dissidents," or more formally as "Inuit Tungavingat Nunamini" (ITN). The Naskapi Indians, relocated by the government in 1948 to Schefferville, a mining centre, from Fort Mackenzie, were invited by the Cree and Inuit to participate in the negotiations. As it turned out, the Naskapi did not become signatories until 1978 and thus had to negotiate their considerable land claims after the agreement was signed. Their agreement was known as the "Northeastern Quebec Agreement." Although not an issue at the time, a ninth Cree band (the Oujé-Bougoumou) came to be recognized by the two levels of government only in June 1985, and their claims (land and compensation) are still being stalled by the federal government.

The protection of Cree and Inuit aboriginal rights by the process of negotiation rather than through a court-imposed solution has produced in the agreement some far-reaching and innovative provisions. An adequate discussion of all of these, along with the subsequent problems faced by the Cree in their implementation, would require a book-length manuscript in itself. Readers wishing more details and analysis of the agreement should consult, as a beginning, Vincent and Bowers[52] and Feit.[53] The most important component of the agreement is the guarantee of aboriginal rights to the land, the maintenance of a lifestyle based on hunting and fishing, and a large measure of autonomy or self-government.

The land issue was resolved by a division of the land into three categories. Category I land is land allocated to the Cree and Inuit for their exclusive use and is the land in and around their communities, that is, reserve land. The extent of this land is actually small, a total of 5600 square kilometres for the Inuit and 3500 square kilometres for the Cree. Category II lands are those over which the native peoples have exclusive hunting, fishing, and trapping rights but no exclusive occupancy. These were lands surrounding the villages. For the Cree some 40 000 square kilometres were so designated, and for the Inuit, 56 000 square kilometres. The government of Quebec may permit development on Category II lands without the consent of the natives, as long as the land used for development is replaced. However, the activities the government authorizes must not interfere unreasonably with the hunting, fishing, and trapping activities of the native peoples. Finally, Category III lands are all the rest, surrendered by the Cree and Inuit and over which they can hunt everywhere except in areas of development/building, much as the customary use of crown lands has been elsewhere. However, as for the rights to hunting and fishing, these are to be controlled, in terms of quotas and allocation, by a coordinating committee made up of natives and government representatives, with natives given precedence over non-native hunters and outfitters.[54] In all cases, mineral rights belong to the provincial government.

The main principle behind the novel land division is, of course, the recognition of the primacy of hunting, fishing, and trapping as a way of life for both Inuit and Cree. This principle was further developed for the Cree in a unique program called the Income Security Program (ISP), a program that manages the wildlife and also ensures a guaranteed income for the hunters and their families, according to the amount of time they spend in the bush. This program is self-administered in each village by the Cree Trappers Association, a body that not only regulates the hunting and marketing of animals but also conducts the research necessary to the making of its decisions. Feit, commenting on the ISP in 1988, found that increased numbers of Cree were participating in a hunting economy and that this activity has enhanced traditional social forms and practices. However, as effective as the program is, it has not been able to control external influences, particularly those caused by development. It has also been handicapped by the lack of credibility of local-level management in the eyes of government administrators and scientists.[55]

The third far-reaching provision in the agreement was local and regional government. Twenty-one municipalities were created, thirteen of which were Inuit. The Cree and Inuit were given control over all local matters, including education and health services. To coordinate these services and inter-village affairs, the Inuit and Cree each opted for a regional government, known as the Kativik Regional Authority and the Cree Regional Authority. In addition, there were a host of lesser agencies created, such as the Cree Board of Health and Social Services, the Cree School Board, the Cree Construction Corporation, the Kativik School Board, the Makivik Corporation (which manages the Inuit compensation money), the Avatuq Cultural Institute, and so on. The culmination of these processes and steps towards self-government was the establishment in 1988 of responsible self-government, decided by referendum in the whole of the Inuit territory, now known as Nunavik.

In his study of regional development among the Cree, Richard Salisbury[56] asks whether this regionalization would have taken place anyway and suggests that the benefits of regionalism have developed through the judicial and negotiation processes. Since this issue is too complex to summarize briefly, readers are directed instead to Salisbury's work as well as to that of La Rusic[57] for an analysis of the bureaucratic structures that have emerged among the native people of James Bay.

The native agencies and bodies that were established to oversee the implementation of the agreement have had a difficult job right from the beginning. According to the Cree, many of the obligations of the governments spelled out in the agreement were not implemented without a "fight." The Cree and Inuit have had to press, often unsuccessfully, for the fulfillment of these commitments, from environmental measures to health services to finances.

Negotiated under pressure in a phenomenally short time, the agreement is obviously flawed in a number of respects. One such flaw, in the opinion of other Quebec-based native peoples, is that the signatories to the agreement extinguished the land claims of *all* others in the James Bay and northern Quebec regions, thereby releasing Canada and Quebec from their obligations of 1898 and 1912. Those affected are Montagnais from Quebec and Labrador, Naskapi and Inuit from Labrador, as well as the Algonquin, Atikamekw, and the dissident Inuit.

By the terms of the agreement, these other peoples are considered a "third party" with which Quebec is required merely to attempt negotiations. This is, as Robert Pratt, lawyer for the Naskapi, notes, a rather vaguely worded undertaking.[58]

The Atikamekw-Montagnais

It is under these constraints that other Indian groups of central Quebec have tried to establish their claims. The one that is the most advanced is that of the Conseil Atikamekw-Montagnais (CAM), which signed with the two levels of government a "framework agreement" in September 1988 and an "agreement on interim measures" in 1989. Still to be negotiated is the agreement-in-principle and the final agreement. The framework agreement just sets forth the procedures to be followed in the negotiations as well as their *modus operandi*. The agreement on the interim measures concerns the protection of native land rights while the negotiations are proceeding, that is, the right to be consulted and participate in development projects, such as the establishment of a park or wildlife reserve. The final agreement was to have been signed in April 1991 but negotiations broke down because the Quebec government offered what the CAM viewed as pitifully meagre, a total of 1200 square kilometres of territory.[59] The negotiations resumed later in 1991.

The forging of a political organization to represent the interests of both nations occurred in 1975. The Atikamekw are a people numbering about 4000 in three communities in the Haute-Mauricie region and the Montagnais are 11 000 people divided into nine communities located in the Lac St-Jean and lower north-shore regions. Their joint ancestral homeland covers an area of about 550 000 square kilometres[60] and includes territory in Labrador, just as the Innu of Labrador have ancestral claims to portions of Quebec. The Montagnais, like the Innu, suffer from the overflights of the low-flying aircraft of NATO. As for decision-making within CAM, negotiators were appointed but a series of workshops were held in the communities to determine the issues and finally resolutions were passed at an Estates General.[61]

The report by Bernard Cleary, the chief negotiator for CAM, sets out the points of interest that CAM has been stressing in negotiations. First on the list is the recovery of full ownership rights to a large part of ancestral lands and then a series of requirements that seem to parallel the James Bay Agreement—self-government on a local and national level, a national constitution, economic development, a guaranteed minimum-income plan, and adequate funding, including "catch-up" funds. Another major concern is the establishment of a new social contract that defines the relationship between native and non-native governments on a equal basis.[62]

The Algonquins, too, are developing their claim. They, today, live in nine Quebec-based communities (one other, Golden Lake, is in Ontario) in the Outaouais and Abitibi-Témiscamingue regions and number some 5000 people. The core of their original homeland was the Ottawa valley.[63] As warfare, caused by the fur trade, intensified, the Algonquins relocated northward. There are also references to Algonquins being located around the town of Trois Rivières in the early seventeenth century,[64] suggesting that the Algonquin land claim may well stretch from its centre in the Ottawa valley eastward to Trois Rivières and northward to the Abitibi region.

The Algonquin claim is in the early stages of the long process required by the Department of Indian and Northern Affairs. It is a pressing claim because much of their ancestral land base is now occupied by cities and farms and because their hunting lands are being turned into deserts as clear-cutting by logging companies continues unabated, much of it in La Vérendrye Park, classified as a provincial wildlife reserve. The Algonquins are particularly critical of the conservation methods being employed, saying that clear-cutting, herbicide spraying, and reforestation procedures will produce a "monoculture" forest with insufficient diversity to meet the needs of the various animal species.[65] Not only is their comprehensive land claim not being given full recognition but the Algonquins are being shut out of the decisions being made about the management of their dwindling forests, forests they have inhabited for centuries. Negotiations with Quebec to set up an integrated, renewable resource-development plan covering the forest wildlife have been underway since 1988 but in 1991 no agreement had yet been reached.[66]

Responses of Québécois

There are no studies indicating how the non-natives in the province view the land-claim efforts of the various native groups. The one settled claim, the James Bay and Northern Quebec Agreement, did not encounter any non-native opposition; however, that tells us little since few non-natives were directly affected. A more significant fact is that the opposition to the proposed project (based primarily on environmental concerns) in the early 1970s came more from within the much smaller anglophone community than from the francophone one. This is not surprising since Bourassa, as earlier indicated, draped the whole enterprise in nationalistic rhetoric.[67] Thus, all aspects of the hydroelectric project, including its enabling legislation, met little opposition within government circles and beyond. More recently, the Crees' opposition to the new proposed hydroelectric project at Great Whale River has generated considerable hostility in Quebec.

In other parts of the province, Indian claims to the land are meeting resistance. A good example is the claim of Kanesatake, the Mohawk community at Oka. The municipal government has wished, for some time, to lease land for the expansion of a private nine-hole local golf course, the course and expansion area being on white-pine forested land claimed by the Mohawks as part of the original seigneury of Oka.[68] Confrontations between the Oka residents and the Mohawks have been taking place for more than one hundred years and erupted again recently on 11 July 1990 when the Sureté du Québec attempted to dismantle the barricade erected by the Mohawks a few months earlier. This latest confrontation lasted seventy-eight days and the action of the Kahnawake Mohawks in closing off bridge access to Montreal provoked some threatening demonstrations by local white residents. This pent-up racism spilled into the streets of Montreal, where native-looking people were harassed by citizens and police.[69] After the armed conflict ended, the pine forest was returned to the Mohawks by the federal government. Still unresolved, however, is the issue of ownership of the seigneury.

Similarly, Kahnawake is preparing its land claim for much of its old seigneury, now housing suburban developments. No one expects the local population to welcome this claim, especially since the two governments, federal and provincial, have themselves been confrontational over each and every land claim or claim to wildlife resources in the province. The federal government has not been assuming the responsibilities of the trusteeship invested in it. When school textbooks or historical documentaries aired on television fail to mention that the land on which the Québécois are living has not yet been ceded by the Indians, can one expect the larger population to react any differently?

The Future of Land Claims

Every part of this province except Nunavik is under some form of Indian claim. Although the Cree signed the James Bay and Northern Quebec Agreement in 1975, they are now reopening many of the issues, via court challenges, as the provincial government forges ahead with its plans to develop, for hydroelectric purposes, the Great Whale River system and later the Nottaway–Broadback–Rupert rivers system. The grounds on which the Cree are contesting these new developments are basically environmental because the environmental requirements set out in the agreement have been too often breached by governments and the Cree fear for the viability of their traditional hunting economy. They may also argue in the courts that the government needs their consent to go ahead with any new projects since, as their lawyer James O'Reilly stated in 1988, all that they gave up in the 1975 agreement was "the right to exclusive possession and occupation of the territory, no more."[70]

Inasmuch as Quebec did not meet the requirements of the 1912 Boundaries Extension Act and the federal and provincial governments negotiated the James Bay and Northern Quebec Agreement only because there was "a gun to their head" in the form of possible court delays to the project, and, inasmuch as there are no land treaties signed for other regions, the future does not augur well for the signing of other land-claims agreements, as witnessed by Quebec's offer of a paltry 1500 square kilometres to the Atikamekw-Montagnais. Governments, with the seeming backing of their citizenry, do indeed settle land claims only when forced. It is not an action that flows from any sense of good will or desire to try to compensate native people for all they have lost.

Documents

A. Northern Quebec Inuit Association: Letter to Jean Chrétien, Minister of Indian Affairs, 5 May 1972

On behalf of the communities of Inoucdjouac, Povungnituk, Ivujivik, Sugluk, Wakeham Bay, Koartak, Payne Bay, Tasiujaq, Fort Chimo, and George River, all in the province of Quebec, the Northern Quebec Inuit Association hereby demands that the James Bay Development Project, be halted, immediately.

The reasons why this project has to be stopped are the following:

1.   We fear much of the wildlife we depend on for livelihood will be damaged permanently. Our way of life will also be altered permanently. We do not want this.

2.   The James Bay area is a major migration route for geese, which is our major source of food for geese in spring. If this area is destroyed, so will part of our food supply—the geese.

3.   We do not want the Great Whale and Fort Chimo Rivers to be dammed up. If this is done, it will affect ice break-up and freeze-up processes, damaging hunting conditions.

4.   If Fort Chimo River is dammed up, this could affect our weather conditions. It will definitely change the tide level and flow in Ungava Bay, which is among the highest in the world. We fear for destruction of mammal life. It is our food.

5.   If this big mistake is allowed to proceed, Indians living in James Bay will be wiped out. You say there will be many jobs for them, and can you tell us for how long? Can you not find other means for producing electricity? Indians in James Bay do not want this project or this "progress" which destroys our land. We fully support the Indians in opposition to this project.

6.   We do not want our land to be raped and defaced for any reason. If dams and projects were meant to be in that land, we believe that he who created the earth is the only one who has right to do so. No one else has.

Written resolutions passed by each of the Inuit councils in the above mentioned communities will be forthcoming as soon as transportation conditions permit. Petitions, signed by the general population in each community will also be submitted with the resolutions.

B.   The James Bay Agreement

Section 2: Principal Provisions

2.1   In consideration of the rights and benefits herein set forth in favour of the James Bay Crees and the Inuit of Quebec, the James Bay Crees and the Inuit of Quebec hereby cede, release surrender and convey all their Native claims, rights, titles and interests, whatever they may be, in and to land in the Territory and in Quebec, and Quebec and Canada accept such surrender.

2.2   Quebec and Canada, the James Bay Energy Corporation, the James Bay Development Corporation and the Quebec Hydro-Electric Commission (Hydro-Quebec), to the extent of their respective obligations as set forth herein, hereby give, grant, recognize and provide to the James Bay Crees and the Inuit of Quebec the rights, privileges and benefits specified herein, the whole in consideration of the said cession, release, surrender and conveyance mentioned in paragraph 2.1 hereof.

Canada hereby approves of and consents to the Agreement and undertakes, to the extent of its obligations herein, to give, grant, recognize and provide to the James Bay Crees and the Inuit of Quebec the rights, privileges and benefits herein.

2.3   In consideration of the rights and benefits herein set forth in favour of the Inuit of Port Burwell who are ordinarily resident of Killinek Island, the Inuit of Port Burwell hereby cede, release, surrender and convey all their Native claims, rights, titles, and interests, whatever they may be, in and to land in the Territory and in Canada, and Quebec and Canada accept such surrender.

Quebec and Canada, the James Bay Energy Corporation, the James Bay Development Corporation and the Quebec Hydro-Electric Commission (Hydro-Quebec) to the extent of their respective obligations as set forth herein, hereby give, grant, recognize and provide to the Inuit of Port Burwell the rights, privileges and benefits specified herein, the whole in consideration of the said cession, release, surrender and conveyance mentioned in this paragraph.

For purposes of the Agreement a person of Inuit ancestry who was or will be born on that part of Killinek Island within the Northwest

Territories shall be deemed to have been born or to be born in Quebec, or if such person is ordinarily resident in Port Burwell he shall be deemed to be ordinarily resident in Quebec.

. . .

Canada or the Government of the Northwest Territories, as the case may be, will continue to be responsible for providing programs and services to the Inuit who are ordinarily resident in Port Burwell in accordance with criteria that may be established from time to time.

2.4   In consideration of and subject to the rights, benefits and privileges in favour of the James Bay Crees and the Inuit of Quebec, the James Bay Crees and Inuit of Quebec consent by these presents to the settlement out of court of all legal proceedings relating to the James Bay project or to the claims, rights, titles and interests in land that they may have. The James Bay Crees and the Inuit of Quebec further undertake not to institute any further proceedings relating to the matters contemplated in the said legal proceedings already instituted which are presently before the Supreme Court of Canada in virtue of leave to appeal granted by the Supreme Court of Canada on February 13, 1975.

. . .

2.5   Canada and Quebec shall recommend to the Parliament of Canada and to the National Assembly of Quebec respectively, forthwith upon the execution of the Agreement, suitable legislation to approve, to give effect to and to declare valid the Agreement and to protect, safeguard and maintain the rights and obligations contained in the Agreement. Canada and Quebec undertake that the legislation which will be so recommended will not impair the substance of the rights, undertakings and obligations provided for in the Agreement.

Both the federal and provincial legislation approving and giving effect to and declaring valid the Agreement, if adopted, shall provide that, where there is an inconsistency or conflict between such legislation and the provisions of any other federal or provincial law, as the case may be, applicable to the Territory, the former legislation shall prevail to the extent of such inconsistency or conflict.

. . .

2.6   The federal legislation approving, giving effect to and declaring valid the Agreement shall extinguish all native claims, rights, title and interests of all Indians and all Inuit in and to the Territory and the native claims, rights, title and interests of the Inuit of Port Burwell in Canada, whatever they may be.

2.7   During the Transitional Period of two (2) years referred to herein, Canada and Quebec shall to the extent of their respective obligations, take the measures necessary to put into force, with effect from the date of execution of the Agreement, the Transitional Measures referred to in the Agreement.

Except for such Transitional Measures, the Agreement shall come into force and shall bind the Parties on the date when both the federal and provincial laws respectively approving, giving effect to and declaring valid the Agreement are in force.

Upon the coming into force of the said federal and provincial legislation the Transitional Measures shall be replaced by all the other provisions of this Agreement. All acts done by the Parties in virtue of the said Transitional Measures shall then be deemed to have been ratified by all the Parties hereto.

2.8   In the event that the legislation referred to in paragraph 2.5 hereof does not come into force within a period of two (2) years from the execution of the Agreement, all compensation paid to or for the benefit of the James Bay Crees and the Inuit of Quebec by Quebec or Canada pursuant to Sub-section 25.1 shall be repaid to, revert to or remain with, as the case may be, the said governments. However, during the transitional period, the James Bay Crees, the Inuit of Quebec and the Inuit of Port Burwell shall be entitled to receive, retain and use any interest earned thereon when due under the provisions of paragraphs 25.1.6 and 25.2.6. Such interest payments shall be made to the Grand Council of the Crees (of Quebec) for the benefit of the James Bay Crees and to the Northern Quebec Inuit Association for the benefit of the Inuit of Quebec and the Inuit of Port Burwell.

2.9.1   During the period between the date of execution of Agreement and either the coming into force of the legislation referred to in paragraph 2.5 or two (2) years from the date of execution of the Agreement, whichever is the earlier (which period is herein referred to as the "Transitional Period"), Quebec undertakes, in the case of the James Bay Crees, from the date of the execution of the Agreement and in the case of the Inuit of Quebec and the Inuit of Port Burwell, from the respective dates that agreements are reached with Quebec in accordance with Section 6 for the selection of Category I lands, not to alienate, cede, transfer or otherwise grant rights respecting the lands which are to be allocated as Category I lands to or for the benefit of the James Bay Crees, the Inuit of Quebec and the Inuit of Port Burwell, except for those rights which Quebec could grant under Sections 5 or 7. Such lands are described in the Territorial descriptions annexed to Section 4 and to be annexed to Section 6 as selections are made and shall include the lands known as Category IA and Category IB lands.

2.9.2   During the transitional period, the James Bay Crees, the Inuit of Quebec and the Inuit of Port Burwell shall be permitted to occupy, enjoy and use the Territory in accordance with present practice, subject to the rights of the other parties to the Agreement to act in such a manner as not to jeopardize rights which the James Bay Crees, the Inuit of Quebec and the Inuit of Port Burwell will have when the Agreement comes into force and effect. Nonetheless, this shall not be deemed to be a recognition nor a waiver of any right in or to the Territory in favour of or by the James Bay Crees, the Inuit of Quebec and the Inuit of Port Burwell.

2.9.3 Moreover, during the transitional period, and subject to acquired rights, the James Bay Crees, the Inuit of Quebec and the Inuit of Port Burwell when they will have selected their lands as aforesaid, shall be granted by regulations of Quebec and Canada, to the extent of their respective jurisdictions, which Quebec and Canada hereby undertake to adopt to give effect to these presents, the exclusive right to hunt, fish and trap in the lands which are or shall be described as Category I and Category II lands and to grant the right to trap and to hunt and fish in Category III lands, the whole subject to such limitations on the Native people as are contained in Section 24 of the Agreement. These regulations shall also provide that the Inuit of Quebec and the Inuit of Port Burwell (through their Community Councils) and the James Bay Crees shall be authorized to allow other persons to hunt, fish, and trap in Category I and Category II lands in the manner set forth in Section 24. Moreover, subject to acquired rights, the said regulations shall also provide for the same rights to the Native people in respect to outfitting as would have applied had the Agreement come into force on the date of its execution, except that notices relating to the right of first refusal with respect to outfitting facilities during the Transitional Period shall be given to the interested Native parties in respect to their respective areas of primary interest and to both interested Native parties in respect to areas of common interest.

2.9.4 From the date of execution of the Agreement, Canada and Quebec shall pay for the benefit of the James Bay Crees, the Inuit of Quebec and the Inuit of Port Burwell the amounts of compensation to which they shall be entitled upon the coming into force of the Agreement in accordance with the provisions of Sub-section 25.1. However, during the transitional period, such amounts of compensation shall not be paid to the legal entity or entities contemplated by Sections 26 and 27 but shall instead be paid to financial institutions in Quebec mutually acceptable to Quebec, Canada and the Cree and Inuit parties, for the benefit of the James Bay Crees, the Inuit of Quebec and the Inuit of Port Burwell, pursuant to trust arrangements acceptable to Canada, Quebec and the interested Native parties. It is recognized that there may be separate trust arrangements for each of the interested Native parties.

2.9.5 During the transitional period, the James Bay Energy Corporation and Hydro-Quebec undertake that they will carry out all measures respecting Le Complexe La Grande 1975 in the manner provided for in Section 8 as if the said Section were in force and effect from the date of execution of the Agreement. Furthermore, the James Bay Energy Corporation and Hydro-Quebec undertake that during the said transitional period Le Complexe La Grande 1975 which is being built will substantially conform to the provisions contemplated by the "Description Technique—Le Complexe La Grande 1975" (dated October 20, 1975) referred to in Section 8 of the Agreement.

The James Bay Crees, the Inuit of Quebec and the Inuit of Port Burwell undertake that during the Transitional Period, no legal proceedings will be instituted having as an object the halting of works being carried out substantially in conformity with the said Le Complexe La Grande 1975.

2.9.6 In addition to the foregoing, the provisions of the Agreement relating to Health and Social Services, Education and Justice and Police shall be implemented to the extent possible within existing legislation, during the Transitional Period. In respect to the income security program for the Crees and in respect to the support program for Inuit hunting, fishing and trapping the transitional measures during the transitional period shall be as described in Sections 30 and 29 respectively. Subject to the provisions of said Sections, at the termination of said Transitional Period the Native parties shall be obliged to render an account to Quebec concerning the use of such moneys for such programs and to repay and remit to Quebec any portion of such moneys not used for the said purposes.

. . .

2.9.9 The Transitional Period may be extended by consent of all parties.

2.10 The parties hereto recognize and declare that all lands other than Category IA lands are and shall remain under the exclusive legislative jurisdiction of the Province of Quebec.

In the event that a final judgment of a competent court of last resort declares that the whole or any part of Categories II and III lands fall under the legislative jurisdiction of Canada, because of rights granted to the Native people with respect to all or any such lands or because such lands are held to be lands reserved for Indians, then any rights given to the Native people with respect to such lands shall cease to exist for all legal purposes.

Quebec and Canada undertake as of the date of the said judgment, both one to the other, as well as individually and collectively, in favour of the Native people to do all things necessary and to introduce such legislative or other measures needed to enable Quebec and/or Canada, in their respective jurisdictions, to grant anew the same rights that ceased to exist but with provincial jurisdiction in the said lands.

Nonetheless, in order to avoid hardship to the native people and notwithstanding the above, the effect of the preceding provisions with respect to the termination of the rights of the native people shall be suspended for a period of two (2) years following the date of the judgment.

During such period of suspension, Quebec and Canada undertake that they will not do anything or permit anything to be done which would prevent the granting or restoration to the Native people of any rights so nullified.

At the expiration of the period of suspension of two (2) years mentioned above, should no measures have been taken which would make possible, under provincial jurisdiction, the restoration of rights to the Native people, Canada and Quebec shall continue to endeavour to take the measures necessary which will make possible the restoration under provincial jurisdiction of the said rights over Categories II and III lands.

Should any Category I lands, exclusive of Category IA lands of the Crees, be held by a final judgment of a competent court of the last resort to fall under federal legislative jurisdiction, none of the rights of the Native people in regard to such lands shall be affected. However, Canada and Quebec undertake to diligently do all things necessary and to introduce such legislative or other measures required so that such lands and rights of the Native people related to such lands fall under provincial legislative jurisdiction.

The termination of any rights in virtue of this paragraph and the circumstances described herein shall not be deemed to be nor be construed as nullifying in any manner whatsoever any other rights or provisions of this Agreement.

2.11 Nothing contained in this Agreement shall prejudice the rights of the Native people as Canadian citizens of Quebec, and they shall continue to be entitled to all of the rights and benefits of all other citizens as well as those resulting from the Indian Act (as applicable) and from any other legislation applicable to them from time to time.

2.12 Federal and provincial programs and funding, and the obligations of the Federal and Provincial Governments, shall continue to apply to the James Bay Crees and the Inuit of Quebec on the same basis as to the other Indians and Inuit of Canada in the case of federal programs, and of Quebec in the case of provincial programs, subject to the criteria established from time to time for the application of such programs.

2.13 The rights of the Crown in right of Canada in respect to Federal properties and installations in the Territory and the rights of the Crown in right of Quebec in respect to provincial properties and installations in the Territory, which are now or hereafter owned by the Crown or used for the purposes of the Federal or Provincial Government, as the case may be, shall not be affected by the Agreement, except as otherwise specifically provided for herein.

Subject to the provisions of this Agreement the rights of persons not parties hereto shall not be affected.

2.14 Quebec undertakes to negotiate with other Indians or Inuit who are not entitled to participate in the compensation and benefits of the present Agreement, in respect to any claims which such Indians or Inuit may have with respect to the Territory.

Notwithstanding the undertakings of the preceding sub-paragraph, nothing in the present paragraph shall be deemed to constitute a recognition, by Canada or Quebec, in any manner whatsoever, of any rights of such Indians or Inuit.

Nothing in this paragraph shall affect the obligations, if any, that Canada may have with respect to claims of such Native persons with respect to the Territory. This paragraph shall not be enacted into law.

2.15 The Agreement may be, from time to time, amended or modified in the manner provided in the Agreement, or in the absence of such provision, with the consent of all the Parties. Whenever for the purposes of, or pursuant to, the Agreement, unless otherwise expressly specified, consent is required in order to amend or modify any of the terms and conditions of the Agreement, such consent may be given on behalf of the Native people by the interested Native parties.

2.16 The Agreement shall, within four months from the date of execution, and in a manner satisfactory to Canada, be submitted to the Inuit and the Crees for purposes of consultation and confirmation. The transitional measures provided for herein and the provisions of Sub Sections 25.5 and 25.6 shall take effect only from the time of such confirmation but retroactive to the date of the execution of the Agreement.

2.17 Canada and Quebec shall recommend that legislative effect be given to the Agreement by Parliament and the National Assembly, subject to the terms of the Agreement and the legislative jurisdiction of Parliament and the National Assembly.

· · ·

Notes

[1] James V. Wright, *Quebec Prehistory* (Toronto: Van Nostrand Reinhold 1979), 23.

[2] Marcel Laliberté, *La forêt boréale*, in C. Chapdelaine, ed., *Images de la préhistoire de Québec* (Recherches amérindiennes au Québec 1978), 7 (1-2):87–98.

[3] Moreau S. Maxwell, "Pre-Dorset and Dorset Prehistory of Canada," in W. Sturtevant, ed., *Handbook of North American Indians. Arctic* (Washington, D.C.: Smithsonian Institution 1984), 5 (David Damas, vol. ed.):360.

[4] Adrian Tanner, "The Significance of Hunting Territories Today," in *Cultural Ecology*, ed. B. Cox (Toronto: McClelland and Stewart 1973), 105.

[5] Although there were no land-cession treaties, there are at least two recognized treaties, granted by the British authorities, affecting some of the Indians in Quebec. One, Jay's Treaty of 1794, provided that Indians living on both sides of the border (between the United States and the Canadas, but not including the Indians of the Hudson's Bay Company's territory) were to be exempt from levies on personal goods and entitled to pass freely across the border; see Derek G. Smith, *Canadian Indians and the Law: Selected Documents, 1663–1972* (Toronto: McClelland and Stewart 1975), 14. The other is a document signed by Governor Murray in 1760 granting the Hurons of Lorette the "free Exercise of their Religion, their Customs, and Liberty of trading with the English." A recent Supreme Court decision held that this document constituted a treaty which is still in effect; see Supreme Court of Canada, *R.* v. *Sioui*, 1990, 1 S.C.R. 1025.

[6] Richard J. Diubaldo, "The Absurd Little Mouse: When Eskimos Became Indians," *Journal of Canadian Studies* 16, 2 (1981), 34.

[7] Peter Cumming and Neil Mickenberg, eds., *Native Rights in Canada* (Toronto: Indian and Eskimo Association 1972), 81.

[8] Ibid., 76.

[9] R. Cole Harris, ed., *Historical Atlas of Canada: From the Beginning to 1800* (Toronto: University of Toronto Press 1987), 116; and J.M.S. Careless, *Canada: A Story of Challenge* (Toronto: Macmillan 1953; repr. 1974), 100.

[10] Cumming and Mickenberg, *Native Rights in Canada*, 85.

[11] Ibid., 30.

[12] Ibid., 86.

[13] Paul-André Linteau, René Durocher, and Jean-Claude Robert, *Quebec: A History 1867–1929*, trans. Robert Chodos (Toronto: James Lorimer 1983), 6.

[14] Morris Zaslow, *The Opening of the Canadian North, 1870–1914* (Toronto: McClelland and Stewart 1971), 150, 154.

[15] Cumming and Mickenberg, *Native Rights in Canada*, 89.

[16] *Statutes of Canada*, 1912, Chap. 45.

[17] Larry Villeneuve and Daniel Francis, *The Historical Background of Indian Reserves and Settlements in the Province of Quebec* (Ottawa: Department of Indian and Northern Affairs, Research Branch 1984), 6.

[18] Ornstein, *The First Peoples in Quebec: A Reference Work on the History, Environment, Economic and Legal Position of the Indians and Inuit of Quebec* (3 vols., Montreal: Native North American Studies Institute 1973), 3:108.

[19] Brian Deer, personal communication, March 1991.

[20] Ornstein, *The First Peoples in Quebec*, 3:108, 118.

[21] Ibid., 166-8.

[22] Francis, *A History of the Native Peoples of Quebec, 1760–1867* (Ottawa: Department of Indian and Northern Affairs Research Branch 1983), 29.

[23] National Archives of Canada, RG 10 (Indian and Northern Affairs), vol. 6759: 420-10, 17 July and 18 August 1924 (Quebec Game Laws).

[24] Ornstein, *The First Peoples in Quebec*, 3:133.

[25] Province of Quebec, *Native Peoples of Quebec* (Quebec: SAGMAI 1984), 78.

[26] Ornstein, *The First Peoples in Quebec*, 3:125–6.

[27] Villeneuve and Francis, *The Historical Background of Indian Reserves and Settlements*, 60–5.

[28] Province of Quebec, *Native Peoples of Quebec*, 79.

[29] Francis, *A History of the Native Peoples of Quebec*, 32.

[30] *R. v. Sioui*, 1990.

[31] Francis, *A History of the Native Peoples of Quebec*, 32.

[32] Louise Tremblay, "La politique de gestion de terres amérindiennes au Lac de Deux Montagnes 1725–1825." Paper presented to the Canadian Historical Association meetings, Kingston, Ontario, 3 June 1991, 12.

[33] R. Daniel, *A History of Native Claims Processes in Canada, 1867-1979* (Ottawa: Department of Indian and Northern Affairs, Research Branch 1983), 77–83.

[34] Supreme Court of Canada, *Simon* v. *Regina*, 1985, 2, *S.C.R.*, f.387.

[35] Frank G. Speck, *Naskapi: The Savage Hunters of the Labrador Peninsula* (Norman, Oklahoma: University of Oklahoma Press 1977; first published 1935); Adrian Tanner, *Bringing Home Animals: Religious Ideology and the Mode of Production of the Mistassini Cree Hunters* (St. John's: Memorial University Institute of Social and Economic Research 1979), 105.

[36] RG 10, vol. 8620:1/1–15–15, pt.1, f.5, 1933.

[37] Ibid., vol. 6750:420–10 A, Emile Saindon to D.C. Scott, 29 October 1931.

[38] Ibid., vol. 6750:420–10, 7 October 1898.

[39] Ibid., vol. 6750:420–10 A, 22 July 1926.

[40] Ibid., vol. 6750:420–10, 17 December 1925.

[41] Toby Morantz, "Dwindling Animals and Diminished Lands: Early Twentieth Century Developments in James Bay," in W. Cowan, ed., *Papers of the Eighteenth Algonquian Conference* (Ottawa: Carleton University 1987), 220.

[42] RG 10, vol. 3033:235, 225, pt.1, 17 August 1903.

[43] Boyce Richardson, *Strangers Devour the Land* (Toronto: Macmillan 1975), 9.

[44] Sylvie Vincent and Garry Bowers, eds., *Baie James et Nord Québécois: Dix Ans Après* (Montreal: Recherches amérindiennes au Québec 1988), 221.

[45] James O'Reilly, "The Role of the Courts in the Evolution of the James Bay Hydroelectric Project," in Vincent and Bowers, *Baie James et Nord Québécois*, 34.

[46] Ibid., 36.

[47] Daniel, *A History of Native Claims Processes in Canada*, 221.

[48] Harvey Feit, "Negotiating Recognition of Aboriginal Rights: History, Strategies and Reactions to the James Bay and Northern Quebec Agreement," *Canadian Journal of Anthropology*, 1980 (2):160.

[49] Vincent and Bowers, *Baie James et Nord Québécois*, 224–5.

[50] Province of Quebec, *The James Bay Agreement* (Quebec: Editeur officiel 1975), section 25–2.

[51] Feit, "Negotiating Recognition of Aboriginal Rights," 159.

[52] Vincent and Bowers, *Baie James et Nord Québécois*.

[53] Feit, "Negotiating Recognition of Aboriginal Rights," and "Legitimation and Autonomy in James Bay Cree Responses to Hydro-Electric Development," in Noel Dyck, ed., *Indigenous Peoples and the National-State* (St John's, Nlfd: Memorial University, Institute of Social and Economic Research 1985), 27–66.

[54] Province of Quebec, *The James Bay Agreement*, sections 5–7.

[55] Harvey Feit, "The Power and the Responsibility: Implementation of the Wildlife and Hunting Provisions of the James Bay and Northern Quebec Agreement," in Vincent and Bowers, *Baie James et Nord Québécois*, 74–9.

[56] Richard F. Salisbury, *A Homeland for the Cree: Regional Development in James Bay, 1971–1981* (Montreal: McGill- Queen's University Press 1986), 147.

[57] Ignatius La Rusic, *Negotiating a Way of Life* (Montreal: SSDCC 1979; report prepared for Research Division, Dept. of Indian and Northern Affairs).

[58] Robert Pratt, "Third Party Native Rights and the James Bay and Northern Quebec Agreement," in Vincent and Bowers, *Baie James et Nord Québécois*, 67.

[59] Alain Bissonnette, *Examen des faits nouveaux: bilan de la situation chez les Atikamekw et les Montagnais* (Report to the Commission des droits de l'homme, Montreal, 22 July 1991); Bernard Cleary, *Un bilan de quartre ans de négociations* (Report presented to the Working Group on Indigenous Peoples, Geneva, 23 July–3 August 1990).

[60] Conseil Atikamekw-Montagnais, *La négociation de la revendication territoriale des Atikamekw et des Montagnais* (Quebec [1989]; pamphlet).

[61] Bernard Cleary, "The Estates General of the Atikamekw and Montagnais Nations," *Rencontre* 11, 2 (December 1989), 4.

[62] Ibid., 4–5.

[63] The Algonquins protected their control of the Ottawa River system by levying tolls in 1632; see Reuben Gold Thwaites, *The Jesuit Relations and Allied Documents*, (73 vols., Cleveland 1896–1901), 5:239n57.

[64] Ibid., 8:247, re. 1635.

[65] *Gazette* (Montreal), 12 April 1990.

[66] Lucie Dumas, "Negotiations Under Way," *Rencontre* 12, 3 (1991), 14.

[67] Sylvie Vincent, "Hydroelectricity and Its Lessons," in Vincent and Bowers, *Baie James et Nord Québécois*, 247.

[68] Michel Girard, "Some Thoughts on the Environmental History of the Oka Forest." Paper presented to the Canadian Historical Association Meetings, Kingston, Ontario, 3 June 1991.

[69] Ida Williams, "Discussion of Events at the Montreal Native Friendship Centre." Paper presented to a Teach-In on Human Rights among Native Peoples, Montreal, McGill University, 7 February 1991.

[70] Vincent and Bowers, *Baie James et Nord Québécois,* 48.

Aboriginal Land Claims
in the Atlantic Provinces

Adrian Tanner

Sakej Henderson

$\mathbf{T}$he homelands of the aboriginal nations of the Atlantic region are not identical with the area covered by the present Atlantic provinces. In fact, these provinces' very existence is based on questionable claims of jurisdiction and land title, given that aboriginal sovereignty or ownership was never brought to an end. The provinces are constructs of the European imagination, their illusory existence dependent on actions that overlook or suppress the rights of the aboriginal nations. In our view, an aboriginal-rights perspective must begin with a serious challenge to the legitimacy of these actions.

The national lands of the Mi'kmaq, called Mi'kma'ki, became sectioned among all four Atlantic provinces, as well as Quebec. They were surrounded by the lands of the Mi'kmaq's allies: the Malacite, who over time were split between New Brunswick and Maine, the Beothuk in Newfoundland, and the Innu (Montagnais and Naskapi) in Labrador and Quebec. Since the middle of the eighteenth century aboriginal tenure to all of these lands has been constitutionally protected by treaties, proclamations, and instructions. They were labelled the "Hunting Grounds" and explicitly reserved to the Indian nations in the Royal Proclamation of 1763.

However, the establishment of colonial, and later provincial and national, regimes created an artificial division of the aboriginal dominion. The Beothuk, a small group who prehistorically probably had social contacts with natives across the Straits of Belle Isle, became island-bound as the result of European contact and were unable to survive the impact of colonial settlement. The Innu were separated between Quebec and Labrador, a boundary that also divided the Inuit of Labrador from those of the Ungava peninsula. As we will see, the formation of these boundaries often came to interfere with aboriginal land rights.

The provinces of Newfoundland, Nova Scotia, New Brunswick, Prince Edward Island, and Quebec were originally part of Mi'kma'ki. The Mi'kmaq Compact, both the central treaty of 1752 with the grand chief and delegates and the various accession treaties by the Mi'kmaq district chiefs between 1753 and 1793, established a permanent and continuing political relationship between the Mi'kmaq and the crown. The compact became the foundation-stone on which the Atlantic provinces were created. After representative government was extended to the new provinces, the crown affirmed the constitutional position of the compact in 1761 royal instructions to Nova Scotia, which then included the modern provinces of New Brunswick and Prince Edward Island, and the broader 1763 proclamation. The compact also became part of the constitution of Canada and the federated provinces in accordance with sections 132, 109, and 92(24) of the original British North America Act, and sections 25 and 35 of the Constitution Act, 1982. The 1763 proclamation also applied to Innu and Inuit territory in modern-day Labrador.

Most of the territory of Atlantic Canada, therefore, derives from aboriginal treaties with the crown. It was a consensual treaty order affirmed by instructions and proclamations. These royal commands became the explicit legal, prerogative order that protected the First Nations from both the representative assembles and the immigrants. The imperial crown intended that the existing coastal British settlements and reserved aboriginal hunting grounds in Atlantic Canada would remain undisturbed. Both were to govern themselves under separate sources of authority and the protection of the crown. Each community, British and aboriginal, was to continue to function under its own distinct, customary constitution, while the 1763 proclamation provided the constitutional arrangement for managing relationships between these two autonomous communities.

In their path to representative, then responsible, government, the colonial settlers in Atlantic Canada ignored the prerogative treaties, instructions, and proclamation. Their goal was to have the same relationship with the crown that the First Nations enjoyed. Through various devices, the colonial authorities replaced the prerogative order with one based on their own self-interest. When the crown refused to justify their instrumental order, the colonials transformed colonialism and racism into local legislative power, creating an alternative order that was valid only within British settlements. Eventually they extended their colonial order to the Mi'kmaq. The colonial order allowed the immigrants to take the land and rights that the crown had reserved for the Indian nations and tribes. In particular, the 1763 proclamation reserved all the lands in Atlantic Canada as the "Hunting Grounds" of the Indian nations and tribes, the only exemption being for land that was either ceded or purchased. This proclamation is still in effect.

Since they have continually taken reserved lands, each successive government has lived in fear of being exposed. This fear has cemented itself into governmental policy, and sometimes into legislation. No popularly elected government wants to "give back the land" to the aboriginal peoples. To conceal its self-interested and *ultra vires* actions, governments have been forced to accord racism a higher legal status than that of the prerogative order.

Herein lies the unity of the historical backgrounds of Newfoundland and Labrador, Nova Scotia, New Brunswick, and Prince Edward Island. No land-cession treaties have ever been signed, with the possible exception of the relatively small Moravian land grants in Labrador and agreements with the Malacites of the Saint John River valley. Government intervention to restrict the immigrants' desire for aboriginal land, in some cases as a result of pressure by the aboriginal groups and associations, might in theory have influenced this situation. But apart from the small reserves established in the Maritimes as family estates for farming, there has been little unified government action in this direction.

Aboriginal tenure in all the Maritime provinces and in Newfoundland and Labrador has a common status under British law: the land is constitutionally reserved for the First Nations as "Hunting Grounds." Very little aboriginal tenure has been legally extinguished by any formal treaty or purchase, and as a result native land has always been protected by the United Kingdom's constitutional law. Nevertheless, the present federal policy on land claims treats the Maritimes differently from Labrador. While in Labrador the aboriginal peoples had their formal statements of land claim accepted as valid for comprehensive settlements, claims by groups in the Maritime provinces have all been rejected on the grounds that they were "superseded by law."

In the following section the argument is made that this difference does not, as is asserted by the Department of Justice, result from any valid difference in the legal basis for aboriginal title between the two areas. We might speculate that the different approach is instead based on an unstated federal policy of wishing to recognize comprehensive claims that can be settled with grants of unassigned land, but not those that would require compensation for land already assigned. Whatever the reason, there are important practical differences in the situation of aboriginal land rights and claims in the two parts of Atlantic Canada, so in this chapter we will look at them separately. But recognizing the distinctions made by federal policy must not be equated with validating the federal illusion.

The Maritimes

In a claims-policy statement of 8 August 1973,[1] the federal government pledged that lawful obligations under the treaties, the 1763 proclamation, and the BNA Act of 1867 would be honoured. It affirmed the queen's commitment that Canada would "recognize the importance of full compliance with the spirit and terms" of its treaties with native people. The 1763 proclamation, "which, whatever differences there may be about its judicial interpretation, stands as a basic declaration of the Indian people's interest in land in this country," was officially acknowledged as the starting-point of the crown's responsibility towards Indians and the lands reserved to them. While establishing a new broader negotiation process for settling land claims, the government emphasized that "nothing in the following policy enunciated is intended to alter" its legal responsibilities under either the treaties or the proclamation. Issues dealt with under the prerogative acts were called "specific claims."

In its claims-policy statement, the government announced that beyond these specific claims it was also establishing a new category of claims. After the Supreme Court of Canada had affirmed, independent of treaties and the proclamation, the existence of a valid common-law title to aboriginal lands because of long historical use (the Calder case), the government stated that it was "ready to negotiate with authorized representatives of the native peoples on the basis that where their traditional interest in the land concerned can be established, an agreed form of compensation or benefit will be provided to native people in return for their interest." These claims were called "comprehensive."

Overall, the government acknowledged that there were some variations in the claims. To remove the sense of grievance and injustice that hindered Canada's relationship with the Indians, the government stressed that the claims process required a flexibility of response. Two of the areas of Canada where such flexibility was needed, it said, were the Atlantic provinces and southern Quebec—the ancient territory of Mi'kma'ki. The government admitted that "no treaties of surrender were entered into" in these parts of the country. It also declared "that land claims in these areas are of a different character from those referred to earlier in this statement," that is, British Columbia, northern Quebec, the Yukon, and the Northwest Territories—all areas where Indian peoples did not have treaties with the crown.

In 1975 the Court of Appeals for Nova Scotia, in *Isaac* v. *The Crown*, ruled that the Royal Proclamation of 1763 applied to Nova Scotia and that the aboriginal lands of the Mi'kmaq had not been ceded to the crown. The Province did not appeal the decision. Armed with this judicial determination of the highest court in Nova Scotia, the Sante Mawi'omi wjit Mi'kmaq (Grand Council of the Mi'kmaq) requested submission of a Mi'kmaq position paper to the federal government.

On 25 April 1977, four years after the policy statement, the Mawi'omi, through the Union of Nova Scotia Indians, formally submitted the first stage of its national land claim, dealing with the imperial reservation created by the 1763 proclamation in Nova Scotia, the oldest province, to the minister of the Department of Indian Affairs. Since Prince Edward Island, New Brunswick, and parts of northeastern Quebec had originally been parts of Nova Scotia, their claims were collaterally involved. On 23 June 1977, the minister, Warren Allmand, asked the Office of Native Claims, Department of Indian and Northern Affairs, and the Department of Justice for a "thorough evaluation" of all the facts and documentation within the Nova Scotia Mi'kmaq Aboriginal Rights Position Paper. On 2 October 1978, a little over a year and a half later, Indian Affairs rejected these land claims on the advice of the Department of Justice. Hugh Faulkner, the new minister of Indian Affairs, explained the reasons for the rejection:

> The Government's 1973 policy on comprehensive claims provides for the negotiation of those claims where Indian title has not been extinguished by treaty or superseded by law. We have concluded, after careful study of your claim, that Indian title, in Nova Scotia has effectively been superseded by law, thus placing your claim outside the terms of this policy. In Nova Scotia, the actions of successive pre-Confederation and post-Confederation governments in opening up the lands of the Province to settlement, in granting such land by letters patent, in granting various rights to third parties, and in setting apart other lands as Indian reserves, have had the effect of superseding Indian title in all areas other than reserve lands.[2]

This was another formal admission that the ancestral lands were not extinguished by treaties with the British crown between 1726 and 1761. The assertion that the 1763 proclamation had been superseded by colonial legislation was not supported by any United Kingdom precedent.

No explanation was provided by the minister why the Mi'kmaq claims were no longer regarded as different from other comprehensive or specific claims. In the government's earlier view, there was no concept of claims "superseded by law" because of the existence of a treaty with the crown. The Mi'kmaq had entered into treaties that had not ceded any land to the crown; on the contrary, the crown had reserved the Mi'kmaq's unceded lands as their reserved hunting grounds pursuant to the 1763 proclamation. These imperial documents established the Mi'kmaq claim, as well as the cornerstones of the federal obligation. Thus the new claims policy was changing the government's own legal obligations.

The Mi'kmaq leaders rejected the concept that either the provincial or federal authorities had the power to pass laws contrary to the crown's treaties, instructions, and proclamation. Alexander Denny, grand captain of the Mawi'omi and president of the Union of Nova Scotia Indians, stated to the government that provincial law could not supersede the Mi'kmaq aboriginal title protected in the proclamation. Any laws of Nova Scotia and Canada that superseded the Mi'kmaq aboriginal title were of "questionable validity," he said, since the government saw their sole purpose as protecting land title and treaty rights for the crown. Under the explicit terms of the proclamation, the provincial assembly had no authority to abrogate imperial obligations or modify them without a public treaty with the Indians.

The deputy minister of Indian Affairs, Arthur Kroeger, refused to fund a court challenge to the decision. On 22 May 1979 Kroeger wrote that purchase through a public treaty with the Indians was not the only way the crown could acquire lands reserved under the proclamation:

> While [cession by treaty] is one means by which interests in lands traditionally used and occupied can be ended, it is the Government's position that such interests may also be legally terminated by other means. More specifically, native title may be superseded by the legal exercise of powers by a provincial or federal government in a manner adverse to continuation of the traditional use and occupancy of lands by native people. . . . Regardless of whether the Royal Proclamation of 1763 did or did not have application in Nova Scotia, it is the Government position that any Mi'kmaq title to land in Nova Scotia outside of the reserves has been superseded by law subsequent to 1763.[3]

On 18 September 1979, the associate deputy minister of justice, P.M. Ollivier, responded for the Justice Department. He characterized the claim as asserting "the continued existence of aboriginal title throughout Nova Scotia," rather than just lands reserved by both treaty and the 1763 proclamation. Ollivier explained:

> The position is that under the St. Catherines Milling Case Indian title is a personal and usufructuary right, dependent upon the good-will of the Sovereign, and which may be extinguished by surrender or otherwise, whereupon the Crown's underlying title becomes absolute. In the Calder Case, Judson, J. acknowledged the right of the Sovereign to extinguish that title "whether it be done by treaty, by sword, by purchase, by the exercise of complete dominion adverse to the right of occupancy or otherwise." Prerogative acts of the Sovereign authority such as setting apart reserves and opening the rest of the land for homestead grants and settlements can bring about extinguishment of Indian title. These views were adopted by MacKeigan, C.J.N.S., in the Isaac Case who found that lands reserved as hunting grounds had gradually been restricted by white occupation under Crown grant which extinguished the Indian right in the land. In Nova

Scotia, in fact, there has been, over the years, a consistent pattern of exercising complete dominion over Crown land adverse to the right of occupancy by opening the land for settlement and alienating and disposing of those lands in a manner inconsistent with the continuation of any aboriginal title and this has brought about the extinguishment of any Indian title that may have existed.[4]

The Mi'kmaq leaders pointed out, however, that Nova Scotia settlements were not creations of the sovereign. Moreover, grants are not irrefutable evidence of ownership, especially in the case of conflicting imperial reservations for Indians and colonial grants to settlers. According to the opinion of the Department of Justice, private acts of British settlers could supersede the 1763 proclamation. Justice refused to review the claim on its own merits.

The federal government has never found any specific legislation that extinguished Mi'kmaq title. Instead it created a new theory to justify the taking of reserved hunting grounds. On 11 August 1980, the minister of Indian Affairs, John Munro, stated

> In reviewing the matter, I find that there is no single piece of legislation explicitly extinguishing native title in Nova Scotia. Rather, this occurred through the generally *uncontested and continuous exercise* of power by the colonial governments to grant lands within their respective domains subject to such limitations as were imposed upon them from time to time. There is also the undisputed fact that settlements did take place. In Nova Scotia, various pieces of pre-Confederation legislation provided for the opening of public lands for settlement, for the making of surveys, the sale or lease of the land itself or timber, quarries, and mines thereon and for the reservation of other lands for Indians. Some of these are reproduced in the "Consolidation of Indian Legislation, Volume 3" prepared under contract for this Department and distributed to Indian Associations, including UNSI in 1979. To be noted particularly are "An Act Relative to the Crown Land Department" S.N.S. 1851 Chapter 4, "Of the Crown Lands" R.S.N.S. 1851 Chapter 28, "An Act Concerning Indian Reserves" S.N.S. 1859 Chapter 14, "Of the Crown Lands" S.N.S. 1864 Chapter 26. There are others which can be readily identified in the above-noted volume. Of course, the process of selling, leasing, alienating and setting aside Crown lands for various purposes has continued since Confederation and is dealt with, at least in part, by the current Provincial Lands and Forests Act. The basis of the legal opinion of the Department of Justice is that *opening Crown lands for settlements, alienating it or otherwise dealing with it in a way inconsistent with the continuation of aboriginal title, and the setting aside of reserves for Indians operates to extinguish any aboriginal title that may have existed.* This is consistent with Mr. Justice Judson in the Calder case and applying it to Nova Scotia, Chief Justice Mackeigan, in the Isaac case, noted that "only a few thousand widely scattered acres have never been granted, placed under mining or timber licenses or leases, set aside as game preserves or parks, or occupied prescriptively". He found that as a result, Indian reserves may be the only place in which native or aboriginal title may still subsist. [Emphasis added][5]

This letter transformed the test from the legal exercise of power to a new standard—the uncontested and continuous exercise of power by a colonial government that opened up reserved lands for settlement even though they were protected by prerogative treaties and the 1763 proclamation.

In three different explanations, the ministers had relied on three different standards to explain "superseded by law." Each letter created a broader test than the previous one had, and each minister's explanation contained the same central imbalance. Each appeared to assume that the Indian Affairs interpretation of the statutes concerned was correct, but this interpretation was not borne out by the wording of the statutes themselves, legislative history, or general imperial-colonial law. And each explanation conveniently overlooked the fact that the government's 1973 land-claims policy was to provide compensation for the taking of reserved lands. The Department of Justice has refused to present its rationalization to the courts.

The positive acknowledgment and affirmation of "existing aboriginal and treaty rights" in the Constitution Act of 1982 reinforced the Mi'kmaq position. Justice's interpretation of Mi'kmaq rights was rendered inconsistent with the supreme law of Canada by section 52 of the new constitution and thus of no force and effect as law. Moreover, in 1984, in *Guerin* v. *The Queen*, the Supreme Court of Canada gave a clear legal description of the crown's obligation to lands reserved for Indians. In the absence of a treaty, Justice Estey found that the crown in the 1763 proclamation accorded special rights to the Indians. The various pre-Confederation laws and the federal Indian Act "all reflected a strong sense of awareness of the community interest in protecting the right of the aboriginal population in those lands to which they had a longstanding connection" (346). Justice Bertha Wilson, on behalf of three members of the court, found that the Indian Act "recognizes the existence of a fiduciary obligation" but did not create it (346). This obligation was to "protect and preserve the band's interests from invasion and destruction" (357).

Chief Justice Dickson, speaking for four members of an eight-jury panel, took a broader view. He concluded that the crown's obligation under the Indian Act was of an historical fiduciary nature. Its existence as an independent legal interest was *sui generis* and predated the 1763 proclamation. It became legally effective with the crown's undertaking in the proclamation (and in subsequent legislation) of a responsibility to protect Indian property interest from exploitation in relation to land dealings (358).[6]

In 1985 an undivided Supreme Court of Canada, in *Simon* v. *The Queen*, held that the 1752 treaty with the Mi'kmaq constituted a positive source of protection against infringement on aboriginal hunting rights, and that the treaty continued to be effective as an enforceable obligation between the Indians and the crown. The 1986 report of the Task Force to Review Comprehensive Claim Policy also affirmed the Grand Council position. It noted that "claims of a different character" were mentioned in the policy statement but the federal government had not identified any mechanism for dealing with them. Because of the Guerin and Simon decisions, the task force argued that the "superseded by law" concept was no longer supported by case law, and concluded that it "should no longer be applied to exclude from the comprehensive claims process those aboriginal societies that have not been a party to a treaty or the subjects of extinguishment legislation. Nor should it exclude those aboriginal societies that have engaged in treaty relationships, but that have not specifically dealt with lands in those treaties."[7]

On 13 March 1987 Grand Captain Denny formally wrote the minister of Indian affairs requesting that the Department of Justice review its 1978 opinion in light of the new constitution, decisions of the Supreme Court of Canada in *Guerin* and *Simon*, and the task force's conclusion. In 1988 the Grand Council asked for an independent review of Justice's decision, arguing that "superseded by law" was inconsistent with the decisions of the Supreme Court of Canada and had become an arbitrary and capricious concept. The council pointed out that the methods that Justice asserted could legally terminate the recognized and protected Mi'kmaq tenure—successive pre-Confederation and post-Confederation governments opening up the lands of the province to settlement, granting such lands by letters patent, and granting various rights to third parties, as well as setting apart other lands as Indian reserves—had not been accepted as valid by the Supreme Court of Canada in the Guerin and Simon decisions.

The council requested a review of whether Justice had properly exercised its discretion under the 1973 policy statement. Four points were raised: (1) Justice failed to consider and give proper weight to explicit prerogative treaties and instruments that recognized the Mi'kmaq's tenure and the crown's obligations to them; (2) Justice arbitrarily failed to apply the "different character" standards to its review of the Mi'kmaq land claim; (3) Justice utilized a judicial theory irrelevant to the legal history of the 1977 claim; (4) Justice's decisions were inconsistent with the current decision law of the Supreme Court of Canada.

Under the *prima facie* evidence of prerogative treaties and acts establishing the reserved hunting lands, the important question in the Mi'kmaq claim is the authority of Nova Scotia officials or private settlers to confiscate these lands without compensation. The reserved hunting grounds were vested property rights that the crown directly granted to the Mi'kmaq. These property rights created legally enforceable fiduciary obligations on the part of both Nova Scotia and Canada. The acts by which Justice attempted to prove extinguishment were unlawful—they could not constitutionally limit the Mi'kmaq's reserved lands.

The federal government's position that pre-Confederation provinces and Canada had the right to confiscate vested Mi'kmaq rights is also contrary to the main rules of constitutional law regulating the colonial relationship between the United Kingdom and overseas territories. These rules postulate the supremacy of the king-in-council and the king-in-parliament, not only in the initial establishment of legitimate government and law in the territories, but also for the supervision thereafter of colonial governments and the legal system. Neither the provinces nor Canada had a right to amend these constitutional orders.

The crown's recognition of the reserved lands under prerogative treaty and the 1763 proclamation, coupled with the absence of a treaty of surrender, the Grand Council argued, ought to have secured and vested the Mi'kmaq tenure in the constitution of Nova Scotia (as well as New Brunswick, Prince Edward Island, Quebec, and Newfoundland) and later in that of Canada. The government clearly acknowledged and understood this unique and different situation in the 1973 policy statement. Indian Affairs or Justice had arbitrarily placed the 1977 claim in the wrong category under the policy statement. Either of these agencies of the federal government, the council asserted, had confused lands recognized under the 1763 proclamation with common-law aboriginal title.

With explicit constitutional protection of their aboriginal lands in the prerogative acts, the Grand Council argued that it did not seek to, or need to, deny that British settlement had taken place within their reserved lands in Nova Scotia prior to Confederation. The council pointed out, however, that this fact was irrelevant to the issue of extinguishment since it had long been recognized that aboriginal title is not incompatible with the establishment of private estates or interest in the land. British settlement of reserved land was an argument for compensation, not for denial of the claim.

Moreover, the 1977 claim did not seek to establish possessory rights to land owned by private individuals, because that was not the remedy of the 1973 policy statement. The policy statement provided only for an agreed form of compensation or benefit to be enshrined in legislation in return for the unburdening of the private estates from the existing Mi'kmaq interest, easements, profits, covenants, and servitude under the prerogative treaties and instruments. As to crown land, the claim sought to show a continuing and vested joint interest of the Grand Council with the sovereign. After the Guerin and Simon decisions confirmed the points raised concerning the validity of the treaties and the fiduciary responsibility of the crown, the council argued that Justice could not ignore its arbitrary mistake, which had deprived the Mi'kmaq of a remedy for the confiscation of their vested property rights under the proclamation.

In addition to selecting the wrong category for the 1977 claim, Justice used a wrong judicial theory to examine the claim. The basic question raised by Justice's rejection of the Nova Scotia claim was the failure to distinguish the protection of Mi'kmaq tenure under the treaties and the 1763 proclamation from the common-law aboriginal title recognized in *Calder*. An unrecognized or common-law aboriginal title is one not confirmed by treaty or the proclamation. The 1977 claim of the Mi'kmaq rested on positive reservation of aboriginal lands by the British sovereign.

Mi'kmaq tenure, therefore, is the opposite of the Nisga'a tenure recognized in *Calder*. The courts have ruled that the Mi'kmaq nation constituted one of the several nations and tribes of Indians who lived under British protection in 1763 and were directly connected to the crown by the 1752 treaty. Both of these laws are still valid in Nova Scotia law. Mi'kmaq tenure was also protected in the commission and instructions to Lord Cornwallis in 1749, the French Articles of Capitulation in 1760, the Additional Instruction of 1761, the Nova Scotia Proclamation of 1762, the Treaty of Paris, the Proclamation of 1763, and other instructions. These prerogative acts not only reserved a well-defined Mi'kmaq hunting ground, but also declared an exclusive extinguishment test—the crown could purchase the reserved lands of the Mi'kmaq nation only "at some public Meeting or Assembly . . . held for that purpose by the Governor in Chief of the Colonies where the Land shall lie."[8]

Justice's broad propositions concerning Nova Scotia's complete extinguishment of Mi'kmaq tenure are thus indefensible and unjustifiable in light of the actual legal history of Nova Scotia and the rest of Atlantic Canada. It must also be noted that, even though Justice applied the Judson theory to reject the Mi'kmaq claim, that same theory was not sufficient to deny the Nisga'a's comprehensive claim—the Nisga'a's claim to the minister was accepted as valid. The Mi'kmaq argued that this fact alone illustrated the arbitrary and political nature of Justice's decision in the 1977 claim.

It was the position of the Grand Council that the Nova Scotia assembly had no beneficial interest in the reserved Mi'kmaq hunting grounds under either the treaties or the 1763 proclamation. Nova Scotia remained a prerogative colony prior to Confederation and thus subject to prerogative treaties and acts that protected these hunting grounds. The same argument is applicable to the rest of the Mi'kmaq hunting grounds in Atlantic Canada. In contrast to the situation in the province of Canada (Ontario and Quebec), there never was an imperial act granting the crown's beneficial interest in the lands to Nova Scotia or to New Brunswick, Prince Edward Island, or Newfoundland. In the history of the Maritime provinces there is no Act of Union of 1840, upon which the Privy Council and Supreme Court of Canada placed such reliance in the St Catherine's Milling decision.

Clearly, under article 8 of the 1752 treaty as well as other prerogative acts, the Mi'kmaq were entitled to judicial protection in their reserved lands from interference by the Nova Scotia assembly or any other legislative body. The Department of Justice failed to give the treaty or the proclamation a fair, large, and liberal construction as it was required to do by the Simon decision. Instead, it placed the burden of proof on the Mi'kmaq.

The arbitrary nature of the claims process is its essential unity. The initial promises of fulfilling the crown's lawful obligations under the treaties and 1763 proclamation have been ignored. The Department of Justice refused to affirm the queen's and the federal government's commitment to honour the treaties and "recognize the importance of full compliance with the spirit and terms" of treaties. In fact, its review of Mi'kmaq treaties is stricter than the courts'. Originally, in its 1973 policy, the government's recognition of its responsibility was dated back to the proclamation, "which, whatever differences there may be about its judicial interpretation, stands as a basic declaration of the Indian people's interest in land in this country."[9] But these differences of interpretation have become a cover under which the government ignores its lawful obligation. To the Department of Justice, ambiguity is an excuse not to admit claims, rather than to clarify obligations. Moreover, in the claims processes, Justice has sought to alter its legal responsibilities, as defined by the courts, under the treaties and the proclamation. Faced with its breaches of the fiduciary obligation, the department has become a rigid instrumentalist and an official apologist for the status quo.

The Department of Justice's decision in the Nova Scotia case prevented the Mi'kmaq and other First Nations in the Maritimes from submitting comprehensive claims to the federal government. Instead they agreed to allow the Mi'kmaq Grand Council, through the Union of Nova Scotia Indians, to challenge the government's position.

After the initial rejection of its argument by the Government of Canada in 1980, the Grand Council decided to take its concerns to the United Nations. Grand Captain Denny initiated the Grand Council's original communication to the UN's Human Rights Committee on behalf of all the Mi'kmaq in Atlantic Canada from Newfoundland to Quebec. Part of the claim argued that Canada's denial of Mi'kmaq self-determination and the rejection of their land claims violated the Optional Protocol to the International Covenant on Civil and Political Rights. In the covenant, the United Nations member states recognized the "sovereign right of every State to dispose of its wealth and its natural resources." This right was classified as "permanent" and "inalienable" and "in no cases may a people be deprived of its own means of subsistence." The covenant also held, however, that any state appropriation of private property must be accompanied by compensation to the original owners.[10] The Grand Council asked the UN to affirm its right to the possession of all the territory reserved in the treaty of 1752 and the Royal Proclamation of 1763 as Mi'kmaq "Hunting Grounds." Its communication stated:

Canada in the British North America Act, and the Mi'kmaq Nationimouw in its Treaty, both recognise the dominion of the British Crown. Canadian territory resides in "the Crown in right of Canada" or the "Crown in right of a Province." Compatible with our Treaty, the territory of the Mi'kmaq Nationimouw should have been held, since 1752, by "the Crown in right of the Mi'kmaq Nationimouw." We will abide by our Treaty and respect the integrity of Canada's federal and provincial Crown territories if Canada gives assurances that it will respect the integrity of our "Mi'kmaq Crown" lands. We ask the forum of nations to declare that "except where settled by British subjects prior to 1752, the ancient territory of the Mi'kmaq Nationimouw is property vested in the British Crown in right of the Nationimouw, and cannot be taken or occupied by Canada or any other State without the consent of the Santeoi Mawaiomi.[11]

On 21 July 1981 the Government of Canada challenged the jurisdiction of the Human Rights Committee under the Optional Protocol. The government argued that the Mi'kmaq communication was inadmissible because it affected the national unity and territorial integrity of Canada, that treaties with North American native peoples are not valid international documents, and that sections 24, 34, 36, and 55(c) of the constitutional resolution tabled in the House of Commons on 24 April 1981 resolved the issue of aboriginal and treaty rights.

Answering the argument regarding territorial integrity, the Grand Council in October 1981 pointed out that Canada's position was inappropriate because it assumed a disputed fact, that is, whether the reserved territory of the treaties recognized by the 1763 proclamation ever lawfully became part of the territory of Canada, and failed to deal with the rights to property. In its supplemental communications of October and November 1981, Canada reaffirmed its position that the Grand Council's communication was inadmissible.

In 1985 the UN Human Rights Committee ruled that the collective rights of the Mi'kmaq were admissible under the covenants, and in 1990 it asserted jurisdiction over the dispute.

At the time of this writing, the Grand Council along with the Union of Nova Scotia Indians and the Native Council are in the middle of preparing to take the land claim to the civil courts. They have rejected federal land-claim policies.

Newfoundland and Labrador

Official actions of both pre-Confederation and post-Confederation Newfoundland governments have, with some exceptions, tended to avoid recognition of the aboriginal peoples and their land rights. The main reason is that the First Nations were protected directly by the imperial crown or federal crown, under the 1763 proclamation, and not by colonial or provincial governments. Their lands were also reserved to them as their hunting grounds, distinct from the small British coastal settlements.

The Mi'kmaq treaties and the 1763 proclamation protected the Mi'kmaq on the island of Newfoundland, as well as the Innu and Inuit of Labrador. The aboriginal population in Labrador was largely ignored by Britain, and the issue was beyond the delegated authority of the colony. The Inuit were effectively made the responsibility of the Moravian Church, and the Innu were for most official purposes treated as "Canadian Indians" until the Labrador boundary dispute was resolved in 1927. For at least part of the year some Innu occupied the area known as "Rupertsland" (the watersheds of rivers flowing into Hudson Bay), reserved to the Hudson's Bay Company (HBC) under its 1670 charter, but those occupying the Atlantic and St Lawrence watersheds, including what is now Labrador, were outside the HBC's domain.

Newfoundland, like all the other Atlantic provinces, has not been consistent in applying the 1763 proclamation and protecting the reserved hunting grounds of the Indian nations from the encroachments of non-aboriginals. Some cases of limited recognition of aboriginal peoples can be cited, but such recognition is derived from imperial law rather than colonial legislative authority. The colony, and later the province, could thus, legally speaking, neither legitimize nor restrict aboriginal land rights. Yet that was exactly what it did, imposing its will by force on aboriginal peoples.

In 1769, soon after the royal proclamation, the first of four grants of land in northern Labrador was issued by special order of the Privy Council in Britain to allow the Moravian Church to establish mission communities among the Inuit. The following year, the Moravians went to Labrador to select their first site, and in doing so sought and obtained from as many of the local Inuit as they could formal consent to the purchase of the land. A payment was also made for the land. When they reported to the British what they had done, Lord Barrington of the Privy Council said that he thought the Moravians had acted prudently, because the conveyance they got from the Inuit was "a firmer Grant to you than the King's . . . [who could only give] such as he himself had from the King of France."[12] Thus there was some official awareness of aboriginal land title in Newfoundland and the crown's interest in international treaties and law.

Between 1897 and 1903 Newfoundland issued questionable grants of land, timber, minerals, and water rights along the lower Hamilton (now Churchill) River, and woodcutting began there in 1901. Quebec began pressing a counterclaim to the area in 1906. There is also evidence that territorial claims were made in the early 1900s by some Innu, in response to trapping incursions into the interior by Labrador "settlers."[13] A boundary dispute ensued between Canada and Newfoundland, which was not finally settled until the Privy Council decision of 1927. However, the Innu claims against both Canada and Newfoundland were not resolved by this decision.

In fact, prior to the decision only a few Europeans had penetrated the interior, mostly HBC employees trading with the Innu and mixed Inuit-European settlers trapping along the watershed of the Churchill and Naskapi rivers. Aboriginal land-use patterns were one of the main forms of evidence presented in the boundary-dispute case, indicating some awareness that the rights of the states involved were to some degree dependent on the prior rights of the aboriginal peoples.

In 1907 another questionable grant was made by the Newfoundland government, involving timber-cutting rights over 550 square miles of land near Davis Inlet, on the north coast of Labrador. However, Governor McGregor withheld his approval, noting that it would be an infringement on the rights of the native people of the region. The grant was indefinitely deferred by the government, an action that McGregor interpreted as a recognition of native rights.[14]

Two protective statutes were passed by Newfoundland during the period of responsible government specifically referring to aboriginal people. One forbade sales or gifts to them of intoxicating liquor, and the other prevented them from being paid to leave the colony. After Confederation, the provincial Alcoholic Liquors Act included a section that was far more sweeping in its treatment of aboriginal people than was the Indian Act of the time. While non-status Indians and all Inuit were exempt from the provisions of the then-current Indian Act, which included a ban on alcohol, paragraph 69 (1) (i) of the Newfoundland legislation stated that liquor could not be sold or given to "an Indian or Esquimaux, whether or not such a person is an Indian under any provision of any Statute of the Parliament of Canada."

While today Newfoundland usually applies provincial game laws to aboriginal people in the same way as to the general population, in the past certain exceptions were made, particularly in Labrador. For example, much of the western part of Labrador is the traditional hunting grounds of Innu who have become based in the communities of Sept Îles, Schefferville, and Natashquan, in Quebec, and who might thus be considered "non-residents" under Newfoundland laws. Official recognition was given to their need to hunt in Newfoundland when, in 1961, an order was issued under the wildlife regulations stating that "the term 'resident' shall include Indians registered with the Seven Islands Indian Reservation who live in or are tending traplines in Western Labrador." This recognition was discontinued in the early 1970s, however, and in the mid-1980s was replaced with a statute permitting residents of Quebec, whether aboriginal or not, to apply for licences to hunt in Labrador. In the past ten years there have been frequent arrests of Quebec-based Innu hunting on their traditional lands within Labrador. This application of provincial game laws to aboriginal people has been a major factor restricting the ability of the Innu to use and occupy their lands.

During the 1947 pre-Confederation negotiations between Canada and Newfoundland on the terms of entry, a sub-committee on Indians and Eskimos was formed and its report concluded that after union Indians and Inuit were to be administered by the federal government in the same way as they were in the rest of Canada.[15] Yet this is not what happened. Indian bands were not declared, status Indians were not registered, Inuit were not assigned tag numbers, and no federal programs of the Department of Indian Affairs (or of the separate Department of Northern Affairs which, at the time, administered the Inuit) were made available. Elsewhere in Canada reserves were either established under the provisions of treaties or, where no treaties existed, were created to protect aboriginal communities and to allow the federal government to spend money on government programs for Indians, such as housing. In Newfoundland no reserves were created, except in 1986 when, in response to a threatened legal suit, the Conne River Mi'kmaq were registered as status Indians, and the community land was officially recognized as a reserve.

The 1949 terms of union transferred "lands reserved for Indians" (their reserved hunting grounds) to Canada, just as if Newfoundland had joined Canada in 1867. In other words, Indians—including Inuit—and Indian lands became an exclusively federal constitutional responsibility. However, not until 1954 did the federal government take any action to fulfil this responsibility. It did so first by direct payments from the budget of Indian Affairs to the provincial government to cover health costs, but not until 1965 to cover education and administrative costs. Over the years these funding agreements have become more complex, but negotiation of them is a private matter between the federal and provincial governments, and control over how the funds are spent rests largely with the Newfoundland government. Eligibility for these funds is based not on the ethnicity or status of an individual, but on whether or not he or she happens to reside in one of a list of designated communities.[16] Conne River was added to the list in 1973, but Mi'kmaq outside Conne River have never had access to these funds.

Using these same funds, the Newfoundland government resettled the Inuit of the northern-most Labrador communities without their consent to Nain and Makkovik in the 1950s, and settled the hitherto nomadic Innu to Shesatshit (North West River) and Utshimashit (Davis Inlet) in the 1960s. Today each of these Labrador Innu communities has an elected band council with a chief, who deal with the provincial and federal governments, although the legal status of these bodies is unclear since they are not covered by statute at either level of government. In

1980 the province agreed to participate in the negotiation of the Innu and Inuit claims, which had already been accepted as valid by the Office of Native Claims, and in 1987 it issued a formal policy on land claims.

In summary, Newfoundland has followed an inconsistent policy, most of the time denying recognition of aboriginal people as having any distinct legal rights, but at other times putting them in a legally distinct category, placing special restrictions on their rights as ordinary citizens, giving limited recognition to their need to hunt, and recognizing a list of "native" communities in order to obtain access to federal Indian Affairs funding.

Ktaqamkuk Mi'kmaq

Traditionally the Mi'kmaq in Newfoundland were under the jurisdiction of the district chief of Unamakik ("The Foggy Lands"), which covered Cape Breton Island, St Pierre and Miquelon, and the island of Newfoundland. Anticipating the division of Unamakik under Confederation, the Grand Council recognized Ktaqamkuk as a special district.

The question of the origin of the Mi'kmaq of Newfoundland is now a significant legal matter. In 1986 the federal government rejected the 1980 claim of the Newfoundland Mi'kmaq on the grounds that the claimant group did not enjoy exclusive use and occupation of the territory under claim since time immemorial, which, one assumes, means prior to the establishment of British sovereignty. This is a strange twist in the legal mentality. In the rest of Mi'kma'ki, the Department of Justice's position is that the immigrants had a right to take the constitutionally vested property of an aboriginal group, but in Ktaqamakuk is it asserted that to do this the immigrants had to be of a certain race. This decision underscores the racial politics behind the land-claims policy. It also illustrates the incoherence of the process.

The Mi'kmaq's oral history states that they were living in Newfoundland long before European contact. Whether or not this can be proved with substantial evidence, the federal rejection means that a test has been applied to the Newfoundland Mi'kmaq claim that was not previously used in settling claims and land-cession treaties in Canada. In the region from Ontario to the Rockies it was well known at the time of the treaties that substantial movements of aboriginal populations had just previously been taking place, although the exact extent and timing of these movements remain a matter of controversy among specialists even today. Rather than attempting to make treaty settlements on the basis of the actual locations of groups in question at the time when British sovereignty was first established, a more pragmatic approach was taken of simply assuming that a group could surrender the title of the area of land it was actually using and occupying at the time when the treaty negotiations occurred.

Moreover, this kind of pragmatic, if technically imprecise, approach to defining the area covered by aboriginal title, and to whether the aboriginal beneficiaries or their forebears had actually used and occupied the area since before the establishment of British sovereignty, has continued to be used in modern land-claims negotiations (as distinct from recent land-rights court cases), as can be seen in the wording of the two settlements that have been finally concluded, the James Bay and Northeastern Quebec Agreement and the Inuvialuit Agreement. There, a precise definition of beneficiaries as only those whose forebears had occupied the area in question since time immemorial is not used, nor is it even established what was the precise area where the aboriginal groups concerned actually had valid aboriginal title. The second of these agreements includes recent immigrants as beneficiaries.[17] In the first, a boundary line is set down between Cree and Inuit territory, not on the basis of an historically accurate demarcation between the two groups; instead, the 55th parallel was negotiated, based on convenience.[18] In fact, the federal government has pointed out with pride that political negotiation was chosen as a better way to settle modern land claims rather than a formal land-claims commission, on the grounds that this would avoid the arbitrariness and hairsplitting of a court process.[19]

For the Newfoundland Mi'kmaq, the test of proof of exclusive use and occupation of the area has been applied in a narrower and more arbitrary way than with other Canadian treaties and claims. Yet the Mi'kmaq argue that it is a test they can pass. In their 1980 statement of claim they presented evidence of their use and occupation of Newfoundland before British sovereignty. It is not clear on what basis this evidence was disregarded, since no analysis was provided, despite the stated policy that when a claim is denied a full explanation is to be given.[20]

We must therefore turn to an earlier report in which the Newfoundland government, straying into an area beyond its authority, reviewed the claim and, like the later federal decision, concluded that it was invalid.[21] Critics of this report have pointed out that, based on present archaeological knowledge, its conclusion that the Beothuk were the exclusive prehistoric occupants of area of the claim is unwarranted. They also point out that the report takes account of only some of the historical evidence and makes questionable interpretations of the material it does use (for example, in finding that Cape Breton Mi'kmaq made merely infrequent use of Newfoundland prior to 1670).[22]

The report, moreover, bases itself on the requirements for proof of aboriginal title laid down by Justice Mahoney, in the Baker Lake case, another common-law title case in which neither a treaty nor the 1763 proclamation is involved. It is the wrong test for the Mi'kmaq. The Newfoundland report appears to ignore Justice Mahoney's conclusion in his judgment that a discontinuous use of an area by nomadic hunters, such as the report appears to believe was made by Cape Breton Mi'kmaq before they took up full-time residence in Newfoundland, does not in itself diminish aboriginal title to the area in question.

The hard evidence of Mi'kmaq occupation of Newfoundland can be briefly summarized as follows. European documents indicate that the proto-contact Mi'kmaq were a seagoing people who were crossing at least to the Magdalene Islands without European craft. From at least the sixteenth century onwards they had a significant presence in Newfoundland, which they incorporated into their territory.[23] By at least 1695 they are reported to have been there in considerable numbers and had a detailed knowledge of the interior, acting as guides for the French when overland raids were made on British establishments on the Avalon peninsula and the northeast coast. After the fall of New France in 1763 a treaty of peace and friendship was signed with the British at Codroy Island, off Bay St George, on the west coast of Newfoundland. The Mi'kmaq view this agreement as an accession treaty to the 1752 Mi'kmaq Compact. There is some evidence that in 1782 the Mi'kmaq were given a land grant in Bay St George, although specific details have yet to be found. Detailed evidence of the extent of Mi'kmaq occupation of the interior of Newfoundland is found in the reports of British expeditions into the interior in the late eighteenth and early nineteenth centuries. In 1870 land grants were made to the Mi'kmaq residing at Conne River. During the nineteenth century many Mi'kmaq acted as big-game guides for visiting sportsmen, a role they continued to fill until the caribou population declined in the early 1900s. The ethnographer Frank G. Speck visited the Newfoundland Mi'kmaq in 1914, and his published account includes a description of their family hunting territories, which at that time covered the greater portion of the island.[24]

Since the rejection of their claim, some of the Newfoundland Mi'kmaq have worked towards gaining formal recognition as status Indians. This has effectively divided those at Conne River, who have been successful in this objective, from those elsewhere, who so far, under the Federation of Newfoundland Indians, have not. The latter group is now seeking recognition as status Indians through the courts, under a Charter of Rights argument, on the grounds that they were not treated equally with the people of Conne River. The case is pending. They are also part of the case presented to the UN Human Rights Committee, noted above. As of early 1992, Conne River is in the process of preparing to take its case for aboriginal land rights to court.

Inuit

In comparison with the land claims of the Mi'kmaq and the Innu, the Labrador Inuit land claim is relatively straightforward. While Inuit territory historically included the south coast of Labrador, two hundred years ago, under Moravian tutelage, the Inuit abandoned this region for residence closer to the mission stations along the north coast, and the area of their claim is limited to central and northern Labrador. An overlap exists with the Innu claim. A framework agreement was signed in 1990, and negotiations have begun.

Apart from the land grants to the Moravian Church, mentioned previously, the claim does involve one special aspect. Historically, the Labrador Inuit are unusual in having become more socially integrated within the wider community, including people of part-European descent, at a relatively earlier stage than virtually any other aboriginal group in Canada. Starting in the early 1800s some Inuit intermarried with Europeans, and the offspring group, known as "settlers," or Kablunangajuit, developed a culture made up of a combination of Inuit and European traits. Most of the communities in northern Labrador today include separate "Inuit" and "settler" groups, as well as others without any aboriginal ancestry.[25]

Settlers and Inuit thus have close ties, a degree of common heritage, and similar lifestyles and household economies, based on a mixture of subsistence hunting and commercial fishing. It is in many ways a worthwhile relationship, and there are strong reasons for both groups not to wish to allow the land-claims process to create a division between them. The Labrador Inuit Association (LIA) has up to now recognized this fact, using a broad definition of who it represents. Membership in the association is open to all residents of northern Labrador, providing they or their ancestors were residing there before 1940, although the president is required to be able to speak Innuktitut. However, the land-claims process may now make necessary the difficult exercise of distinguishing who is or is not an Inuk.

Although it was not then the focus of much attention, a similar issue arose forty years ago. Starting in 1954, contributions to the federal–provincial cost-sharing agreements for the Labrador Inuit were calculated on the basis of a working assumption that the population of the north Labrador coastal communities was made up of two-thirds Inuit and one-third non-Inuit.[26]

The issue of who is or is not an Inuk may now arise in the context of the Labrador Inuit claim because the agreement will have to define who is entitled to benefit from its terms. Several Canadian draft or final land-claims agreements have calculated some benefits on a per-capita basis, including land allotments and compensation payments, so that in comprehensive land-claims settlements the exact number of beneficiaries can become a very important issue, with the government side attempting to impose as narrow a definition as possible. Even if the size of the benefits in a Labrador Inuit settlement is arrived at without reference to the number of beneficiaries, each side in the negotiations will need to have in their heads a theoretical figure of the number of beneficiaries involved, in order to compare the generosity of any proposal with the terms of previous land-claims settlements.[27] The LIA will probably want settlers to be counted for the purpose of establishing the amount of land and compensation, but if it is unsuccessful on this point it must then decide whether it wants them to share such benefits with them, as well as share in any hunting rights that are gained.

Still more problematic will be the rights of settlers living in the urban-industrial Goose Bay and Upper Lake Melville area. Because they have a somewhat different recent history from those on the coast, and are more dependent on the wage economy, it is not clear whether their interests can be represented by the LIA. They may ask to share benefits of any settlement to the same extent as the coastal settlers, or they may pursue their own claims. Some have formed the Labrador Metis Association, although nothing formal has yet been undertaken towards a separate claim.

Innu

The Innu (also known as Montagnais-Naskapi), together with the East Cree, with whom they are closely related, occupy the boreal-forest interior of the Quebec Labrador peninsula. Although the Labrador coast faces towards Europe, and it was probably the Labrador Innu who had some of the initial fleeting contacts with the first Viking, Portuguese, Basque, Breton, and Dutch arrivals to the coast, their significant contacts with Europeans did not occur until later and were the result of the fur trade. Fur-trade posts became established on the Labrador coast only in the late eighteenth century, but previously the Innu had, directly or indirectly, been in contact with the St Lawrence posts since the fifteenth century.

While the scientific evidence of Innu occupation of the interior of Labrador since well before first European contact is now indisputable, the suggestion that they are only recent migrants to the region still surfaces from time to time. There are three main sources for this misconception. First, from the eighteenth century onwards, English observers on the Labrador coast identified the Innu who came out from the interior with the French of Canada.[28] Secondly, a number of sources quote Innu oral history or legend as stating that they originally came from further south and west.[29] Thirdly, several maps produced in the seventeenth and eighteenth centuries show a large part of the interior of what is now southern Labrador as being occupied by the "Esquimaux," information apparently based on a 1730 map by the missionary Pierre-Michel Laure. In the 1930s the anthropologist Frank G. Speck assembled this evidence and concluded that the Innu must have migrated to Labrador recently, in the seventeenth and eighteenth centuries, pushing out a group of interior-dwelling Inuit. He theorized that this migration had been caused by attacks on them from the south and west by the Iroquois.[30]

We now know that Speck's theory has no basis in fact. The English accounts of "French" Innu who came out to the Labrador coast to trade were made at a time when there was no established border between Canada and Labrador, and by observers who did not know how far inland the Innu actually lived. There were then few fur traders on the Labrador coast, and the fact that the Innu occasionally travelled to the French posts on the St Lawrence River does not tell us where they resided. Many Innu were converted to Roman Catholicism while at the posts, and some even learned French. But their territory was primarily the vast interior, including most of what is now Labrador.

Secondly, the accounts given by Innu themselves stating that they originally came from the south and west are, no doubt, historically true; but none of these accounts indicates a specific time when this migration occurred, and the archaeological evidence, which was not available in Speck's time, seems to suggest that these movements into Quebec-Labrador actually happened several thousand years ago. Other Innu accounts of migrations may refer to recent movements, but of groups moving (in some cases, with the encouragement of fur traders) into areas already occupied by other Innu with whom they had kin ties, in line with their established land-tenure practices.

Finally, it has been recently shown that the term "Esquimaux" was used in the seventeenth and eighteenth centuries by Innu in the Saguenay River region to refer, not to the Inuit, but to outlying Innu groups, including those inhabiting the interior of Labrador. It is to these Innu groups that the Laure and other map references to "Esquimaux" refer.[31] Moreover, any evidence of attacks on Innu by the Iroquois indicates that these incidents were limited to the region north of Montreal and Quebec, and thus there is no reason to believe that they would have caused migrations to places as far away as Labrador.

The early perception of the Innu as "outsiders" to Labrador, however, seems to have influenced European treatment of them. To the Newfoundland colonial authorities, the Innu were essentially interlopers from Canada. For example, after 1867 any bills for the rations occasionally issued to starving Innu at trading posts in Labrador were sent for payment to Ottawa, even though St John's did pay for the same kind of rations issued to Labrador Inuit.[32] In the early twentieth century disputes broke out in the interior as the Innu continued to hunt in the face of incursions by settlers trapping in their territory. Regardless of Innu priority or rights, the few such disputes that found their way to the Labrador magistrate were settled in favour of the settlers.

As noted earlier, the 1927 Quebec–Labrador border cut through the heart of traditional Innu territory, with some bands having their community of trade, and later of residence, located on one side of the border but much of their traditional hunting lands on the other. Traditional Innu land tenure permitted people to move freely between bands, providing they had established kinship links. The Innu found themselves moving between what has become two separate products of the

European imagination, Quebec and Newfoundland. Serious problems have thus been created for them, especially in the application of provincial game laws and in the land-claims process.

Land claims are a federal responsibility, yet the federal government has recognized only claims made by organizations that it has funded explicitly to represent the aboriginal people, not of a particular aboriginal nation, but of a particular province. The Innu are thus represented by two organizations, the Conseil des Attikameg et des Montagnais (CAM) for those based on Quebec, and the former Naskapi Montagnais Innu Association (NMIA), now renamed the Innu Nation (IN), for those based in Labrador. The claims process requires claimant groups to specify a clear boundary around the area of claim. For the Innu, such a specification of two areas of claim is unrealistic, especially since aboriginal tenure encompassed population movements between the recently superimposed territories of two provinces. The process causes each organization to be pitted against the other, since each must either include a large area within its claim which overlaps the claim of the other, or fail to represent fully the actual history and interests of its own members.

One result of these two claims is that the Innu are involved in an overly complex negotiation process, for the two organizations must deal with three governments, two provincial and one federal. These so-called "overlapping" claims are, in reality, another figment of the European imagination.

The "divide and conquer" implications of this situation run deep, since the artificial competition imposed on the two aboriginal organizations is a seriously unbalanced one. Only the Quebec-based organization has in the past been recognized by the federal government as having legal "status," and thus has had access to federal programs. Only it has been on the federal government's "short list" for land-claims negotiations. Given that a late-coming group to a negotiation process is usually at a disadvantage, this will undoubtedly lead to tensions between CAM and IN when negotiations of overlapping issues begin. In cases such as the Lubicon and Dene land claims the government has proved only too willing first to foster, and then to exploit, a lack of unanimity among aboriginal negotiators to its own advantage.

The above situation faced by the Quebec-based and Labrador-based groups in land claims also explains why each group has developed quite different political strategies towards the negotiations. CAM opposed the James Bay Agreement, later pursuing its own settlement. Until recently, the Labrador-based group rejected the claims process as constituted, because of the extinguishment clause, the lack of self-government provisions, the disunity among Innu that it imposes, and the presence of the two provinces as full participants. They preferred instead to assert their land rights, not by negotiation, but by the exercise of sovereignty and by public actions opposing activities that they saw as interfering with their land rights. Most notably, this included a campaign of civil disobedience in opposition to the multinational military flight-training activities centred at Goose Bay, as well as a campaign against provincial game laws.

The success the Innu had with these campaigns in pressuring the federal government appears to have had some unexpected repercussions for their land claim, in the form of a federal offer to expedite negotiations. For their part, the Labrador Innu have agreed to begin negotiations towards a framework agreement. One of their first aims will be for interim protection measures against the development of their lands while negotiations are underway.

Conclusion

The discussion of land claims in Atlantic Canada points to the substantive bias underlying federal land-claims policy and decisions. These biases are dangerous for all Canadians, and need to be articulated.

The bias that pervades the land-claims decisions in the Nova Scotia and Newfoundland Mi'kmaq cases is the view that aboriginal claims are inferior to immigrants' rights. This is a colonial and racist concept, one that is emphasized by the federal Indian Act. The federal administration of land or assets is based on the assumption that aboriginal peoples of Canada, either because of their genetic make-up or culture, are incapable of managing their own lands. Under this selective use of the federal legislation, Indians are perceived as dependent on the immigrants to manage their lands.

A related bias in the decisions regarding the validity of the Nova Scotia and Newfoundland Mi'kmaq claims is the belief that the First Nations' right to continued possession and enjoyment of their protected hunting grounds under the treaties and the 1763 proclamation is subordinate to the needs of the immigrants. The traditional land-extensive economies of First Nations are viewed as a problem for the immigrants. That is, regardless of the treaties and the 1763 proclamation, no tribe or people have a right to withhold from others more than is necessary for their own support and comfort.

Land-claims decisions in Atlantic Canada gives significance to these third-party rights by rewarding the trespassers. After all, one cannot remain in possession of land except with the assistance of the legal and administrative process. If neither the courts nor Indian Affairs under the Indian Act will eject the immigrant trespassers and squatters, can it be said that the government has done nothing to "take" the land, a situation it was suppose to correct?

The federal government is not concerned about protecting its constitutional obligation to the crown and the First Nations. The decisions to reject the Mi'kmaq claims illustrate no concern for the social stability of aboriginal people or their tribal society. The losses to First Nations of protected tenure and territory are seen by the Department of Justice as questions of morality rather than of law. This position clearly articulates how poverty is imposed on aboriginal people.

The lack of concern for either the social stability or material conditions of aboriginal people begins with the concept that aboriginal people, in distinction to Europeans, never had any rights to their lands. Imperial treaties and proclamations protecting the Indians were temporary measures that colonial legislation and immigrants' actions could unilaterally terminate. The British common law supports this distinction with a legal presumption—all ungranted land in a settled colony belongs to the crown rather than to indigenous people. Thus, all obligations of the crown to indigenous people are matters of "honour" rather than of law.

These biases have no support in either law or reason. In the Human Rights Covenants, geopolitical "science" and population-imperative theories of national rights have been condemned by twentieth-century nations. Maximizing their population density is not what makes the immigrants' legal right to the land better than that of the First Nations in Canada. This proposition could be reversed by the First Nations, to fault the European societies for so overpopulating themselves that they were forced to steal other peoples' land to survive. Moreover, the same concept would deny any of Canada's claims to the Arctic.

In practice, these biases are disclosed in the Department of Justice's invocation of technical defences against Mi'kmaq claims, as well as in its overt concern for third parties (immigrants). Its attitude revolves around the concept of social stability. It believes that Canadian (that is, immigrant) social stability depends on not disturbing immigrants' claim to land, based on use and occupation, even if they obtained the land by theft. Simply stated, the government's position is that immigrants have rights, aboriginal people do not. Any specific rights aspired to by First Nations under imperial treaties and proclamations are mere "grievances" and "claims." The First Nations' claims are not to be allowed to disturb the immigrants' rights, or their conception of progress.

Experience has shown that, in the land-claims process, the Department of Justice values aboriginal uses of the lands less than those of the immigrants. This is so not because the First Nations value their land less, but rather because their land uses are considered legally and morally inferior. Their uses of land are seen as limited to the perpetuation of traditional, economically inferior lifestyles.

The concept that the vested property rights of certain people under imperial treaties, instructions, and proclamations are not to be protected by the rule of law is dangerous. It is not the same as expropriation, which, in the interest of natural justice, ordinarily requires a hearing, some reasonable purpose, and compensation. A federal agency can take vested aboriginal property rights without a hearing, for any purpose, with no compensation required.

Neither is the taking of vested property rights supported by the "command" theory of the law. This version of legal positivism sees all law as the "will" or "command" of a sovereign. The positivist axiom of John Austin holds that the law is what the sovereign says it is. Since 1761 the British sovereign in imperial instructions and proclamations has legally protected the reserved hunting grounds and Indian country of the First Nations. Nevertheless, their reserved lands were abolished by actions of immigrants. In some cases, immigrants simply squatted on protected lands. The crown's servants ignored these actions, thus denying the aboriginal people the protection the crown promised, until the land or assets were lost through theft. In other cases, the crown's servants actually protected the immigrants, perfecting the trespass by giving grants to the squatters. In still others, the governments summarily abolished by statute aboriginal or treaty rights. Thus, colonial legislation and even the actions of trespassers were treated as a kind of subsidiary sovereign, with the authority to supersede imperial law and the sovereign command.

The Canadian government has chosen to call these acts lawful, but in so doing it is only validating colonialism and racism.

Documents

A. Micmac Treaty, 1752

Treaty or
Articles of Peace and Friendship Renewed

between

His Excellency Peregrine Thomas Hopson Esquire Captain General and Governor in Chief in and over His Majesty's Regiments of Foot, and His Majesty's Council on behalf of His Majesty.

AND

Major Jean Baptiste Cope chief Sachem of the Tribe of Mick Mack Indians, Inhabiting the Eastern Coast of the said Province, and Andrew Hadley Martin, Gabriel Martin and Francis Jeremiah members & Delegates of the said Tribe, for themselves and their said Tribe their heirs and the heirs of their heirs forever. Begun made and Concluded in the manner form & Tenor following, viz.

1.   It is agreed that the Articles of Submission & Agreements made at Boston in New England by the Delegates of the Penobscot Norridgwolk & St. John's Indians in the Year 1725 Ratifyed and Confirmed by all the

Nova Scotia Tribes at Annapolis Royal in the Month of June 1726 and lately Renewed with Governor Cornwallis at Halifax and Ratifyed at St. John's River, now read over Explained & Interpreted shall be and are hereby from this time forward renewed, reiterated and forever Confirmed by them and their Tribe, and the said Indians for themselves and their Tribe and their Heirs aforesaid do make and renew the same Solemn Submissions and promises for the strict Observance of all the Articles therein Contained as at any time heretofore hath been done.

2.   That all Transactions during the late War shall on both sides be buried on Oblivion with the Hatchet, And that the said Indians shall have all favour, Friendship & Protection shewn them from this His Majesty's Government.

3.   That the said Tribe shall use their utmost Endeavours to bring in the other Indians to Renew and Ratify this Peace, and shall discover and make known any attempts or designs of any other Indians or any Enemy whatever against his Majesty's Subjects within this Province so soon as they shall know thereof and shall also hinder and Obstruct the same to the utmost of their power, and on the other hand if any of the Indians refusing to ratify this Peace shall make War upon the Tribe who have now Confirmed the same; they shall upon Application have such aid and Assistance from the Government for their defence as the Case may require.

4.   It is agreed that the said Tribe of Indians shall not be hindered from, but have free liberty of hunting and Fishing as usual and that if they shall think a Truck house needful at the River Chibenaccadie, or any other place of their resort they shall have the same built and proper Merchandize, lodged therein to be exchanged for what the Indians shall have to dispose of and that in the mean time the Indians shall have free liberty to bring to Sale to Halifax or any other Settlement within this Province, Skins, feathers, fowl, fish or any other thing they shall have to sell, where they shall have liberty to dispose thereof to the best Advantage.

5.   That a Quantity of bread, flour, and such other Provisions, as can be procured, necessary for the Familys and proportionable to the Numbers of the said Indians, shall be given them half Yearly for the time to come; and the same regard shall be had to the other Tribes that shall hereafter Agree to Renew and Ratify the Peace upon the Terms and Conditions now Stipulated.

6.   That to Cherish a good harmony and mutual Correspondence between the said Indians and this Government His Excellency Peregrine Thomas Hopson Esq. Capt. General & Governor in Chief in & over His Majesty's Province of Nova Scotia or Accadie Vice Admiral of the same & Colonel of One of His Majesty's Regiments of Foot hereby promises on

the part of His Majesty that the said Indians shall upon the first day of October Yearly, so long as they shall Continue in Friendship, Receive Presents of Blankets, Tobacco, some Powder & Shott, and the said Indians promise once every year, upon the said first of October, to come by themselves or their Delegates and Receive the said Presents and Renew their Friendship and Submissions.

7. That the Indians shall use their best Endeavors to save the Lives & Goods of any People Shipwrecked on this Coast where they resort and shall Conduct the People saved to Halifax with their Goods, and a Reward adequate to the Salvadge shall be given them.

8. That all Disputes whatsoever that may happen to arise between the Indians now at Peace and others His Majesty's Subjects in this Province shall be tryed in His Majesty's Courts of Civil Judicature, where the Indians shall have the same benefits, Advantages & Priviledges as any others of His Majesty's Subjects.

In Faith & Testimony whereof the Great Seal of the Province is hereunto appended, and the Partys to these Presents have hereunto interchangeably Set their Hands in the Council Chamber at Halifax this 22nd day of Nov. 1752 in the 26th Year of His Majesty's Reign.

B. Proclamation by Governor Shuldham, 1772

BY HIS EXCELLENCY MOLYNEUX SHULDHAM, ESQR.
Governor and Commander in Chief in and over the Island of
Newfoundland, the Coast of Labrador, &c. &c.

WHEREAS I am informed that the Esquimaux Savages inhabiting that part of the Coast of Labrador where the Unitas Fratrum and its Society have formed a Settlement for the furtherance of the Gospel among the Heathen have lately strolled from the said Settlement to the Southward with a View of Trading with the shipping which touch upon that Coast. AND WHEREAS many Barbarous Murders have been committed on both sides by the English upon the Savages and the Savages upon the English, occasioned by Disputes and Misunderstandings in Bartering their Traffick. For the putting a stop thereto for the future I do hereby desire and require the said Unitas Fratrum to use every fair and gentle means in their power, to prevent the said Esquimaux Savages from going to the Southward without first obtaining their Permission in writing for so doing, and till such time as other Settlements shall be formed and extended down along the Coast. Given under my hand this 10th of April 1772.

C. Newfoundland Governor William McGregor's Visit to Labrador, 1908

31. One important duty in respect to the Esquimaux devolves on the Government of Newfoundland, a duty that is beyond the power of the Moravian Mission to perform for the natives; that is, to protect them in their rights to their own territory. They are in danger from the concession seeker; and they are threatened by division through the action of Canadian Officers in the settlement of the Labrador Boundary. Applications are made to this Government for timber concessions wherever it is thought any useful timber exists. To grant any timber concessions north of Cape Harrison, the point that is recognised as the southern limit of the Moravian Mission-field, would be a great injustice to the Esquimaux. Such grants would not only reduce their supplies of timber and fuel, but would most seriously diminish the available game and fur which hitherto have been of such great importance to them. The moral influence on the Esquimaux would also be very prejudicial to them as a community. On this matter of concessions there clearly can be no compromise between right and wrong.

This has been practically recognised by the late government, as will be gathered from the letter of the Deputy Minister of Agriculture and Mines, dated 20th October, 1908, and addressed to myself by that gentleman in answer to my letter to Mr. Long, of 17th October, asking for information. Some additional information on this important question is given in Dr. Hutton's letter of 13th November, 1908, which shows how dependent the Esquimaux are on the remnants of forest on the Labrador Coast. . . .

It is also undesirable that the Esquimaux and the Mission should be separated into two divisions by an artificial and unnatural boundary line between Newfoundland and Canada. Both the natives and the mission have always, in practice, been under Newfoundland; and it does not appear that they have any desire for a change. Their hunting lands, it now seems, extend further from the coast than I had formerly understood to be the case; this is, however, a question that admits of precise definition on the spot. But with respect to Killinek, at Port Burwell, I know of no reasonable claim that can be urged against its remaining under Newfoundland, except the erroneous idea that Cape Chidley had been at some date or other authoritatively and officially declared to be the boundary of Newfoundland on Labrador.

If the Government of Newfoundland will protect the Esquimaux in their natural rights to their own coast, the Moravian Mission, with very little other assistance, will no doubt continue to watch over the natives in the future as faithfully as they have done in the past. As long ago as 1793 Chief Justice Reeve suggested as a means of saving the then existing remnant of the Beothuk race of Newfoundland, that the Moravian Mission should be invoked to establish a branch of their Mission among the Beothuks. Had this suggestion been followed, there might have been some survivors of that doomed and unfortunate race today, if one may judge from the way that the Moravians have preserved the Esquimaux. In any case such an effort honestly made would to some extent have softened the deep and dark stain that rests on the Europeans that hunted the helpless Beothuk to death. The service the Moravians have rendered in preserving the Esquimaux will be much more fully appreciated when the work written by my friend, Mr. James P. Howley, on the Beothuk, is published, the manuscript of which I have had the privilege of perusing.

The close attention the Mission gives to the vital statistics of the Esquimaux is well seen. . . . To elucidate the question whether the child-bearing capacity of the race was failing, Bishop Martin has shewn that at Nain the 53 Esquimaux married women living there had borne 248 children, or a mean of 4.6 each. But of the 248 children only 68, that is hardly 28 per cent, are alive.

A similar return, prepared for me by the Reverend S. Waldmann at Killinik, shews that sixteen women have had 52 children, or a mean of 3 1/4 each. Of these, however, 45, or 86 per cent, are alive. There is still much to learn in respect of the manners and customs, &c., of the Esquimaux. . . .

D. Statement of Claim of the Naskapi Montagnais of Labrador Ungava Presented to the Government of Canada, 1977

Agreement in Principle Between the
Naskapi Montagnais Nation and Her Majesty
the Queen, in Right of Canada

Whereas prior to the coming of the Europeans the Naskapi Montagnais or Innots, the aboriginal people of the Labrador Ungava peninsula with their traditional homeland stretching from the Gulf of St. Lawrence to Ungava Bay to the Atlantic coast, have lived in this their country since time immemorial;

And whereas the Naskapi Montagnais have certain national property rights to their country;

And whereas Europeans and the descendants of European settlement elsewhere have settled upon and undertaken developments in the country of the Naskapi Montagnais without the consent of the Naskapi Montagnais and without treaty between the Naskapi Montagnais and the European settlers or their sovereign;

And whereas the national integrity of the Naskapi Montagnais has been violated by such unauthorized settlement and interference on the lands of the Naskapi Montagnais;

And whereas there are in international law certain political, human and universal rights such as the rights to self-determination, non-discrimination, and enjoyment of culture which are witnessed in the practice of nations and international instruments such as the United Nations Declaration of Human Rights;

And whereas the Naskapi Montagnais have survived as a people;

And whereas both the Naskapi Montagnais and the federal government of Canada have expressed a desire to see clarification of the rights of the Naskapi Montagnais people and the negotiation of an agreement on the terms and conditions of non-aboriginal presence in the territory of the Naskapi Montagnais, at the earliest possible occasion;

It is therefore agreed between the Naskapi Montagnais and Her Majesty the Queen in the right of Canada that negotiations do commence forthwith to resolve the aforesaid according to the following principles:

1. The Naskapi Montagnais have the right to recognition, self-determination and all the rights and privileges due other sovereign nations including the right to growth and development as a people.

2. The Naskapi Montagnais, as an aboriginal nation have the right to retain ownership of their national territory, and under such terms, as to ensure their independence and self-reliance, traditionally, economically and socially, and the maintenance of whatever other rights they have, whether specified in this agreement or not.

3. Canada agrees to respect the national integrity of the Naskapi Montagnais and to do nothing to violate the national rights of the Naskapi Montagnais and in so doing to respect the precepts of international law.

4. Unless and until the cession or surrender by the Naskapi Montagnais of any of their country to Canada, Canada agrees to prevent any further settlement or industrial development on the unceded territory of the Naskapi Montagnais.

5. The Naskapi Montagnais have the right to practise and preserve their languages, traditions, customs, and values.

6. The Naskapi Montagnais have the right to develop their own institutions and enjoy their rights as a people in the framework of their own institutions.

7. There will therefore be a Naskapi Montagnais government with jurisdiction over a geographical area and over subject matters now within the jurisdiction of the government of Canada or the government of Newfoundland, and subject to a *freely negotiated* final agreement

embodying the principles herein set out, such a Naskapi Montagnais jurisdiction shall join the Confederation of Canada.

8. Following a final agreement, the government of Canada hereafter in the exercise of matters within its jurisdiction will:

A. abandon the "last frontier" mentality and all attempts to colonize and settle the country of the Naskapi Montagnais; and

B. guarantee that no provincial government will continue to prosecute attempts to colonize, settle, or violate the national integrity of the country of the Naskapi Montagnais; and

C. do everything in its power to assist in the recognition, survival, and development of the Naskapi Montagnais as a people.

9. The government of Canada will finance the establishment of new Naskapi Montagnais communities in cases where existing communities are inhabited by significant numbers of non-aboriginal people and a significant proportion of the Naskapi Montagnais community wishes to reestablish themselves elsewhere.

10. The Naskapi Montagnais will be compensated by Canada for past use of, damaged to and destruction of Naskapi Montagnais lands.

11. Within six months of the signing of this agreement negotiations will commence for a final agreement or treaty, and within six months of the signing of the final agreement:

A. legislation incorporating the terms of the final agreement will be submitted to the National Assembly of the Naskapi Montagnais.

B. legislation incorporating the terms of the final agreement will be submitted to their Parliament by Canada.

12. It is recognized and accepted that negotiations must allow for the continuing day-to-day involvement of all Naskapi Montagnais.

13. In the interim period between the signing of this agreement and the passing of legislation by both parties, the Naskapi Montagnais nation and Canada will not take any action which violate either the terms or the spirit of this agreement.

And whereas the Naskapi Montagnais recognize that there are non-aboriginals who have come to live among the Naskapi Montagnais and the Naskapi Montagnais wish to be fair to them;

And whereas both the Naskapi Montagnais and Canada wish to recognize and respect the rights of these settlers;

And whereas both parties recognize that unauthorized immigration and settlement without surrender of the Indian national property right to the territory of Labrador Ungava does not constitute under international law a legitimate extinguishment of Indian title, power and authority over the Naskapi Montagnais homeland;

And whereas while the Naskapi Montagnais nation cannot be asked to yield up its prerogative to decide on the destiny of its country, both parties accept the right of non-aboriginals to all the individual freedoms guaranteed by the United Nations Charter of Human Rights, and all such other rights to self-determination as free individuals;

And whereas both parties accept that these settlers on Naskapi Montagnais territory specifically should not have the right, individually or collectively to restrict or infringe upon the national rights of the Naskapi Montagnais to self-determination as a people;

It is therefore agreed that the following principles are recognized by the Naskapi Montagnais nation and the government of Canada;

14. The Naskapi Montagnais agree that non-aboriginals have the right to individual self-determination and the use and development of their own institutions and the use and enjoyment of their own languages and cultures; and the Naskapi Montagnais pledge their support to the non-aboriginals residing in the country of the Naskapi Montagnais in the pursuit of their rights.

15. The government of Canada will establish a regime to compensate all non-aboriginals who suffer hardship because of, or non-aboriginals who wish to leave Labrador Ungava because they are unable to adjust to, changes ensuring the viability of the principles herein contained and particularly measures introduced to guarantee the recognition, self-determination, and development of the Naskapi Montagnais as a people.

16. The Naskapi Montagnais agree that all non-aboriginal individuals holding lands in estate fee simple as of October 31st, 1977 will not be deprived of their property rights, but after that date all lands will be subject to the terms of this agreement.

In witness whereof, Her Majesty Queen Elizabeth II and the Naskapi Montagnais nation, through their representatives have hereunto set their hands.

Notes

[1] Canada, "Policy Statement on Native Land Claims" (Ottawa: Department of Indian Affairs and Northern Development 1973).

[2] Hon. H. Faulkner, letter to the Union of Nova Scotia Indians.

[3] A. Kroeger, letter to the Union of Nova Scotia Indians.

[4] P.M. Ollivier, letter to the Union of Nova Scotia Indians.

[5] Hon J. Munro, letter to the Union of Nova Scotia Indians.

[6] *Guerin* v. *The Queen* (1984).

[7] *Simon* v. *The Queen* (1985).

[8] Royal Proclamation of 1763.

[9] "Policy Statement on Native Land Claims."

[10] United Nations, *International Covenant on Civil and Political Rights* (1966).

[11] Grand Captain Alec Denny and Mi'kmaq Nationimou Communication. Document G/S0 215/51 CANA (18) R. 19/78. (Geneva: United Nations Human Rights Committee 1980).

[12] James Hiller, "The Moravian Land Grants" in Labrador Inuit Association, *Our Footprints are Everywhere: Inuit Land Use and Occupancy in Labrador* (Nain: Labrador Inuit Association 1977).

[13] See, e.g., Great Britain, Privy Council, Judicial Committee, *In the Matter of the boundary between the Dominion of Canada and the Colony of Newfoundland in the Labrador Peninsula, between the Dominion of Canada of the one part, and the Colony of Newfoundland of the other part* (London: W. Clowes and Sons 1927), 2318.

[14] Newfoundland, *Reports of Governor William McGregor of Official Visits to Labrador, 1905* (St. John's: Government of Newfoundland 1980).

[15] Edward Tompkins, *Pencilled Out: Newfoundland and Labrador's Native People and Canadian Confederation, 1947–1954*. Report prepared for Hon. Jack Harris, M.P. (Ottawa: House of Commons 1988), 14–15.

[16] Royal Commission on Labrador, *Report of the Royal Commission on Labrador*, 6 vols. (St. John's: The Royal Commission on Labrador 1974), 6:1166–98.

[17] *The Western Arctic Claim: A Guide to the Inuvialuit Agreement* (Ottawa: Indian and Northern Affairs 1984).

[18] *The James Bay and Northern Quebec Agreement* (Quebec: Éditeur Officiel du Québec 1976).

[19] Canada, *In All Fairness. A Native Claims Policy. Comprehensive Claims* (Ottawa: Indian Affairs and Northern Development 1981), 21–2.

[20] *In All Fairness*, 14.

[21] Newfoundland, *Assessment and Analysis of the MicMac Land Claim in Newfoundland* (St. John's: Government of Newfoundland 1982).

[22] Indian and Inuit Support Group, *The Newfoundland Government's Rejection of the Micmac Land Claim* (St. John's: Indian and Inuit Support Group 1982).

[23] Charles A. Martijn, ed., *Les Micmacs et la Mer* (Montreal: Recherches amérindiennes au Québec 1986).

[24] Frank G. Speck, *Micmac and Beothuk*. Indian Notes and Monographs (New York: Heye Foundation, Museum of the American Indian 1922).

[25] Shmuel Ben-Dor, *Makkovik: Eskimos and Settlers in a Labrador Community* (St. John's: Institute of Social and Economic Research 1966); John C. Kennedy, *Holding the Line: Ethnic Boundaries in a Northern Labrador Community* (St. John's: Institute of Social and Economic Research 1982).

[26] *Report of the Royal Commission on Labrador.*

[27] See, e.g., Keith Crowe, "Claims on the Land 1," *Arctic Circle* 1, 3 (1990).

[28] See, e.g., George Cartwright, Letter to Lord Dartmouth, 1774, quoted in Great Britain, *In the Matter of the boundary*, 2672, 2675; Palliser, Newfoundland Governor, 1766, quoted in Great Britain, ibid., 1253; Edward Chappell, *Voyage of His*

Majesty's ship Rosmund to Newfoundland and the southern coast of Labrador . . . (London: J. Mawman 1818).

[29] See, e.g., Henry Y. Hind, *Exploration in the Interior of the Labrador Peninsula: The Country of the Montagnais and Nasquapee Indians* (London: Longman, Green, Longman, Roberts and Green 1863); Lucien M. Turner, "Ethnology of the Ungava District, Hudson Bay Territory" in *Eleventh Report of the Bureau of Ethnology, Smithsonian Institution, 1889–1890* (Washington: Smithsonian Institution 1894), 267; Frank G. Speck, "Culture Problems in Northeast North America," *Proceedings of the American Philosophical Society* 65, 4 (1926), 300.

[30] Frank G. Speck, "Montagnais-Naskapi Bands and early Eskimo Distribution in the Labrador Peninsula," *American Anthropologist* 33 (1931): 557–600.

[31] José Mailhot, Jean-Paul Simard, and Sylvie Vincent "On est toujours l'Esquimau de quelqu'un," *Études Inuit Studies* 4, 1–2 (1980).

[32] Great Britain, *In the Matter of the boundary*, 2681–88.

Aboriginal Land Claims in the Canadian North

William R. Morrison

The aboriginal claims of the native people of the Yukon and Northwest Territories are "comprehensive" claims. That is, they deal not with specific grievances, such as infringements of treaties, but with a spectrum of issues ranging from land use to political rights to financial compensation. Only one treaty was signed between the First Nations of the two territories and the government of Canada—Treaty 11 of 1921, which covered most of the Mackenzie valley[1]—and this agreement proved largely abortive. The result was that, when the modern period of treaty negotiating began in the mid-1970s, both the Yukon and Northwest Territories were in effect clean slates on which a new record of claims negotiation could be written. Yet, though the slate is new, the people of this land have inhabited it for a very long time, since the Canadian north, specifically the Yukon, is the longest continually inhabited part of Canada. The Dene people of the region have lived there for at least 4000 years, and some would claim a great deal longer.

Four comprehensive claims have been the subject of negotiation in the territories: that of the Council of Yukon Indians (CYI), of the Inuvialuit of the western Arctic, of the Dene and Metis of the Mackenzie valley, and of the Inuit of the eastern Arctic.[2]

The Yukon

Canada acquired what is now the Yukon in 1870 as part of a transfer from Britain that included the Prairie west and the continental section of the Northwest Territories. For decades, however, the Canadian government ignored the native people of the Yukon River valley and the rest of the country north of the line of agricultural settlement. Ottawa was prepared to negotiate treaties only with those native people who lived in areas that seemed likely to be settled by whites. In the southern Prairies, for example, the government was most anxious to sign treaties and assign the Indians to reserves so that the land could be opened to agricultural settlement. In the northern parts of the provinces and in the territories, however, the government saw no reason to go to the trouble and expense of taking the native people into treaty. Rather, they should be left alone, to pursue their traditional hunter-gatherer way of life.[3] When on occasion the indigenous people of the region asked for the protection and benefits of treaty, as Jim Boss of the Yukon did in 1902, their requests were ignored.

This began to change after the end of the Second World War with the advent of the modern welfare state. Because the new social programs were universal, they were extended to the native people of the north as well as to the rest of Canadians. As well as giving various kinds of assistance, these programs provided an irresistible opportunity for social engineering. A good example was the mothers' allowance, a cash payment that was given to the mothers of school-age children. In order to get the monthly payments, the parents had to ensure that the children were in school, meaning that the natives of the Yukon had to send their children to residential schools, which many were reluctant to do, or come in from the bush camps and settle in communities, a process that was incompatible with their traditional way of life. Moreover, the government, not trusting the natives to use the payments wisely, paid in kind rather than in cash, which gave bureaucrats considerable control over native purchasing and eating habits.

Within twenty years of the end of the war, a new generation of young native leaders had emerged in the Yukon as elsewhere in the north. Their desire to secure more control over the lives of their people coincided with a new interest in the north on the part of Canadians, fuelled by the energy crisis and an increased social awareness—legacies of the material wastefulness and the social dynamics of the 1960s. It was also influenced by the model of the Alaska Native Claims Settlement Act, which had given the 55 000 native people of that state 40 million acres of land and almost a billion dollars in payments—a deal that seemed at the time an incredible bonanza.[4]

The first salvo from the Yukon indigenous people came from the Indians of Old Crow, who in 1972 sent a petition to the House of

Commons calling for a halt to the geological activity in connection with oil and gas exploration that was taking place on their traditional hunting lands.[5] This was followed in 1973 by a document entitled "Together Today for our Children Tomorrow," presented to the federal government by the Yukon Native Brotherhood (YNB), soon to become the Council of Yukon Indians. This was a "comprehensive" claim, based on the premise that native rights in the Yukon had never been extinguished by treaty and were thus intact, and that these rights had to be addressed before any further economic development in the territory could take place.

What the indigenous people wanted was a land base—that is, land to live on, land on which to operate traplines, land for hunting and fishing. Chief Elijah Smith, president of the YNB, said that the basic demand was "Land. Land that was left behind by our ancestors to us. We are staking our claims on our land."[6] They also wanted compensation for land already lost and a high degree of control over the future of the territory. Finally, and most difficult to resolve, the native people resisted the government's wish to "extinguish" their rights as part of a treaty, as had been done in all other treaties signed with the natives of the southern provinces. Rather, they insisted that their aboriginal rights should remain intact, a position that the government would not accept since it feared that the result might be new demands in the future.

Nevertheless, Ottawa accepted the claim for negotiation, and meetings began, resulting in the spring of 1976 in an agreement-in-principle, which was approved by negotiators from both sides. Under this agreement, the federal government secured its basic requirement of extinguishment of aboriginal title to the Yukon. In return, the First Nations, who then numbered about 6000 status and non-status Indians, acquired control of 3100 square kilometres of land, with another 44 000 square kilometres reserved for hunting, fishing, and trapping. Seventy to ninety million dollars was to be paid over a number of years in royalties for natural resources, and there were additional provisions for job training, management preparation, and other social benefits.

To the surprise of those who did not realize how deeply felt the natives' position was, when the agreement-in-principle was taken to the communities, it was rejected, and the native negotiators were repudiated. The objection was that the agreement, though more generous in terms of money, was essentially no different in principle than the older treaties signed with the Indians of the southern provinces: it bought out aboriginal rights in return for cash, certain services, and the establishment of reserves. The native people had not secured any control over the economic and social future of the Yukon.

Negotiations began again, this time with the participation of the territorial government, which had watched with some alarm as the Yukon's future was decided virtually without the participation of the non-native population of the territory. By 1977 a "settlement model" had been agreed upon by all sides, defining three goals to be achieved in the final agreement:

1. To restore, protect, preserve and guarantee the identity of the Yukon Indians and their freedom to choose a way of life in harmony with their cultural heritage.

2. To provide land and other forms of compensation to Yukon Indian people, to compensate them for lands traditionally used and given up under the settlement, so that they may have the opportunity to build an economic base equal with that of other Yukon citizens.

3. To provide Yukon Indian people with the incentive and opportunity to have their rightful say, within the context of a one-government structure, in the decision-making authority which governs their everyday life.[7]

These were all laudable goals, but implementing them would take many more years of negotiation. Moreover, they did not address the vexed question of aboriginal rights. These the native people refused to surrender, yet the government insisted on extinguishing them. When the word "extinguishment" proved too provocative, the government began to use the word "certainty"—that is, the agreement must give the government certain assurance that the native people would not try to reopen negotiations at some future date, but the principle was essentially the same.

In 1980, then Minister of Indian and Northern Affairs John Munro stated that it was time "to get down to some hard, serious negotiating on the substantive issues . . . specific matters such as land, compensation, and clarification of rights."[8] In the next year, an agreement was signed outlining the "broad parameters" for the greater involvement of the native people in controlling their education system.[9] Yet more years were to pass before an agreement was finally negotiated. The delay was in large measure caused by the reluctance of the native people, who were the ones who would have to live with it, to sign a document that would end forever their right to reopen the question of their aboriginal rights. The Indians of the southern Prairies had signed their lands away in the 1870s for a pittance, and along with their lands the right to reopen negotiations. The abortive agreement-in-principle of 1976 had guaranteed a cash payment of about $12 000 per capita, a sum not to be sneezed at in 1976 dollars, but the payments were spread out over a long and undefined period and, unlike the annuities, were not to be paid in perpetuity.

What the native people wanted was not a land-for-cash deal, which is essentially what the Alaskan natives had agreed to, nor an updated version of the old annuity system, but an agreement that provided a large measure of control over the future of their land. The woman who wept when being interviewed by a TV crew at the thought of surrendering her aboriginal claim expressed the feelings of many Yukoners.

In the late 1980s there was an important change in the negotiating process. The election of an NDP government in the Yukon, headed by Tony Penikett, replaced an administration that had at best an ambivalent and at worst a hostile attitude towards the CYI claim with one that was sympathetic to it. The federal government about the same time decided as a matter of courtesy and political expediency to involve both territorial governments more closely in the negotiating process. In 1989 a final agreement-in-principle was announced, followed in April 1990 by the signing of a curiously named "Umbrella Final Agreement," which still must be ratified by each of the Yukon First Nations, a process that began in June 1991 with the signing of the final agreement at Mayo.

As is the case with other claims that have been settled, or are close to being settled, it is impossible for an outsider to judge whether the agreement-in-principle of 1989 is a "good" deal for the native people; it is for them to decide, as they will do in the near future. From the government point of view, it would seem to be a success, since by its terms the Yukon First Nations "agree to cede any aboriginal title to non-settlement lands and waters within Canada. . . . "[10] After nearly seventeen years of intermittent negotiations, the government seems to have won its point of extinguishment, at least of land title. (Aboriginal rights remain in effect on lands granted to native people; those rights have been surrendered on other lands.)

The Inuvialuit Claim

This is the claim of the Inuit, or Inuvialuit, living in the western Arctic communities of Sachs Harbour, Holman Island, Paulatuk, Tuktoyaktuk, Inuvik, and Aklavik. Though they are, like the Indians to the south of them, indigenous peoples, they have not lived in the Mackenzie Delta-Beaufort Sea region for a particularly long time. There were apparently about 2000 Inuit living in the region at the time of first European contact in the 1830s, but the anthropologist Diamond Jenness reported that by 1930 there were only twelve living descendants of these people, as well as about 300 Inuit living in the area who had migrated from Alaska.[11] The rest had died of virgin-soil epidemics, many introduced by the American whaling ships that penetrated the region in the late 1880s.[12] Despite this near-extinction, however, their numbers have rebounded to more than 2500, partly because of in-migration from elsewhere in the Arctic.

In May 1977 the Inuvialuit, organized as the Committee for Original People's Entitlement, or COPE, presented a comprehensive claim to the federal government entitled "Inuvialuit Nunangat," or "Land of the People of the Western Arctic." Like the Council of Yukon Indians' claim, Inuvialuit Nunangat asked for a land base, control of natural resources, and a strong voice in the future development of the region.

Unlike the Yukon claim, however, the COPE claim was settled fairly swiftly; it was, in fact, the first of the northern comprehensive claims to be settled, largely because the Inuvialuit did not raise insurmountable objections to the principle of extinguishment. By late 1977 an agreement on the provisions concerning wildlife had been reached, by October 1978 an agreement-in-principle was signed, and in the spring of the next year an agreement was reached on which lands the Inuvialuit would claim under the final agreement.

After a breakdown in negotiations in 1979 and again in 1980, discussions began again early in 1983, and a final agreement was signed on 5 June 1984. In return for substantial benefits of various kinds, the Inuvialuit agreed to the extinguishment of their claims to large sections of the western Arctic. The basic provision was for ownership of 11 000 square kilometres of land with surface and subsurface rights, and another 78 000 square kilometres of land with rights to everything but gas and oil. A total of $45 million would be paid between 1984 and 1997, and a variety of other benefits were also provided.

The Dene/Metis Claim

The claim of the native people of the Mackenzie River valley is undoubtedly the best known outside the north, partly because of the economic importance the region assumed in the 1970s as the route by which new oil and gas reserves from the Arctic were to flow southward to energy-hungry (or energy-wasteful) southerners, but more because the claim was the subject of possibly the most famous royal commission in Canadian history—the Berger commission.[13]

There are two First Nations groups in the Mackenzie valley south of its delta—the Dene and the Metis. To a degree they are ethnically and culturally different from one another—the Dene are indigenous people whose ancestors have lived in the region since time immemorial, while the Metis are the descendants of unions between the Dene and Europeans in the region[14]—yet because their economic circumstances are similar, their claims were, at the insistence of the federal government, negotiated as a single claim.

About 8000 Dene and 5000 Metis live in twenty-seven communities in the Mackenzie valley. The Dene are Athapaskan people living in a large area of the sub-Arctic from the Mackenzie on the east to Alaska on the west. The Canadian Dene comprise five Dene tribal groups and a group of northern Cree. In early historical times they lived in small groups with no rigidly defined territorial boundaries, speaking a number of different dialects. Europeans gave them European names—Hare, Slavey, Dogrib, Loucheaux. But to themselves they were always Dene, which is the Athapascan word for their own people, and their land is Denendeh—land of the Dene.

Contact between the Dene and Europeans began in the eighteenth century, especially after the establishment of a fur-trade post on Lake Athabasca by Peter Pond in 1778. By 1840, with the founding of the Hudson's Bay Company post at Fort McPherson, the Mackenzie valley was firmly linked with the world of European commerce. The arrival of Roman Catholic and Anglican missionaries in mid-century forged spiritual and cultural links with Europe.

Like that of the native people of the Yukon, the Dene way of life was largely unaffected by the industrial revolution of the late nineteenth century and by the political and economic growth of the Dominion of Canada. Despite the appalling mortality caused by epidemics of diseases ranging from smallpox in the 1830s to influenza after the First World War, the Dene way of life did not change much until after the Second World War, when the heavy hand of the federal government was laid upon them. As in the Yukon, the family allowance and other programs drew the Dene from bush camps into a string of small communities along the Mackenzie, a process that has been called the "micro-urbanization of the North."[15] The irony of the process is that the Northwest Territories is now the mostly sparsely settled region of Canada, and yet one in which few people live permanently on the land.

In 1921 the Dene signed a treaty with the federal government, for the usual reasons—Ottawa had discovered that the land of the Dene had economic potential and wished to extinguish their aboriginal rights so that development could proceed. In this case it was the discovery of oil deposits at Norman Wells and the promise—an illusory one, as it proved—of an oil boom that spurred the treaty. Treaty 11 was different from the ten that preceded it in that some of its native signatories survived into an age when native affairs came to be viewed much differently than in the nineteenth century, and when their contention that they had been tricked by the government negotiators found a sympathetic audience in southern Canada. In the 1970s their chronicler and champion was Father René Fumoleau, who advanced their position that the Treaty of 1921 (and the part of Treaty 8 of 1899 that applied to the NWT) were agreements of peace and friendship, and that the Dene had never agreed to surrender their land or any of their aboriginal rights: "They saw the white man's treaty as his way of offering them his help and friendship. They were willing to share their land with him in the manner prescribed by their tradition and culture. The two races would live side by side in the North, embarking on a common future."[16]

The comprehensive claims of the native people of the Mackenzie valley are complicated by racial factors absent elsewhere north of the sixtieth parallel, for there is a substantial Metis population in the region—about 5000 as compared to the 8000 Dene. At the time the treaty was negotiated, many of the mixed-blood people of the Mackenzie were given the choice of signing it, which would make them legally

Indians, or accepting scrip entitling them to land or a cash payment, which would exclude them and their descendants from the benefits of the Indian Act.[17] There was also a non-status Indian population; that is, indigenous people who did not think of themselves as Metis but were not covered by the provisions of the treaty, for various reasons, including marriage of a native woman to a non-native man.[18] This legal division of people whose way of life was substantially similar tended to weaken their bargaining position, especially when they formed separate groups to present their positions to government.

Although it was and is the position of the federal government that Treaties 8 and 11 as they apply to the NWT are valid land surrenders, it agreed in 1976 to accept a comprehensive claim for negotiation with the Dene. The government did not of course accept the Dene position that they had been misled at the time of the original negotiations, but the fact that the treaties had not been fulfilled by Canada—in particular, no reserves had ever been established under Treaty 11 and only one in the NWT under Treaty 8—permitted the government to accept the idea that the Mackenzie valley treaties had been abortive.

Although in theory the government refused to recognize Metis land claims in the territories, it did accept a claim from the Metis Association of the NWT in 1977 "because it constitutes an integral part of the Native community and many of its members would quality as Dene beneficiaries."[19] In 1983 the Dene and Metis agreed to negotiate together.

The era of modern negotiations in the Mackenzie valley began when in 1973 a number of Dene leaders filed a caveat claiming aboriginal interest in crown lands in the region. The Supreme Court of the NWT upheld the caveat, ruling that the chiefs might be able to establish an aboriginal interest. Since planning was well underway for an energy corridor linking the Arctic oil and gas deposits with consumers in the south, this development was of more than academic interest. Though the caveat was later struck down by the NWT Court of Appeal and by the Supreme Court of Canada, it had served its purpose in delivering a shock to the government and to public opinion in southern Canada. The result was the establishment in the spring of 1974 of the Mackenzie Valley Pipeline Inquiry, chaired by Justice Thomas Berger of the Supreme Court of British Columbia.

The Berger commission, as it was popularly known, sat at a time of tremendous interest in the north, and tremendous tension as well. The price of petroleum products was rising, the Organization of Petroleum Exporting Countries (OPEC) was flexing its muscles, there were shortages of oil all over the western world, and there seemed to be a vast supply in the Canadian Arctic. Hundreds of millions of dollars were being spent on drilling, compressor stations, and various facilities, much of it in the land of the Dene. Thus when people came to the Berger commission and threatened to damage any pipeline that was built before their aboriginal claims were settled, the threat carried meaning for the Canadian public that went beyond the usual rhetoric of such occasions. Berger's most important recommendation was that no pipeline be built for ten years, but ironically, by the time his report was issued, the energy crisis had dissipated and southerners were beginning to forget about shortages of energy. A few years later the Norman Wells oil field was linked to the south by pipeline with hardly any public reaction at all.

At the same time that the Berger commission was focusing attention on the Mackenzie valley, the Dene leaders issued the "Dene Declaration," a statement of their aboriginal claims that is probably the best-known document produced by native people in this century, as well as one of the most radical. It begins with the declaration that "We the Dene of the N.W.T. insist on the right to be regarded by ourselves and the world as a nation," and goes on to say: "The government of Canada is not the government of the Dene. The Government of the N.W.T. is not the government of the Dene . . . there are realities we are forced to submit to, such as the existence of a country called Canada, we insist on the right to self-determination as a distinct people . . . We the Dene are part of the Fourth World. . . . What we seek then is independence and self-determination within the country of Canada."[20]

Despite the protestations of such leaders as James Wah-shee, president of what was then called the Indian Brotherhood of the Northwest Territories, the Dene Declaration was a clearly separatist document designed to shock the government into taking the Dene position seriously. It was followed by a document entitled "Recognition of the Dene Nation through Dene Government,"[21] which claimed Dene jurisdiction over virtually every provincial and federal field of authority except the military and the postal service. The Metis claim, on the other hand, which was negotiated separately from that of the Dene from 1977 to 1984, was much less radical in tone and did not ask for any degree of political autonomy.

Negotiating an agreement with the Dene and Metis of the Mackenzie valley proved to be difficult, not least because the federal government insisted that all claims in the region be settled at the same time. When the Dene and Metis balked, the government in March 1978 cut off the funds that had been supplied to their organizations to help them with the research for their claims.[22] Funding began again in April 1980, and in July 1981 negotiations were resumed, but it was not until 1983 that the Dene and Metis leaders were able to agree on common objectives, negotiation strategies, and a common political agenda. In that year the Dene and Metis agreed on criteria for eligibility under an eventual settlement, and in June 1986 a package of agreements and understandings was concluded between the native negotiators and the government concerning the basic elements of a settlement, including financial compensation, the amount of land to be reserved for the First Nations people, eligibility for benefits, wildlife harvesting and management, and benefits from future resource development. This package was presented to the communities for discussion and approval.

After the opinion of the Dene and Metis communities had been secured, negotiations began again in the summer of 1987. On 5 September 1988, after prolonged and tough negotiations, an agreement-in-principle was signed by all parties that provided the Dene and Metis with ownership of 180 000 square kilometres of land and $500 million in cash. It also guaranteed them a voice in the management of land, wildlife, and renewable resources in the region through participation in management boards, as well as preferential hunting and fishing rights and exclusive trapping rights in the region.[23] But as of this writing, the agreement-in-principle seems to have unravelled. Some Dene leaders in the southern Mackenzie valley are balking at the last minute at the principle of extinguishment; other leaders from the Mackenzie Delta, who do not have these qualms, decided to break away and negotiate separately. They successfully concluded negotiations with the federal government. The Metis association continues to pursue a separate agenda. This division, which some argue serves the government's interests, harmed the Dene cause and promises to ensure that negotiations will continue for several years to come.

Nunavut ("Our Land")

This is the claim of the Inuit of the central and eastern Arctic, about 17 000 people living mostly in small communities scattered over a huge region from Eskimo Point to Grise Fiord, and from Coppermine to Iqaluit.

Although the Inuit of the eastern Arctic had met Europeans as early as the sixteenth century, and perhaps as early as the Viking period, the Inuit of the central Arctic coast were the last native people in Canada to come in contact with them—some as recently as the period immediately following the First World War. As with the rest of the north, the native people of the central and eastern Arctic were for the most part left alone, or ignored, by the government until the post-Second World War era. What moved Ottawa to intervene actively in their lives was not a desire to use their lands but the imperatives of the universal welfare state, the wish to emphasize Canadian sovereignty over the region, and to a degree the embarrassment and shame at the revelations of the dismal state of Inuit health made by writers such as Farley Mowat in the 1950s.[24]

Yet the Inuit of Nunavut, though widely scattered and relative newcomers to the arts of politics and public relations, had one great advantage—they made up 80 per cent of the population of their region, and it was evident that they would therefore be in control of its future, at least on the local level, under any agreement that might be negotiated. It was for this reason that the original Nunavut proposal, made in February 1976, had as its main feature the creation of a new territory with the same powers as those of the Yukon and the NWT.[25] The federal government resisted this idea, which was also contentious within the NWT, and in 1980 it was decided to consider the question of a new territory of Nunavut separately from the Nunavut claim itself.

The original Nunavut proposal was somewhat more radical in its political ramifications than the COPE claim, but did not go as far in demanding autonomy as did the Dene. However, this proposal was strongly criticized by many of the Inuit living in the settlements as reflecting too much of the philosophy of the non-native consultants who had helped to draw it up, and was replaced in 1977 by a claim that insisted on a new political arrangement as the basis for a settlement. In this version of the claim, subsurface rights were to remain with the Inuit and an amendment of the Canadian constitution was demanded "to provide for the constitutional recognition and continued assurance of the right of the Inuit to exist as an independent culture within Canada."[26]

In 1981 an agreement was reached on wildlife provisions in a final agreement, but in 1983 negotiations broke down over the degree of political autonomy demanded by the Inuit. There were also problems with the powers of the Nunavut Impact Review Board, a body that was to review oil, gas, and mining proposals and matters relating to the management of Nunavut land and resources—the government wanted it to be an advisory board, and the Inuit wanted it to have the power of veto over development proposals.[27]

However, a number of important subagreements were initialled by 1986, and an agreement-in-principle was signed on 30 April 1990 that, when fully ratified, would provide the Inuit of Nunavut with title to over 350 000 square kilometres of land—an area about half the size of Saskatchewan—$580 million, and a variety of economic and cultural rights and benefits.

Conclusion

In the cases that have been settled so far, the Canadian government has won its basic demand—extinguishment of native title to much of the north, or the "certainty" that the claims will not be reopened in the future. It seems likely that when the Dene/Metis claim in the Mackenzie valley is settled, the agreement will be along the same general lines. But the indigenous people who have concluded these settlements have not necessarily been losers—they have driven hard bargains, receiving a substantial land base, reasonable financial compensation, and, what is more important, a strong degree of control over the future of their region. Many people, including some but not all indigenous people, would consider the agreements to be reasonable compromises.

Whether these events can be taken as auguries of successful settlements of other claims in Canada is uncertain. The federal government found it fairly easy to reserve large areas of land for the Inuvialuit, since the land of the western Arctic was not considered particularly valuable, there were few non-native people in the region, and the territorial government had no real control over the outcome of negotiations. The same is not true in British Columbia, the next battleground of comprehensive claims. Here the land claimed is of immense value, and the provincial government, because it controls crown lands, must be a party to negotiations. It is likely that even the Dene/Metis claim, the most intractable of the four territorial claims, will be far more easily settled than the claims now coming under negotiation.

Documents

A. Together Today for Our Children Tomorrow: A Statement of Grievances and an Approach to Settlement by the Yukon Indian People[28]

The Yukon Native Brotherhood is presenting to the Government of Canada this Statement of our Grievances, and our suggestion about a Settlement on behalf of the Yukon Indian People.

At the same time we want the Government to know that we feel that this is a big responsibility for us. Our people have many deep feelings about our land and about the future of our children.

The Yukon Native Brotherhood has been meeting with their people for several years, to find out what kind of a Settlement we feel will be "fair and just" to both our people and to our White Brothers. Many of our people feel that our grievances are so great that there is no way we can be compensated for what has happened to us. This, we ask you to try to understand and to respect. So that you will better understand our deep feelings, we will tell you something about our past history; then something about the problems we have today; and finally our thoughts about the future.

. . .

Between 1900 and 1930 over half of our people died from Whiteman's diseases. During this time many Indian people returned to the bush. We trapped or worked in the bush with Whitemen and became quite well off. There was no welfare, employment, or housing programs needed.

During this time there was one program which continued to break down the Indian family and the Indian way of life. This was the residential school. They were run by the Church and the Government. This program should never have been allowed to happen. Our children were taken away from their homes when they were six years old. Sometimes we never saw them again until they were sixteen.

We were taught in such a way that we were forced to give up our language, our religion, our way of life, and because of this, we no longer identified with our parents. But what we were taught did not make sense, and it seemed wrong to us. Most of these people gave up the Indian way, but could not accept the Whiteman's way, because we were not taught how to live and work the Whiteman's way. . . . We were caught between the two and didn't know which way to go. . . .

Later on came Indian housing which was (and still is today, even more than ever) used as a bribe to get Indian people to move in from the bush. So the final program of changing the Indian way of life from one of economic independence to a welfare hand-out was complete. . . .

Now in 1973, the only village to escape the Whiteman's rush to get rich at the expense of the Indians is Old Crow, and this is changing every day. The people of Old Crow are scared of the changes the pipeline will bring. They don't want the same thing happening to them as happened to the other Yukon Indian Villages. The Oil Companies and the Government give out paycheques for meaningless jobs which will all disappear when the pipeline is finished. . . .

Many Whitemen say the Indian is lazy. What they do not realize is that the majority of the Indian people have not had an opportunity to provide for his family in the Whiteman's World. The government has not helped to provide this opportunity. . . . The Indian Agent and Welfare Officer have replaced the Indian as head of his own family. Because he is unable to make a living within the changed society, his wife calls the Indian Agent when she needs food, clothing, or firewood.

Many Whitemen say we do not care for our children. They point to Welfare, Truency [sic] and Juvenile Delinquency statistics to prove their point. Nothing could be further from the truth. The main concern of Indian parents today is what is happening to our children. We do not know because you are not telling us what you are doing to them. You take them to school, they go to your movies and dances, they watch your television and hang around your poolrooms. You told us they had to learn to live like Whitemen, so we did not interfere. You said our way of life was dead and that we had nothing to teach them. Please tell us what you are doing to our children, because they are breaking our hearts. We are accused of giving up our children for adoption and foster homes. If you would give us back control over our own lives, no Indian child would be in need of a home. Divorce, adoption, foster homes and illegitimacy are White inventions, not Indian. . . .

Only an Indian can understand, appreciate and feel what it means to be an Indian. If solutions are to be found which will work, it is we the Indian people who must find them. You can only help.

There must be a system set up where the Indian people have some control over the programs that affect us. This control must not be just in the Administration of the program—but in the planning. . . . Our first program must be one of making sure that our Older People benefit from the Settlement. They represent the only living part of our culture. They have suffered through watching the Indian Way disappear. Many will not be here when our programs start to produce results. . . .

The Settlement will only work for our children if we are successful in helping them regain their lost pride. For that reason our cultural program will be our most important one. It will affect all others. . . .

A sick community can only be cured when its members want to be cured. We feel our people have already taken this step. The next step is to encourage the natural leadership of the community to identify problems and propose solutions. This step is now taking place in our villages. . . .

The Yukon Indian people must play an important part in the development of the Yukon. If we are to take part in the Social, Economic and Political Life of this country we must have a solid economic base. We must have a chance to help plan the future of this land if we are going to benefit from its development. . . .

First, we suggest that the Government stop treating the Indian people as labourers, with no management skills. Qualifications for Government jobs must be changed in the Yukon to provide more jobs for our people.

Second, we suggest that the government allow us to plan a self-supporting way of life that will make sense to Indian People. Third, we suggest the government allow us to find out what our own training needs are, and to plan programs to meet these needs. . . . Fourth, we suggest the Government permit us to hire our own experts to help us find the answers we do not have. . . . Fifth, we suggest the Government allow us to control our own corporations, the same as the Whites control theirs. Sixth, we suggest that there be a summer works program. . . .

We have been told that one of our biggest problems with getting the Government to accept this Settlement is that we "are not credible." This is supposed to mean that we cannot be trusted with responsibility. We have heard this for a long time now, and we are fed up hearing this. We now demand a chance to prove you wrong. . . .

We require a temporary land freeze on all unoccupied, unalienated Crown lands to allow enough time for selection, survey, and transfer of control to the Yukon Indian people. . . .

We are saying that we deserve a cash settlement for all our past grievances and for the rights that have been taken away over the past one hundred years. . . . We will not waste this money. It will be invested in our children's future. . . .

Only by an immediate Settlement of all our grievances can the Yukon Indian People obtain Social and Economic Equality with our fellow Yukoners. It will be of benefit to all Canadians when we achieve this equality.

B. The Yukon Indian Land Claim Agreement-in-Principle (1989)[29]

General Provisions

—all settlement agreements negotiated pursuant to the Agreement-in-Principle will be considered land claims agreements as referred to in section 35 of the *Constitution Act*, 1982

—settlement agreements can be amended only by consent of the parties to the agreement

—existing and future programs for status Indians in the Yukon will not be affected by the Umbrella Final Agreement or Yukon First Nation Final Agreements, and will continue to be subject to program criteria

—laws of general application (all federal and territorial laws) will apply on all lands included in the Umbrella Final Agreement and Yukon First Nation Final Agreements, and to all Yukon Indians, except where these laws are inconsistent with the Settlement Legislation or settlement agreements; and

—in return for the rights contained in the Umbrella Final Agreement and Yukon First Nation Final Agreements, Yukon First Nations and all Yukon Indians agree to cede any aboriginal title to non-settlement lands and waters within Canada, except in the Northwest Territories and British Columbia (where Yukon Indians' land claims may overlap).

Eligibility

—In order to vote on and benefit from the Umbrella Final Agreement or a Yukon First Nation Final Agreement, an individual must meet eligibility criteria . . . based on . . . Canadian citizenship, ancestry, residency requirements and community affiliation. . . .

Amount of Settlement Lands (Land Quantum)

—The Agreement-in-Principle entitles Yukon First Nations to 41,439.81 square kilometres (16,000 square miles) of settlement lands in the Yukon. Settlement lands will be allocated among Yukon First Nations prior to approval of the final agreement[s].

—Under the Agreement-in-Principle, Yukon settlement lands will be divided into Category A, Category B and fee simple lands. Any aboriginal title will be surrendered everywhere in the Yukon except to the surface of Categories A and B settlement lands.

—Yukon First Nations will have the equivalent of fee simple title to the surface of Category A lands, and full fee simple title to the subsurface. Category A lands will comprise 25,899.88 square kilometres (10,000 square miles) of the total settlement lands.

—Yukon First Nations will have the equivalent of fee simple title to the surface of Category B lands, but ownership of the subsurface will remain with the Crown. The general public will be permitted access to Category B lands for hunting and fishing . . . most settlement lands that are currently within a community will likely be held in fee simple title.

—An additional 155 square kilometres (60 square miles) may be chosen from existing reserves and lands set aside for Indian use in the Yukon. The reserve land can be held either as a reserve or as settlement lands.

Surface Rights Board

—A Surface Rights Board will be established no later than the date of Settlement Legislation, under separate legislation. This board will have a minimum of one-third representation of Yukon First Nation appointees on panels dealing with settlement lands. It will have jurisdiction over matters relating to surface disputes between holders of surface and subsurface interests in the Yukon, whether native or non-native, as well as to expropriation disputes with Yukon Indians as they relate to compensation.

Land Use Planning

—Under the terms of the Agreement-in-Principle, a land use planning commission will be established in each region of the Yukon. The decisions of the commission will apply to both settlement and non-settlement lands. One-third of the members of each commission will be nominated by Yukon First Nations and one-third by the governments of Canada and the Yukon. The remaining one-third representation will be based on the ratio of Yukon Indians to the total population in the planning region; for example, if Yukon Indians represent a majority of the total population, Yukon First Nations may also dominate the remaining one-third of the planning commission members.

Development Assessment

—The Agreement-in-Principle provides for establishment of a special committee that will define a public process for assessing the impact of development projects in the Yukon. The committee will have one-third native representation. . . . Panels or committees created to assess proposed developments will have:

—one-third Yukon First Nation representation when the development will impact on non-settlement lands;

—two-thirds Yukon First Nation representation when the development will impact on settlement lands; and

—one-half Yukon First Nation representation when the development will impact on both.

Definition of Boundaries

—. . . Training programs will be established to help Yukon Indians participate in employment and economic opportunities arising from the surveying of settlement lands. Employment opportunities in surveying for qualified Yukon Indians will be addressed in each Yukon First Nation Final Agreement.

Heritage

—Under the Agreement-in-Principle, a Yukon Heritage Board will be established with 50 per cent representation from Yukon First Nations. The Board will make recommendations to the appropriate government on the protection and management of Yukon's heritage resources. Yukon First Nations will also be represented on the Yukon Geographical Names Board.

Financial Compensation

—The Agreement-in-Principle provides for financial compensation of $232 million (1988 dollars) to be made for all comprehensive claims by Yukon Indian people in Canada.

—Compensation payments will be allocated among Yukon First Nations prior to the signing of the first Yukon First Nation Final Agreement. Payment to Yukon First Nations will be made over a 15-year period that begins with the signing of the first final agreement.

—Yukon First Nations will repay federal loans that have been made to them and to the Council for Yukon Indians to support negotiations and for the Yukon Elders Program. . . .

Fish and Wildlife

—The Agreement-in-Principle provides for a $3 million (1988) Fish and Wildlife Enhancement Trust Fund to be financed equally by the Council for Yukon Indians, the Government of Canada and the Yukon Territorial

Government. A Fish and Wildlife Management Board will also be established. . . . Thirteen local renewable resource councils will make recommendations on fish and wildlife management matters at the local level to a territory-wide fish and wildlife board. A special sub-committee of the fish and wildlife board will manage salmon resources. . . . Yukon First Nations will appoint 50 per cent of the members of the fish and wildlife board, the local renewable resource councils and the salmon management sub-committee.

—Subject to conversation requirements, Yukon Indians will receive preferential harvesting allocations for some species of wildlife . . . based on a "basic needs" level identified in each Yukon First Nation Final Agreement. . . .

—Yukon Indians will have exclusive hunting rights on Category A lands, and will receive at least 70 per cent of all trap-lines allocated in the Yukon. . . . [D]evelopers will compensate Yukon Indians for any damage they cause to trap-lines. . . . [C]ompensation will be provided to outfitters whose concessions have been reduced by the granting of settlement lands.

Forestry

—Under the Agreement-in-Principle, each Yukon First Nation will manage and allocate timber harvests on settlement lands and will participate in forestry management on non-settlement lands. Forestry management plans will be developed for defined areas in the Yukon. Opportunities for Yukon First Nations to participate in commercial timber operations will be addressed in Yukon First Nation Final Agreements.

Self-government Provisions

—The governments of Canada and the Yukon are committed to negotiating self-government agreements with each Yukon First Nation that requests such negotiations. Self-government agreements will be implemented by legislations separate from Settlement Legislation, and will *not* be constitutionally protected by section 35 of the *Constitution Act, 1982*, unless a constitutional amendment to that effect is in force in the future. . . .

Dispute Resolution

—If disputes arise over interpretation or implementation . . . mediation will be sought before arbitration. Arbitration will occur only with the agreement of the parties to the dispute. Binding arbitration awards will be subject to limited appeal and judicial review. Mediators and arbitrators will be appointed from a panel of 12 persons nominated by the governments of Canada and the Yukon and Yukon First Nations.

C. The COPE/Government Working Group Joint Position Paper on the Inuvialuit Land Rights Claim (1978)

—The Minister of Indian Affairs and Northern Development and the President of COPE have agreed that this Joint Position Paper shall form the basis for a submission to Cabinet requesting authorization for the Minister to execute an Agreement-in-Principle. . . .

—Principles: It is agreed that the four basic goals of the Inuvialuit land rights settlement are to: 1) Preserve Inuvialuit cultural identity and values within a changing northern society. 2) Enable Inuvialuit to be equal and meaningful participants in the northern and national economy and society. 3) Provide specific rights, benefits, and compensation to the Inuvialuit in exchange for any Inuvialuit land rights that now exist. 4) Protect and preserve the Arctic wildlife, environment, and biological productivity.

Eligibility and Enrolment

—The Inuvialuit are best able to determine who should be eligible under the land rights settlement. . . . A person shall be eligible to be enrolled as a beneficiary if, as of the date of the Final Agreement, that person is alive, a Canadian citizen and: i) is of Inuvialuit ancestry, as determined by criteria to be included in the Final Agreement and was born in the Western Arctic Region or Inuvik, or has been a resident of the Western Arctic Region and/or Inuvik for a total of at least ten years, or if under ten years of age, is ordinarily resident in the Western Arctic Region and/or Inuvik; or ii) is of Inuvialuit ancestry and is accepted as a member of an Inuvialuit community corporation; or iii) is an adopted child, under the laws of any jurisdiction or according to Inuvialuit custom, of a male or female person who qualifies. . . .

Corporate Structure

—. . . There shall be an Inuvialuit Investment Corporation; an Inuvialuit Development Corporation, to be a holding corporation carrying on businesses; an Inuvialuit Land Corporation, to hold title to Inuvialuit lands; and a non-profit Inuvialuit community corporation for each community. . . . The Inuvialuit enrolled in the land rights settlement shall share equally in all the benefits received by the various corporations. . . . Control of the corporate entities shall be with the Inuvialuit. . . .

—For greater certainty, it is recognized, in the event of a decision to construct a "Dempster Link" or other pipeline in the Western Arctic Region, there may well be an increase in social problems for the Inuvialuit and as a result new and additional governmental programs may have to be considered and implemented outside the context of this land rights settlement to meet such problems.

Lands and Inuvialuit Ownership

—The settlement shall provide the Inuvialuit with: i) Fee simple absolute title . . . to 4,200 square miles to be selected from traditional lands of the Inuvialuit in the Western Arctic Region . . . to be selected in blocs of 700 square miles near each of the six communities. . . . ii) fee simple absolute title . . . to a single bloc consisting of 800 square miles in Cape Bathurst. . . . iii) fee simple absolute title, less oil, gas . . . to 32,000 square miles to be selected from traditional lands of the Inuvialuit. . . . Inuvialuit lands may not be sold or otherwise transferred except to Inuvialuit individuals or Inuvialuit controlled corporations, or to the Crown. . . .

D.   Dene/Metis Comprehensive Land Claim Agreement-in-Principle (September 1988)

—Subject to the enactment of the settlement legislation, and in consideration of the rights and benefits provided to the Dene/Metis by the Final Agreement, the Dene/Metis hereby agree to indemnify and forever save harmless Her Majesty in Right of Canada from all manner of suits and actions . . . against Canada which any person who is eligible to participate in this Agreement . . . may hereafter have against Canada relating to or in any way arising from the claims, rights, titles and interests described. . . .

Financial Compensation

—The capital transfer payment shall be 453.3 million dollars valued at January 1, 1988. . . .

—The Dene/Metis shall establish a trust fund or funds (hereinafter called "the Heritage Trust") to administer for the benefit of the Dene/

Metis . . . the sum of seventy-five million dollars . . . as part of the capital transfer payment. . . .

Resource Royalty Sharing

—Government shall pay to a designated Dene/Metis organization, annually, an amount equal to: a) 50% of the first two million dollars of resource royalty received by government, and b) 10% of any additional resource royalties received by government. Government may limit the amount to be paid . . . in any one year to the amount which if distributed equally to all participants would result in a Dene/Metis average per capita income equal to the Canadian average per capita income.

Dene/Metis Lands

—. . . a) 66,100 square miles of lands in fee simple, reserving therefrom the mines and minerals. . . . b) 3,900 square miles of lands in fee simple including the mines and minerals . . . 700 square miles of which will be selected by the Dene/Metis of Aklavik. . . . Dene/Metis settlement lands may be conveyed only to government in exchange for other lands, or to Dene/Metis organizations. This section shall not be interpreted to prevent the Dene/Metis from granting leases or licenses to non-participants to use or occupy Dene/Metis lands. . . . Title to Dene/Metis lands shall vest in the designated Dene/Metis organization from the date of settlement legislation. . . . Dene/Metis land selection shall be made so as to leave communities with sufficient land for public purposes and for private, residential and commercial purposes and to leave sufficient land which is reasonably accessible to communities for public use for recreation and harvesting wildlife. . . .

Land Use Planning

—A Land Use Planning Board . . . shall be established and shall have jurisdiction, in accordance with the provisions of this agreement, for the development of land use plans in the settlement area . . . shall have equal membership from nominees of the Dene/Metis and of government. . . .

Environmental Impact Review

—All development proposals in the settlement area . . . shall be subject to a process of environmental impact review. . . . An Environmental Impact Review Board shall be established in the settlement area having equal membership from nominees of the Dene/Metis and of government. . . .

Land and Water Management

—A single Land and Water Management Board shall be established. . . . [E]qual membership from nominees of the Dene/Metis and of government . . . shall have the following powers: i) issue, amend or renew, licences, permits and authorizations and the terms and conditions attaching thereto for all uses of land and water throughout the settlement area . . . ii) oversee compliance with its decisions through inspections or otherwise . . . iii) enforce or secure compliance with its decisions by the suspension or cancellation of licences. . . .

Heritage Resources

—The Dene/Metis shall be actively involved in the manner set out in this chapter in the conservation and management of such heritage resources . . . shall be closely consulted in the formulation of government policy and legislation on Dene/Metis heritage resources . . . shall have preference in employment at public sites, museums and similar facilities in the settlement area related to Dene/Metis heritage resources. . . . The Dene/Metis have traditionally referred to certain lakes, rivers, mountains and other places in the settlement area by traditional or aboriginal names. The official names of such places shall be reviewed, and may be changed to traditional Dene/Metis names. . . . Government recognizes that in appropriate cases artifacts and records relating to the Dene/Metis heritage which have been removed from the settlement area should be returned to the settlement area for the benefit, study and enjoyment of the Dene/Metis and all other residents of the settlement area. . . .

Exploration, Development and Productions of Subsurface Resources

—Prior to opening any lands in the settlement area for oil and gas exploration, Government shall notify a designated Dene/Metis organization, provide it with an opportunity to present its views to Government on the matter. . . . Before any oil and gas exploration takes place, the developer and a designated Dene/Metis organization shall consult on . . . environmental impact . . . location of camps and facilities . . . maintenance of public order including liquor and drug control . . . local Dene/Metis employment . . . any other matter of importance to the Dene/Metis or the developer. . . .

E.   Building Nunavut (1983)[30]

Nunavut is "public government." That is, it is a government for all the people who live in the area embraced by Nunavut whether they were born in Igloolik or Trois Rivieres, Lloydminster or Yellowknife. . . . A special feature of Nunavut is that land claims settlement acts will form important parts of the total "constitution". . . . [S]ome people may feel that there is not enough detail, or that things here are not concrete enough. That is the problem with constitutions. They do not put a seal in anyone's pot on Sunday, nor help bring medical services to people who are sick. They do not say how things are going to be, but rather who will be able to make things happen and what are the limits on their power to do so. Then the people we elect to a Nunavut legislative assembly will actually do the work. . . . [W]e want those people to be as free as possible to do things, and we try to avoid putting too many limits on them in advance. There is no magic in a constitution, but there can be no power for the people of Nunavut without one. . . .

It is recommended that Nunavut bill of rights be entrenched in the Nunavut constitution with the power to take precedence over any other legislation unless a specific Nunavut law provides an exception, and to include rights in the categories of fundamental rights and freedoms, legal rights, social and economic rights, political rights and cultural rights. . . . [I]t is recommended that the Commissioner of Nunavut be chosen in consultation with the first elected Nunavut "MLAs" and before the first session of the Nunavut legislative assembly, and that the Commissioner's instructions from the Government of Canada contain clear guidelines for the performance of duties consonant with the maximum self-government of Nunavut vesting the elected assembly of Nunavut. . . . [I]t is recommended that Inuktitut be an official language of Nunavut and that all public services be available in Inuktitut, and that public bodies including courts and the legislature operate in Inuktitut as freely as in English . . . that Inuktitut be a language of instruction in the Nunavut schools . . . that the Nunavut Constitutional Forum continue to study the application of Inuit customary law in Nunavut. . . .

F.   "Largest Land Claim Agreement-in-Principle Signed Igloolik, NWT" (30 April 1990)[31]

Today, another important landmark was reached in native comprehensive claims. The Tungavik Federation of Nunavut's (TFN) Agreement-in-Principle (AIP) was signed.

The Minister of Indian Affairs and Northern Development, Tom Siddon, TFN President and Chief Negotiator, Paul Quassa, and Northwest Territories Government Leader, Dennis Patterson, signed the AIP.

The AIP covers the largest comprehensive land claim in Canada, representing over 17,000 Inuit and a land area of approximately two million square kilometres in the NWT. The agreement provides for wildlife harvesting rights, participation in management of lands and resources, and a variety of economic and cultural rights and benefits for greater self-sufficiency for Inuit throughout the central and eastern Arctic. The agreement, when finalized in 18 months, will provide the Inuit with $580 million and confirm their title to over 350,000 sq. km. of land—an area about half the size of Saskatchewan.

"Today we are making history and resolving a major issue. After years of extensive negotiations, hard work and dedication, this agreement embodies a settlement which is fair and equitable to all parties," stated Mr. Siddon. "Real progress in claims negotiations is being made. This agreement once again confirms this government's commitment to settling comprehensive claims, improving native/government relations and building stronger native and northern economies."

This agreement will also enhance the climate in the territories for economic and political development by removing legal uncertainty on use and disposition of land and resources in the eastern NWT.

The AIP also reaffirms federal and territorial government support in principle if northerners agree to divide the NWT and create a separate Nunavut Territory. The land claim settlement will not create Nunavut but commits the territorial government and TFN to set up a process for achieving a northern consensus on division outside the claims process.

Third party interests will be protected in the settlement through provisions dealing with wildlife harvesting, and resource management and access to and across Inuit Settlement Lands. Affected third parties will be consulted during the land identification process and provisions have been negotiated to protect any existing third party interest included in these lands.

In ratifying the AIP, the negotiating parties have formally committed themselves to reaching a final agreement within 18 months. This will involve the identification of Inuit settlement lands, the development of an implementation plan and negotiation of agreements regarding overlapping interests with other aboriginal peoples.

Highlights of the Tungavik Federation of Nunavut Claim

—Claimant: Tungavik Federation of Nunavut (TFN)

—Area: over 2 million km^2 claimed in Northwest Territories—central and eastern Arctic

—Population: approximately 17,000 Inuit; 80% of population in settlement area Negotiations

—claim originally presented in 1976 by Inuit Tapirisat of Canada, revised and resubmitted in December 1977

—1979—impasse over proposal to create Nunavut territory

—1980—negotiations resume as agreement reached to deal with creation of Nunavut outside claims process

—1982—TFN replaces Inuit Tapirisat as negotiating body for claim and Tom Molloy appointed as Chief Government Negotiator

—by 1986 a number of major subagreements initialled and federal comprehensive claims policy revised

—1987—government approved mandate for negotiator to proceed on outstanding topics

—December 1989—final elements of AIP negotiated with Minister of Indian Affairs and Northern Development

Highlights of the TFN AIP

Land Title

—approximately 350,000 km^2 of land, 36,257 km^2 with subsurface mineral rights

—access to settlements lands is governed by provisions in AIP

Economic

—$580 million (1989 dollars), $54 million on signing of Final Agreement and remainder over 14 years. $3 million on April 30, 1990, and a further $2 million between the signing of the AIP and Final Agreement (18 months), depending on progress

—Inuit to receive 50 percent of first $2 million of resource royalty received by government and 5 percent of additional resource royalties within settlement area

—increased Inuit participation in government employment in settlement area and government contracting

Wildlife

—Nunavut Wildlife Management Board to be established with equal Inuit and public membership to oversee wildlife harvesting

—specific wildlife harvesting rights and economic opportunities related to guiding, sports lodges and commercial marketing of wildlife products

—compensation where developers cause provable damage to property or equipment used in harvesting wildlife or for loss of income from wildlife harvesting; Surface Rights Tribunal to be set up to determine liability when claims are not settled

—three national parks to be established in settlement area after final agreement

Land and Environmental Management

—detailed provisions ensuring equal Inuit representation on boards with responsibility for land use planning, wildlife management, environmental and socio-economic reviews of development proposals, and water management

Political Development

—reaffirms government support, in principle, for creation of a separate Nunavut Territory subject to northern consensus

—within six months of the AIP, the Government of the Northwest Territories and the Inuit will develop a process to pursue creation of the Territory and government outside the claims process.

Notes

[1] Part of Treaty 8, signed in 1899, extends into the southern part of the Mackenzie valley. See René Fumoleau, *As Long as This Land Shall Last: A History of Treaty 8 and Treaty 11, 1870–1939* (Toronto: McClelland and Stewart 1973), and K.S. Coates and W.R. Morrison, *Treaty Research Report: Treaty 11* (Ottawa: Indian and Northern Affairs Canada 1986).

[2] I have drawn for some of this material on W.R. Morrison, *A Survey of the History and Claims of the Native People of Northern Canada* (Ottawa: Treaties and Historical Research Centre, Indian and Northern Affairs Canada 1983).

[3] K.S. Coates, "Best Left as Indians: The Federal Government and the Indians of the Yukon, 1894–1950," *Canadian Journal of Native Studies* 4, 2 (Fall 1984), 179–204.

[4] Later, however, the deal became the subject of bitter resentment on the part of Alaskan native people. See Thomas R. Berger, *Village Journey: The Report of the Alaska Native Review Commission* (New York: Hill and Wang 1985).

[5] "Petition of . . . members of the aboriginal people of the Old Crow Indians to the Honourable Commons of Canada," 21 February 1972.

[6] Transcript of radio interviews of March and April 1973, provided courtesy of the Treaties and Historical Research Centre, Indian and Northern Affairs Canada.

[7] Treaties and Historical Research Centre, Indian and Northern Affairs Canada, "Planning Council Document #4: Yukon Indian Claim, Settlement Model, July 14 1977."

[8] Treaties and Historical Research Centre, Indian and Northern Affairs Canada, "Dennis O'Connor to Head Yukon Native Claims Negotiations," Indian and Northern Affairs Communiqué, 23 May 1980.

[9] Indian and Northern Affairs Canada, *Annual Review, 1981–82* (Ottawa: Department of Indian and Northern Affairs 1982), 50.

[10] Department of Indian Affairs and Northern Development, *Guide to the Yukon Indian Land Claim Agreement-in-Principle* (Ottawa 1989).

[11] Diamond Jenness, *Eskimo Administration: II. Canada* (Montreal: Arctic Institute of North America 1964).

[12] John R. Bockstoce, *Steam Whaling in the Western Arctic* (New Bedford: Old Dartmouth Historical Society 1977), is a good account of the whaling era in the region.

[13] The report of this commission was published as Mr Justice Thomas Berger, *Northern Frontier, Northern Homeland: The Report of the Mackenzie Valley Pipeline Inquiry*, 2 vols. (Toronto: James Lorimer and Supply and Services Canada 1977).

[14] Or in some cases, descendants of Metis who migrated north from the Prairies late in the nineteenth century.

[15] Alice B. Kehoe, *North American Indians: A Comprehensive Account* (Englewood Cliffs, N.J.: Prentice-Hall 1981), 500.

[16] Fumoleau, *As Long As This Land Shall Last*, 211.

[17] See K.S. Coates and W.R. Morrison, "More Than a Matter of Blood: The Federal Government, the Churches and the Mixed Blood Populations of the Yukon and Mackenzie River Valley, 1870–1950," in L. Barron, ed., *1885 and After* (Regina: Canadian Plains Research Centre 1986).

[18] Until recently, under a provision of the Indian Act that is no longer law, when a native woman married a non-native man, she and her children lost their rights under treaty.

[19] Indian and Northern Affairs Canada, Information Sheet no. 22, February 1989, "Dene and Metis Comprehensive Land Claim."

[20] "Dene Declaration," copy in the Treaties and Historical Research Centre, Indian and Northern Affairs Canada.

[21] Copy in the Treaties and Historical Research Centre, Indian and Northern Affairs Canada.

[22] Substantial sums were involved: from the time the claims process began until the end of March 1978, the Dene received almost $2.4 million; and the Metis Association received $1.1 million between the fall of 1976 and March 1978, the period during which they negotiated separately. Much of this, however, was an advance against the payments that eventually would be made at the time an agreement was reached. "Funding Suspended for Mackenzie Valley Claims Negotiations," Indian and Northern Affairs Communiqué, 27 September 1978, copy in the Treaties and Historical Research Centre, Indian and Northern Affairs Canada.

[23] Indian and Northern Affairs Canada, Information Sheet no. 22, February 1989, "Dene and Metis Comprehensive Land Claim."

[24] Mowat's famous exposé, *People of the Deer* (1952), caused a national scandal, and seriously embarrassed the government of the day.

[25] The original proposal was put forward on behalf of the Inuit by the Inuit Tapirisat of Canada; at first it negotiated for all Inuit, but the Inuvialuit of the western Arctic decided to proceed separately. In 1982 the Tungavik Federation of Canada became the negotiating body for the claim.

[26] The 1976 Nunavut claim is discussed in Peter A. Cumming, *Canada: Native Land Rights and Northern Development* (Copenhagen: International Work Group for Indigenous Affairs 1977), 40–53.

[27] *Nunavut Newsletter*, February 1983.

[28] Prepared by the Yukon Native Brotherhood for the Commissioner on Indian Claims and the Government of Canada, January 1973.

[29] Indian and Northern Affairs Canada, *Guide to the Yukon Indian Land Claim Agreement-in-Principle* (Ottawa 1989).

[30] *Building Nunavut: A Working Document with a Proposal for an Arctic Constitution* (Nunavut Constitutional Forum 1983).

[31] Indian and Northern Affairs Communiqué, 30 April 1990, "Largest Land Claim Agreement-in-Principle Signed."

Metis Land Claims

D.N. Sprague

The promise of economic development was one of the principal incentives for the formation of the Canadian federation in 1867. Advocates of the federation regarded it as an indispensable precondition for railway construction, industrial growth, and, of course, territorial expansion. The prime area of intended colonization by the united colonies was Rupert's Land, a vast expanse of prairie and forest several times larger than the area of the new Dominion, but almost completely uninhabited by "an energetic and civilized race, able to improve its vast capabilities," according to the Canadian "explorer" of the region, H.Y. Hind, reporting in 1860.[1] Nearly all the people Hind found in his travels through Rupert's Land and the North-West Territories in 1857 and 1860 were the "naturally improvident, and perhaps indolent" Indians and "Half breeds" who preferred "the wild life of the prairies to the tamer duties of a settled home."[2] In that sense, neither population was considered an obstacle to Canadian expansion; neither had the strong agricultural orientation of the potential colonizers from Canada. But since the "unsettled" west was still fully exploited within the limits of the traditional subsistence and more recent fur-trade economies, Hind warned that if the native peoples were too abruptly "thrust on one side" by newcomers, the Indians' and Half breeds' "full appreciation and enjoyment of a home in the prairie wilds during the winter and summer would render them a very formidable enemy.[3] On that account, before beginning to exploit the region, Canada would have to satisfy native claims as well as those of the established colonial proprietors, the Hudson's Bay Company (HBC). Moreover, since the new Dominion was still in many respects subordinate to Great Britain, and since the British Colonial Office dreaded expensive "small wars" with aboriginal peoples, Canada had to satisfy the British that Canadians would deal fairly with native peoples before the queen would sanction the transfer.

The first formal request for the territory and statement of benevolent Canadian intent came in the form of an address by parliament to the queen during the initial parliamentary session, December 1867. If Britain would place the territory under the authority of the Dominion, Canada promised that the

> legal rights of any corporation, company, or individual within the same shall be respected. . . . And furthermore, upon the transference of the territories in question to the Canadian Government, the claims of the Indian tribes to compensation for lands required for purposes of settlement will be considered and settled in conformity with the equitable principles which have uniformly governed the British Crown in its dealings with the aborigines.[4]

The Colonial Office responded with encouragement to negotiations between Canada and the HBC. An agreement in principle was reached in 1869 and Canada made preparations to complete the transfer before the end of the year. Unfortunately, the Hudson's Bay Company was the sole claimant to Rupert's Land consulted beforehand. A Canadian statute enacted in the summer of 1869 made plain that the others— "individuals" and "Indian tribes"—would be dealt with in due course, but after the territory had become a crown colony of the Dominion. Such a policy was not acceptable to the residents of the largest settlement in Rupert's Land, the 12 000 people in the District of Assiniboia situated within a 120-kilometre radius of the forks of the Red and Assiniboine rivers. They mounted a popular resistance to the transfer and demanded terms that Great Britain pressured Canada to accept.[5] The result in 1870 was the transfer to Canada of Rupert's Land and the North-West Territories, but with one small corner of the region united to the Dominion as the province of Manitoba.

The statute defining the terms and conditions of the fifth province's entry into Confederation did not mention the claims of "Indian tribes," but the Manitoba Act was seemingly extravagant in the recognition accorded to the land rights of native settlers in the province at the time of the transfer.[6] All such residents won a sweeping assurance that they had pre-emptive claims to the lands they occupied (section 32), and the children of settlers related to Indians had the additional assurance of access to a block of 1.4 million acres to be reserved from other settlement "for the benefit of the families of the half-breed residents" in consideration of the "extinguishment" of their inherited share of the "Indian Title to the lands in the Province" (section 31). Since 80 per cent of Manitoba's population was intermarried with Indian people, the vast majority of Manitobans won a generous dual accommodation, in part attributable to their status as first settlers, and partly owing to their aboriginal ties. Not surprisingly, settlers of similar ancestry elsewhere in the territories demanded the same benefits: title to the lands they occupied, and payment for their aboriginal legacy. Just as predictably, Canada was reluctant to extend the benefit beyond Manitoba, insisting that persons native to the country at the time of the transfer had to choose between "taking treaty" and joining an Indian band, or claiming homesteads and becoming part of the society of the incoming settlers. "Half breeds" could be Indians or homesteaders, but not both.

The reality, however, was that few dual-ancestry original settlers fit easily into either population. Although they spoke one or several Indian languages as well as English or French, and while they usually respected Indian cultural values as they interacted in the fur-trade economy, most native settlers were too Europeanized to merge completely into Indian society. Conversely, their economy, culture, and appearance meant that the "half breeds" were rarely acceptable to "white" society. They remained a group apart, and continued to demand the dual accommodation conceded in principle to "half breed settlers" in Manitoba. Eventually Canada did broaden the concession by statutory amendment in 1879,[7] and brought "North West half breed claims" into administrative routine after 1885.

Thomas Flanagan, a political scientist uncomfortable with the concept of "aboriginal rights" in general[8] and Metis aboriginal rights in particular, suggests that the tortuous history of the extension of Manitoba land rights through the rest of the territories was a matter of "expediency" rather than announced "principle."[9] In that view, the granting of a benefit without an articulated rationale makes the precedent irrelevant to any future discussion of Metis aboriginal rights from a theoretical standpoint; "whatever was done, was done long ago for pragmatic reasons and gives little principled guidance about what Metis aboriginal rights might be in the 1990s."[10] However, Flanagan is wrong for two reasons. In the first place, the distinction between "expediency" and "principle" is entirely irrelevant. By Flanagan's reasoning, the treaties with Indian people are similarly void of "principled guidance" because they were conceded from the beginning as less expensive—expedient—alternatives to purely military forms of subjugation. The legal reality is that every affirmation of an aboriginal right by the government—for whatever reason—relates to principle if only to test the process of extinguishment: was the right, once conceded, extinguished with appropriate compensation and in a manner to do honour to the crown?[11] A negative answer raises another question: what right is breached? Here Flanagan would say, "in the case of the Metis, no right at all, merely an expedient conceded for reasons of policy." That is the second error because Canada's possession of Rupert's Land and the North-West Territories was subject to the terms and conditions of the Britain's Rupert's Land Order of 1870, the obligations in which were no less binding because Canada's compliance emerged through a welter of expedients invented in the 1870s.

By 1879 Canada had decided upon a three-stage process for accommodating Indian people, native settlers, and companies operating in the territories before acquisition by Canada. Stage one was negotiation for extinguishing Indian title in a district of expected colonization. Treaties assured annuities, hunting and fishing rights, reserves, and other benefits to Indian people. At the same time, native settlers related to the Indians (and not members of an Indian band), the "half breeds," would receive a once-and-for-all payment in consideration of their inherited share of Indian title (in the 1880s a "scrip" redeemable for 240 acres of Dominion lands open for homestead, in the 1900s a simple cash payment of $240 per person).[12]

The potentially more valuable consideration of original settler claims occurred at stages two and three of territorial administration. The second stage was making surveys to fit the region into the rectangular pattern specified in the Dominion Lands Act. Surveyors of each six-by-six mile "township" (consisting of thirty-six "sections" one mile square) had instructions to take careful notes on all existing "farm lines . . . all fences, the several buildings and reputed owners" at the same time that they posted the boundaries of each parcel expected to be taken up by newcomers.[13] Stage three of the process was administrative consideration of the claims of settlers before survey. In principle, the older the claim, the more certain the recognition by Canada. Original settlers claiming occupancy from a date before the transfer of Rupert's Land or before Indian treaty were promised free grants. Persons settling later but prior to the date of the Dominion survey had a right of pre-emption, meaning first chance to enter an official homestead or to purchase from the crown (pre-empting either option by a newcomer).[14]

Stage one accommodated Indian peoples and the Indian-title aspect of "half-breed" claims. Stages two and three protected the lands occupied by old settlers. The three together would protect native peoples in general from unrestricted invasion by newcomers. In theory, no conflicts could arise between the competing claims of aboriginal inhabitants and Canadian-sanctioned development because the aboriginal peoples' claims were known and protected by Canada before any lands were granted or sold by the Dominion to individuals or companies. In practice, however, there were major shortcomings and failures at every stage of the process and in every geographical locale overseen by Canada from

1870 to 1930 (the era of the development of crown lands as the property of Canada under the authority of the federal Department of the Interior). And since none of the shortcomings and failures has been remedied or even acknowledged by government in recent times, the legacies of "half breed" or (in more contemporary terms) *Metis* claims are as wide-ranging as those of Indian people. They are *comprehensive* as well as *specific*. There are claims that the aboriginal title of the Metis has not been extinguished (comprehensive claims), and allegations that certain aspects of equitable agreements remain to be fulfilled (specific claims).[15]

The only comprehensive claims of Metis people that the Government of Canada is willing to consider at present involve claimants where Canada is negotiating first agreements with aboriginal groups in general. In other words, Canada does concede that there are certain areas of the country in which stage one was never reached. The present practice is to treat Metis communities the same as Indian bands. The "Comprehensive Land Claim Agreement in Principle" signed with the Dene Nation and the Metis Association of the Northwest Territories in September 1988, for example, abandoned the disparity between the two groups evident in previous "treaty" negotiations. The benefits of the "Dene/Metis Comprehensive Land Claim" were to be divided in proportion to population distribution and land use, rather than by ethnic status. The Metis were parties to the agreement, not recipients of a token gratuity received after exclusion from the undertaking concluded with the Indian people.

Ultimately, however, the Dene-Metis agreement in principle did not come into effect on 31 March 1991, the date by which the settlement was to have been ratified by the 15 000 people affected by its terms. The difficulty was with the largest of the Indian bands signatory to the document. They also had rights under Treaty 8 and Treaty 11 and feared losing them under the new arrangement. In the end, the Department of Indian Affairs refused to reopen negotiations to address such fears. But what remained unchallenged by all parties throughout the unravelling of the agreement between July and November 1990 was the principle that all aboriginal rights—Metis as well as Indian—would be settled on similar terms.[16]

Canada's abandonment of tokenism in the treatment of contemporary comprehensive Metis claims amounts to a tacit admission that the issue of "scrip" or cash in the nineteenth and early twentieth centuries was inappropriate for dealing with aboriginal title claims—precisely what the national and provincial Metis political associations have been contending since the early 1970s. They argue that the Metis have always had a legitimate claim to a share of aboriginal title; and the terms of the transfer of Rupert's Land and the North-West Territories imposed a constitutional obligation upon Canada to extinguish Indian title equitably in every aspect. They point out that the "scrip" and cash disbursements rarely went to the Metis directly, and even where the payment did pass to the nominal recipient, a once-and-for-all gratuity for $240 is trivial payment for value received. Consequently, the Metis National Council and the Association of Metis and Non-Status Indians of Saskatchewan contend that the "aboriginal title of the Metis remains unextinguished." The Government of Canada does not agree; and, to date, no organization or individual has launched a legal action to compel Canada to reconsider the matter, notwithstanding recent Supreme Court decisions that would appear to open the door to such a case.

The role of the Supreme Court has been innovative because the language of the constitution is remarkably unclear. According to section 35 of the Constitution Act (1982):

(1) The existing aboriginal and treaty rights of the aboriginal peoples of Canada are hereby recognized and affirmed.

(2) In this Act, "aboriginal peoples of Canada" includes the Indian, Inuit, and Metis peoples of Canada.

Since the section is silent as to which rights are "existing" and which are spent (or never had any genuine legal reality, notwithstanding possible wisdom to the contrary), section 37 called for a conference of leaders of Canada, the provinces, and native political organizations to consider "constitutional matters that directly affect the aboriginal peoples of Canada, including the identification and definition of rights of those peoples to be included in the Constitution of Canada. . . . " By 1985, however, the conference process had ended in failure. Thus, it remained for the Supreme Court to interpret the meaning of the word "existing" in section 35 and whether such rights were constitutionally protected even though the section 37 process had ended without agreement.

The gains made through the judicial classification of constitutionally protected rights have been more extensive than those even the most optimistic observers had hoped to make in the political arena. Most recently the Supreme Court has declared that any aboriginal right is "existing" if by custom or by treaty an aboriginal group or individual enjoyed a resource or tradition not legally extinguished by 17 April 1982.[17] The test of legal extinguishment is whether the right in question was subject to infringement by a competent authority for a legitimate purpose with compensation to the aboriginal people adequate to do honour to the crown. More important to the court than cataloguing the list of supposed rights is the process for their enforcement: the burden of proving infringement is upon the aboriginal group or individual; the obligation to justify is the government's.[18] In defining the terms for proving infringement and justification of trespass the Supreme Court has removed many obstacles for considering all native claims. Government must become more open to negotiating settlements or face increasing pressure of litigation.

Litigation has already developed in two areas of Metis specific claims. One involves the Manitoba Metis Federation (MMF) against the federal and provincial governments for their roles in the administration of the land-promise provisions of the Manitoba Act. The MMF claims that the protection of settlers' lands along the rivers and creeks by section 32 of the statute meant nothing in the face of amendments that altered the unqualified pre-emptive right to occupied lands; specifically, requirements for "actual occupation and peaceable possession" opened the door to value-of-improvements tests that disqualified most potential Metis claimants.[19] Similarly, various other amendments and Orders in Council narrowed the access of "children of half breed heads of families" to the 1.4 million acres reserved by section 31 "for the benefit of half-breed residents." The same legislation and executive orders limited grants to randomly drawn allotments of bald prairie totally unlike the riverfront land on which Metis people customarily settled. Recipients of squares of empty prairie were understandably eager to sell their grants. Provincial legislation facilitated sales by minors and retroactively legalized otherwise illegal sales.[20]

The MMF claims that the Manitoba statutes purporting to legislate for "half breed lands" are beyond the competence of a provincial legislature because all matters concerning Indian title are within the exclusive jurisdiction of the national parliament under section 91 (24) of the Constitution Act (1982). And the Canadian government's attempts to "amend" the Manitoba Act by ordinary statutes or Orders in Council are unconstitutional because of their inconsistency with a section of a British statute making the Manitoba Act part of the constitution of Canada— section 6 of the British North America Act (1871). Of course, the provincial and federal governments deny both claims.

Manitoba argues that section 91 (24) applies only to "Indians" and "lands reserved for Indians." Consequently, even though the 1.4 million acres was reserved for the Metis "towards the extinguishment of Indian title," the Metis reserve cannot be held to be "Indian land" because the Metis are not "Indians" under the Indian Act. As a result, the provincial legislature was acting well within its power to enact laws affecting Metis property and civil rights. And even if the "Half breed code" were somehow beyond the power of the Manitoba legislature, invalidity does not imply liability. The invalid laws purporting to legalize sales would, at most, invalidate the transactions proven to be irregular, and subsequent actions to recover land illegally sold would have to be against the purchasers of Metis lands, not the province. Either way, the attorney general of Manitoba is confident that there is no "legal basis" for a claim against the province.[21]

The Government of Canada, for its defence, argues that the BNA Act applies only to the sections of the Manitoba Act providing a form of government, not the land-promise provisions in sections 31 and section 32. And even if the Parliament of Canada were prevented from amending the land provisions as well as the rest, officials in the Department of Justice deny that the intent or effect of the "supplementary provisions" was to diminish Metis rights.[22] No claimant was excluded from the 1.4 million acres except persons who ought to have been excluded; persons claiming homesites who passed the value-of-improvements test received more than they were entitled to under a strict interpretation of section 32; and even if there were a few random injustices in the administrative process, too many documents have been lost or destroyed to form an accurate picture of the era. The entire matter is inappropriate for present-day consideration in the land-claims process or for litigation.

The Supreme Court of Canada disagrees. In April 1990 the court ruled that the MMF's quest for "declaratory relief" is neither frivolous nor moot; the case bears directly on the provincial and federal governments' refusal to consider a negotiated settlement of the Metis claim. By rejecting Canada's motion to have the case dismissed on procedural and technical grounds, the Supreme Court is forcing the Manitoba Court of Queen's Bench to hear arguments on the constitutionality of the impugned legislation and Orders in Council. By the same decision, the court seems to have committed itself to making a final judgment of its own in the case after the Manitoba Court of Appeal disposes of the matter in the early 1990s.

One other important aspect of litigation likely to be settled in the 1990s concerns the land rights of Metis settlers in the mid-north, the locality of persons who were supposed to have been accommodated at stages two and three in the administrative process described above. Their case arises from delayed or non-existent surveys. In the vicinity of Norway House, for example, the treaty negotiation for the area dates from 1875, but the surveys to enable free grants to be made did not occur until 1916, and the consideration of claims of settlers identified by the surveyor did not begin until 1924.[23] By then, most of the inhabitants of the district in 1875 were long dead; their heirs, the claimants in the 1920s, were unborn (therefore not occupying ancestral homesites, traplines, and fish camps) at the remote date required by the Department of the Interior for free grants. Consequently, all settlers were required to buy their land (restricted to homesites only) at the rate of $3 per acre. In effect, delay at stage two led to injustice at stage three. Elsewhere in the regions covered by treaties 8, 9, 10, and 11 the surveys were delayed even longer or never occurred at all. As a result, those Metis communities were denied even the limited accommodation accorded the descendants of the original settlers of Norway House. Such a denial would appear to conflict with Canada's solemn promise to respect the usages of the inhabitants of Rupert's Land at the time of the transfer in 1870. As a constitutional obligation, the duty was not to deal with everyone at once, of course, but from time to time as land and resources were required for new developments. The great injustice dealt the Metis settlers of the mid-north was the inexplicable reluctance of Canada to deal with settler claims in a timely manner after concluding the treaties with the Indians: 1875 (Treaty 5), 1899 (Treaty 8), 1905 (Treaty 9), 1906 (Treaty 10), 1908 (extension northward of Treaty 5), 1921 (Treaty 11), and 1929 (extension northward of Treaty 9). Large numbers of descendants of the original settlers in all areas of the mid-north suffered serious interruption of their trapping and fishing economies by twentieth-century mining, hydroelectric development, and logging. Canada denies any responsibility for virtually all such claims given a boundary settlement with Ontario in the 1880s and the formal transfer of Dominion lands to the three Prairie provinces in 1930. Rupert's Land is Dominion land no longer, but crown lands in the right of the provinces. Arguably, each provincial government is bound to honour any unfulfilled terms of the transfer of Rupert's Land from Britain to Canada as a "subsisting trust," but that is the precise point that awaits future judicial consideration.

Adjudication of the major issues of Metis rights and claims has special poignancy in the 1990s because most Metis communities are threatened by a recent change to the Indian Act that makes Metis populations more fluid than ever. With the exception of certain settlements in the Northwest Territories and the province of Alberta (areas in which Metis corporate existence is in process of recognition by the comprehensive-claims process in the Mackenzie Basin and an Alberta initiative regarding its "Metis colonies"),[24] communities reputedly "Metis" are legal anomalies. Where they are self-governing, they enjoy self-government under the same legislation as any other municipality, not as an "aboriginal right." Similarly, residency in a typical Metis community is a purely individual choice. Except in certain parts of Alberta and the Mackenzie Basin, their governing councils do not make decisions concerning community acceptance or rejection of newcomers. Consequently, the ebb and flow of their populations is entirely unrestricted. And yet hundreds of communities in western Canada are still reputedly Metis—even though that distinctiveness has been on the verge of extinction, in some cases for more than a century, by absorption into the society of later-arriving "settlers." The Metis communities have persisted in part because most have deep roots in the history of first contacts between Europeans and Indian people in the fur trade, and to an even larger extent because their "native" ties remain strong. Geographical proximity to Indian people has maintained the working familiarity with aboriginal languages and cultures. Cultural familiarity has meant that Indian and Metis people have continued to find marriage partners on both sides of Indian reserve boundaries. And for more than a century section 12 (1.b) of the Indian Act determined that every Indian woman marrying a non-Indian man lost her Indian status, while every non-Indian woman marrying a status-Indian gained his status. With each generation, Metis and Indian communities have become more closely related, while remaining legally a world apart. Suddenly in 1985, however, the 12 (1.b) effect disappeared by legislative action, the enactment of Bill C-31. The result is that most people in typical Metis communities now have the option of becoming status Indians.

Discouraged by governments having denied their claims so long, a remarkable number of Metis people are becoming "Bill C-31s." When the law was first enacted in 1985, the government imagined that fewer than 12 000 persons would apply, but by the end of June 1990 almost 135 000 applications had been received, and nearly 75 000 were accepted into the new category of status Indians. At The Pas, Manitoba, for example, the band population has increased from 1400 to more than 2000 by the effect of Bill C-31. Overall, two-thirds of the increase in the Indian population nationally for the period from 1985 to 1990 is directly attributable to the inflation of band populations with "Bill C-31s."[25] Metis communities have declined proportionately. The implication is clear: Metis people are one of the aboriginal peoples of Canada whose existing rights have constitutional protection under the reforms of 1982; their statements of rights are becoming more focused and actionable; but as more and more Metis people become Indians within the meaning of the Indian Act, their rights as Metis persons will have vanished by abandonment. Paradoxically, a process of extinguishment is accelerating by reverse assimilation just as the courts are preparing to offer their first-ever clarification of the rights and claims of the Metis. Positive judgments may change the situation, but the decline is so extensive that the assimilation to Indian bands may be irreversible.

Documents

A. Comprehensive Claims

Metis political organizations in Saskatchewan and Alberta contend that "Half breed scrip" was an inappropriate, ineffective means for dealing with aboriginal title; consequently, proper action remains for the future. Clem Chartier, a lawyer who plays leading roles in the Association of Metis and Non-status Indians of

Saskatchewan and the Metis National Council, presents the argument concerning the comprehensive claim of his organizations:

Over 90 per cent of the scrip was delivered into the hands of banks and speculators. The banks received over 52 per cent of the issued scrip. The Department of the Interior, which was responsible for the scrip program, facilitated the transfer of scrip to corporations and individual speculators by keeping scrip accounts for them.

. . .

Most of the speculative activity took place outside the area covered by the Manitoba Act, 1870. Therefore, the constitutional implications of section 31 of that act did not apply. Nevertheless, there is a line of thought that holds that all aboriginal peoples in Rupert's Land and the Northwest Territories had their aboriginal title constitutionally entrenched by virtue of section 146 of the Constitution Act, 1867. That section provided for the entry into confederation of those two areas, and decreed that "the provisions of any Order-in-Council in that behalf shall have the effect as if they had been enacted by the Parliament of the United Kingdom of Great Britain and Ireland. . . . " The British parliament passed an order-in-council on 23 June 1870 making Rupert's Land a part of Canada effective 15 July 1870. . . . "

Incorporated into the order-in-council were addresses to the Queen by the Senate and House of Commons [promising equitable treatment for "aborigenes," individuals, and companies].

. . .

It is argued by the Metis National Council and the Association of Metis and Non-status Indians of Saskatchewan that the action of the federal government [with regard to scrip], coupled with its knowledge of the fraud that was being perpetuated, was illegal, immoral, and inequitable, and that the aboriginal title of the Metis remains unextinguished.[26]

Canada refuses to consider the comprehensive claim of Saskatchewan and Alberta Metis but does accept Metis inclusion alongside the Dene of the Northwest Territories. The "Dene/Metis Comprehensive Land Claim Agreement in Principle" is significant for the parity accorded Metis in the contemporary comprehensive-claims process:

A person shall be eligible to be enrolled as a participant [in the claim] if he or she is a Canadian citizen, resident of the Mackenzie Basin; and (a) a Dene; or (b) a Metis; or (c) a person who was adopted as a minor, under the laws of any jurisdiction or under any Dene or Metis custom. . . .

. . .

Notwithstanding that a person is not eligible to be enrolled . . . he or she shall be eligible to be enrolled if he or she is a Canadian citizen of aboriginal ancestry resident in the Mackenzie Basin, who is accepted by the community... "accepted by the community"... shall mean that a person has been sponsored by a person eligible to be enrolled... and there has been a vote by a majority of those persons resident in the geographic community who are eligible to be enrolled....

. . .

A participant may elect to be enrolled in this settlement as a Dene or as a Metis. The particular rights and benefits described in the Final Agreement may be provided for on an individual or a collective basis.

. . .

The Final Agreement shall describe the Dene/Metis organizations which will receive and manage compensation, benefits and title to lands provided by the Final Agreement....

. . .

Land selections will be fairly representative of the topography and quality of the lands in each region in the settlement area. The lands selected in respect of any community need not be identical in quantity to the lands selected in respect of other communities.

. . .

Land selection shall begin following the approval of this agreement. The parties recognize that prior to land selections: (a) appropriate provisions for interim protection shall be negotiated (b) the Dene/Metis will table their land use and occupancy maps for review by Government (c) the Dene/Metis will advise government as to the regional and community land quantum. . . . [27]

B.   Specific Claims

In 1977 the Government of Canada began funding various Metis political associations to undertake research for a joint committee of Cabinet on Metis and nonstatus Indian land claims. The final report of the Manitoba Metis Land Commission submitted in April 1980 offered detailed analysis of the administration of sections 31 and 32 of the Manitoba Act and concluded with three recommendations:

1.   The government of Canada should recognize that a series of amendments to the Manitoba Act were passed in defiance of the British North America Act of 1871 and the effect of these unconstitutional statutes was the dispossession and dispersal of Metis people from their homeland of Manitoba.

2.   To begin the process of compensating an injured people for the lawlessness of past regimes, the Government of Canada should appoint

an impartial Board of Arbitration empowered to determine: a) the extent of damages b) just and equitable remedies c) appropriate means for implementing remedial action.

3.   To prepare detailed submissions for the Board throughout the period of its hearings, the Metis Associations of Western Canada should be supported with additional funding to defray the costs of participating in the proceedings.[28]

After twelve months without a response from Canada to the documentation of the Manitoba case, the Manitoba Metis Federation filed a statement of claim with the Manitoba Court of Queen's Bench on 15 April 1981. The thrust of the claim was:

The Manitoba Act (SC 1870, c. 3), which created the Province of Manitoba in 1870, conferred certain rights on the Metis people of Manitoba. These rights were set out in Sections 31 and 32 of the Act.

· · ·

For the purpose of clarifying the legal position of the Plaintiffs and the people they represent in these negotiations, it is necessary to determine the constitutional validity of certain alterations and elaborations which the Parliament of Canada and the legislature of Manitoba purported to make to the rights conferred by sections 31 and 32 of the Manitoba Act in the years following their enactment and confirmation.

· · ·

The Plaintiffs contend that all of these purported alterations and elaborations by the Parliament of Canada and the Legislature of Manitoba of the rights conferred by sections 31 and 32 of the Manitoba Act were . . . beyond the competence of both Parliament and the Legislature and were therefore invalid and of no effect.

· · ·

The Plaintiffs therefore claim (a) a declaration that the statutory provisions . . . were ultra vires the Parliament of Canada and the Legislature of Manitoba; (b) such other relief as the Honourable Court may deem appropriate; and (c) the costs of this action.[29]

The minister of justice, Jean Chrétien, responded ten days after the MMF filed its court action—but without mentioning the lawsuit. Chrétien's letter of 27 April 1981 dismissed the land-claim submission of 1980:

Please find enclosed the Government's response to your land claim submission, as prepared by our legal advisors. You will note that it is their considered opinion that the claim as submitted does not support a valid claim in law nor would it justify the grant of funds to research the issue further.

Notwithstanding this opinion, let me state again that the Government is very concerned about the social and economic conditions experienced by many Metis and Non-Status Indians and that those problems will remain a focus of the Government's attention.[30]

The thrust of Canada's answer to the land-claim submission, the "considered opinion" of its legal advisers, was:

Section 6 of the BNA Act, 1871 did not prevent the Parliament of Canada from altering or amending the Manitoba Act, 1870 except insofar as the Act relates to that province. In particular, it did not prevent alternations or amendments to Sections 31 and 32.

. . .

The Report asserts that the "illegal amendments" to Section 31 and 32 of the Manitoba Act deprived Metis claimants of land to which they were otherwise entitled and that these "inchoate rights" remain today with their descendants and could form the basis of legal action.

As described earlier in the review, the legislation objected to was validly enacted and in most instances did not have the effect alleged.

While the first step towards litigation prompted a response to the land-claim submission, the substance of the response showed that litigation would have to succeed before Canada would agree to negotiate a settlement. For a time, the Government of Manitoba, the other defendant, appeared less intransigent, more willing to seek a negotiated settlement. Ultimately, however, the province proved no more accommodating than the federal government and the parties moved towards court action in 1986 with Canada seeking to defeat the plaintiffs on procedural and technical grounds. Ivan Whitehall, the Justice Department lawyer in charge of the defence, told the press on his way into the courtroom on 7 January 1987 that the case was a "side show, the main show is around the negotiating table," adding: "Let us not cloud the issues with a sideshow because with respect that is precisely what this court case is. . . . A case that involves legislation that is long spent in effect is simply not an appropriate case to be litigated on. . . . Clearly the class of people this legislation reaches is very specific and they are people who, I'm afraid, are very long gone.[31]

The judge of the Court of Queen's Bench hearing Canada's motion for dismissal in January 1987 recognized, however, that the "main show" of negotiation was not likely to occur without hearing the case on its merits. Justice Barkman ruled in favour of the Metis:

The applicant (defendant) argues that since the legislation referred to as allegedly unconstitutional in the Statement of Claim is spent, it is not appropriate for the plaintiffs to litigate the question of its unconstitutionality.

. . .

I am of the opinion that the real issues in this action are whether: (1) the Manitoba Act promised a "Metis Reserve," and whether, (2) the alleged measures were unconstitutional and undermined the rights of the descendants of the half-breeds. Those issues are not to be decided on an application of this nature, but are to be decided at trial when all of the evidence is before the Court.

Having decided that there is a real issue or issues to be decided, there remains the question of whether the declaration is capable of having any practical effect in resolving the issues in the case.

I am satisfied that the granting of a declaration, if the plaintiffs are successful, will have the practical effect of supporting the position of the plaintiffs in their negotiations with the Federal Government relating to the Metis land claims. I therefore conclude that this action is appropriate for declaratory relief.[32]

Of course Canada appealed. At the level of the Manitoba Court of Appeal Justice Twaddle argued for the majority in June 1988 that:

The question is . . . whether a decision on the issue has the potential of being useful to the parties in the course of negotiating a political settlement of the Metis land claim . . . . [In Twaddle's opinion] the declaration sought in this case will not decide an issue essential to the resolution of the extra-judicial claim. The settlement of the Metis claim will not be promoted in any real sense by the making of the declaration sought by the plaintiffs.

For these reasons, I am of the opinion that the appeal should be allowed. . . .[33]

The Supreme Court of Canada disagreed unanimously in March 1990:

It cannot be said that the outcome of the case is "plain and obvious" or "beyond doubt."

Issues as to the proper interpretation of the relevant provisions of the Manitoba Act of 1870 and the Constitution Act of 1871 and the effect of the impugned ancillary legislation upon them would appear to be better determined at trial where a proper factual base can be laid.

The Court is of the view also that the subject matter of the dispute, inasmuch as it involves the constitutionality of legislation ancillary to the Manitoba Act, is justiciable in the courts and that declaratory relief may be granted in the discretion of the court in aid of extra-judicial claims in an appropriate case.

We see no reason, therefore, why the action should not proceed to trial.[34]

Thus the Manitoba Metis won the right to their day in court on the merits of the case launched some nine years earlier.

The other specific claim likely to go to trial in the 1990s—that involving the Metis of the Norway House–Cross Lake district of northern Manitoba—is at a much earlier stage of development. A background memorandum on this claim prepared for the Public Interest Law Centre of Legal Aid Manitoba in January 1990 offers a chronology of events and highlights the principal issues:

Chronology

1.   1867–1869: Canada outlines terms and conditions for acceptance of Rupert's Land and the North Western Territory. Among other obligations, Canada accepts responsibility for safeguarding the interests and wellbeing of Indians and old settlers in the region.

2.   23 June 1870: Order in Council of Great Britain accepts Canada's terms and conditions for the transfer, set for 15 July 1870.

3.   1872: Dominion Lands Act (SC 1872, c 23) and its subsequent revisions to the last, 1927, recognize "titles by occupancy" held by persons in the territory before the transfer or settling on Dominion Lands later but still before survey.

4.   1916: Dominion Lands Surveyor completes township surveys encompassing the northern settlements of Norway House and Cross Lake.

5.   1924–1925: Canada notifies residents of Cross Lake and Norway House that their occupancy entitles them to purchase homesites at $3 per acre.

6.   1925–1930: Most settlers agree to pay for at least part of their lots and receive crown patents; others become illegal "squatters" but continue in undisturbed occupancy of their land.

7.   1930: Constitution Act makes transfer of Dominion Lands and resources to the several prairie provinces, shifting crown lands from federal to provincial jurisdiction "subject to any trusts existing in respect thereof and to any interest other than that of the Crown in the same" (paragraph 2), but paragraph 24 provides that "the foregoing provisions may be varied by agreement" and concurrent legislation between the Dominion and the province.

8.   1931–1937: Manitoba seeks final payments on sale contracts and converts "squatters" tenures to leaseholds.

9.   1948: Canada and Manitoba enact concurrent legislation modifying the Natural Resources Transfer Agreement to give the province extended scope for taking lands and waterways for hydroelectric projects.

10.   1948–1987: Revisions of the Manitoba Crown Lands and Water Power Acts reflect the broadened power purportedly transferred in 1948.

11.   February 1966: Nelson River Power Reserve consisting of virtually all crown lands in the Nelson River watershed precludes any but Manitoba–Hydro approved uses of crown lands for six months.

12. June 1967: Nelson River Power Reserve becomes permanent.

13. June 1973: Hydro establishes elevation 690 feet as a severance line, below which any past or future development will be subject to flooding.

14. February 1974: Province of Manitoba concedes that effects of flooding are becoming evident; announces intention of awarding compensation to northern communities in the form of accelerated social and economic development projects.

15. 16 December 1977: Northern Flood Agreement concluded between Manitoba Hydro, the province of Manitoba, and Indian bands within the Nelson River Power Reserve. Representatives of persons on "general permit" or "squatters" are excluded from the negotiations and terms of the agreement.

Notes

[1] H.Y. Hind, *Narrative of the Canadian Red River Exploring Expedition of 1857 and of the Assiniboine and Saskatchewan Exploring Expeditions of 1858* (London 1860), 2 vols., 12:134.

[2] Ibid., 179.

[3] Ibid., 180–1.

[4] Schedule A of *Order in Council of Great Britain Admitting Rupert's Land and the North-Western Territory into the Union* (23 June 1870).

[5] See D.N. Sprague, *Canada and the Metis, 1869–1885* (Waterloo 1989), 55–6, for the decisive impact of British intervention.

[6] Thomas Flanagan, "Metis Aboriginal Rights: Some Historical and Contemporary Problems," in Menno Boldt and J. Anthony Long, *The Quest for Justice: Aboriginal Peoples and Aboriginal Rights* (Toronto 1985), 235 and 240, argues that the settlement was a "matter of policy, not satisfaction of a right." The extravagance, in his opinion, was bending principle to admit the "notion that the Metis were a distinct aboriginal people with rights different from those of either whites or Indians. . . . "

[7] The amendment of the Dominion Lands Act (1872) empowered the Cabinet to set aside land "to such extent, and on such terms and conditions, as may be deemed expedient" to satisfy "half breed" claims. *Statutes of Canada* (1879), chapter 31: *An Act to amend and consolidate the several Acts respecting the Public lands of the Dominion*, section 125(e).

[8] See Flanagan, "From Indian Title to Aboriginal Rights," in Louis Knafla, ed., *Law and Justice in a New Land: Essays in Western Canadian Legal History* (Toronto 1986), 81–100.

[9] The argument, presented in an article entitled "The History of Metis Aboriginal Rights: Politics, Principle, and Policy," *Canadian Journal of Law and Society* 5 (1990), 71–94, completely ignores the Rupert's Land Order of 1870.

[10] Ibid., 90.

[11] *Sparrow* v. *the Queen* (1990).

[12] At the time of the treaty negotiation the division between "Indians" and "half breeds" was so arbitrary in some cases that many native people not members of bands still "took treaty." The first precedent on the Prairies was set in 1871 by "half breeds" of St Peters parish in Manitoba, and was reinforced in 1873 when an entire settlement of "half breeds" at Rainy River became an Indian band under Treaty 3. The practice of taking "half breeds" as "Indians" (and vice versa) continued through the 1900s in the Mackenzie valley and the Yukon. See Flanagan, "History of Metis Aboriginal Rights"; R. Fumoleau, *As Long as This Land Shall Last: A History of Treaty 8 and Treaty 11, 1870–1939* (Toronto 1973); and K.S. Coates and W.R. Morrison, "More than a Matter of Blood: The Federal Government, the Churches, and the Mixed Blood Populations of the Yukon and Mackenzie River Valley, 1890–1950," in F. Laurie Barron and James B. Waldram, eds., *1885 and After: Native Society in Transition* (Regina 1986), 253–77.

[13] Provincial Archives of Manitoba, RG 17 C1, vol. 533, Letter of instruction from J.S. Dennis, surveyor, to George McPhillips, Dominion land surveyor.

[14] See section 114 under "Homestead" and section 6(g) under "Powers of Governor in Council" of the Dominion Lands Act, chapter 55 of *Revised Statutes of Canada* (1906), and the corresponding sections, 10 and 74(c), in the same statute, chapter 113, *Revised Statutes of Canada* (1927).

[15] James S. Frideres, *Native People in Canada: Contemporary Conflicts*, second edition (Scarborough 1983), 81–129, gives an overview of the two streams of the general-claims process.

[16] See *Globe and Mail*, 26 November 1990, A4.

[17] *Sparrow* v. *the Queen* (1990).

[18] Ibid.

[19] Sprague, *Canada and the Metis*, 89–139, elaborates the connection between legislative amendment, bureaucratic intransigence, and Metis dispersal. Gerhard Ens, "Dispossession or Adaptation: Migration and Persistence of the Red River Metis, 1835–1890," Canadian Historical Association, *Historical Papers* (Ottawa 1988), 120–45, suggests that the dispersal had begun before the transfer, and was likely to accelerate even under the most liberal land policy imaginable in the 1870s.

[20] Gerhard Ens, "Metis Lands in Manitoba 1870–1887," *Manitoba History* 5 (1983), 2–11.

[21] Gene Szach, "MMF Land Claims—Overview of Case" (28 March 1984), sent as enclosure with letter from Roland Penner, attorney general of Manitoba, to Don McIvor, president, Manitoba Metis Federation (30 March 1984).

[22] The fullest elaboration of the case for the Department of Justice is Thomas Flanagan, *Metis Lands in Manitoba* (Calgary 1991).

[23] Crown Lands Branch, Manitoba Department of Mines and Natural Resources, Documents concerning lands claims at Norway House and Cross Lake, microfilm reels R–1312 and R–1297.

[24] Recent initiatives follow the recommendations of the report of the MacEwan Joint Metis–Government Committee to Review the Metis Betterment Act and Regulations (1984). The colonies consist of eight blocks of land set aside by the province in 1938 as farming communities for the Metis. At the time of the MacEwan report, their area extended to 50 000 hectares with a population of about 5000 persons. For the details of the implementation of the recommendations of the MacEwan commission concerning self-government and resource ownership, see *Calgary Herald*, 7 January 1989, B4, and 13 April 1989, A14.

[25] A series of page-one feature articles on the subject appeared in the *Winnipeg Free Press*, 12–15 March 1991.

[26] Clem Chartier, "Aboriginal Rights and Land Issues: The Metis Perspective," in Boldt and Long, *The Quest for Justice*, 58–60.

[27] Indian and Northern Affairs Canada, "Comprehensive Land Claim Agreement in Principle between Canada and the Dene Nation and the Metis Association of the Northwest Territories, September 1988" (Ottawa 1988), 14–15, 16, 25, 122–3, and 173.

[28] "Final Report of the Manitoba Metis Land Commission, 18 April 1980," 97.

[29] Statement of claim in *Manitoba Metis Federation and Native Council of Canada* v. *Attorney General of Canada and Attorney General of Manitoba* (15 April 1981), suit 1010/81, paragraphs 5, 8, 11, and 14.

[30] Jean Chrétien, minister of justice, to John Morrisseau, president, Manitoba Metis Federation, 27 April 1981.

[31] *Winnipeg Free Press*, 8 January 1987:1, 4.

[32] Judgment of J. Barkman in *Dumont, et al.* v. *Attorney General of Canada and Attorney General of Manitoba*, suit 1010/81 (18 February 1987), 9, 12.

[33] Judgment of J.A. Twaddle in the Court of Appeal of Manitoba in appeal of *Dumont, et al.* v. *Attorney General of Canada and Attorney General of Manitoba*, suit no. 152/87 (17 June 1988), 16.

[34] Unanimous judgment of the Supreme Court of Canada in *Dumont, et al.* v. *Attorney General of Canada and Attorney General of Manitoba*, suit no. 21063 (2 March 1990).

[35] D.N. Sprague, "Metis Land Rights in Northern Manitoba" (memorandum prepared for the Public Interest Law Centre of Legal Aid Manitoba, January 1990), 1–4.

The Oka Controversy and the Federal Land-Claims Process[1]

J.R. Miller

In their 1961 presentation to the Joint Committee of the Senate and House of Commons on Indian Affairs, the Oka Indians made a simple request: "The Oka Indians wish that the Oka lands be given the status of a reserve. It [*sic*] has all the characteristics of it, with a resident agent of the Department, but it has not the legal status that would enable the band to have a perpetual use vested in it for their enjoyment and that of their children and descendants. What future is there for the Oka Indian?"[2] Nothing was done about the Indians' request through the 1960s, Indian and Northern Affairs Canada taking the view that there was no serious problem because Ottawa was administering the Mohawk lands at Kanesatake as though they were a properly established reserve.[3] As the 1970s opened, there was "still a widespread feeling among Indian people that the problems of Oka [were] far from settled."[4]

As Canadians know all too well, the "widespread feeling among Indian people" was justified, while Ottawa's complacent self-confidence was not. Through the 1970s and 1980s the dispute over title to lands occupied by Mohawk Indians adjacent to the Quebec town of Oka went from bad to worse. The Indians took advantage of a new lands-claim process that the federal government devised after the pivotal Calder decision of 1973 to register a demand, not for the recognition of the lands at Kanesatake as a "reserve," as had been requested in 1961, but as unsurrendered land held by aboriginal title. When that comprehensive claim was rejected in 1975 by the Office of Native Claims (ONC), the Kanesatake Mohawk then initiated a specific claim to the lands. This, too, was rejected by the federal authorities in 1986. However, the federal minister of Indian affairs offered to look for alternative methods of redressing the band's grievance. The federal government "recognized that there is an historical basis for Mohawk claims related to land grants in the 18th century." In 1989 Ottawa proposed a framework agreement for bringing about land reunification.[5] That was rejected by the Kanesatake Indians because it did not seem likely to produce enough land to meet their needs and it appeared not to address either "the long standing problems or unique character of Kanesatake."[6]

Through the later 1980s the unresolved issue of title to the lands occupied by the Mohawk on Lake of Two Mountains rapidly degenerated. On the Indian side, rising frustration was exacerbated by the growing influence of a new form of native militancy, the Warrior Society. On the non-native side, impatience and acquisitiveness combined to produce an attack on a disputed piece of land. In the Euro-Canadian community there was growing exasperation that the continuing dispute over lands adjacent to Oka was thwarting development. Specifically, a plan to expand a privately owned nine-hole golf course to eighteen holes by acquiring and incorporating a forested tract that the municipality owned but the Indians claimed as their own became a source of contention. In preparation for a confrontation over the disputed land some Kanesatake Mohawk erected barricades in the contested area on 11 March 1990. In due course, the town and golf club decided to proceed, securing an injunction from Quebec's Superior Court on 26 April. The Mohawk ignored the court order. A second injunction procured on 26 June was also rejected by the Indians. And on 10 July Oka Mayor Jean Ouellette requested that Quebec's provincial police enforce the injunction to tear down the roadblock. An assault by one hundred police officers the next day resulted in an exchange of gunfire, the death of a police corporal, and an eleven-week standoff that involved Mohawk, police, and 2500 Canadian military both at Kanesatake and Kahnawake. The last of the holdout warriors, their Mohawk supporters, and a few journalists walked out to waiting army and police on 26 September 1990. Canada, Quebec, and the Mohawk of Kanesatake are still evaluating the consequences.

How did a dispute over a relatively small parcel of land culminate in violence, death, and a demoralizing confrontation in a country that prides itself on acceptance of diversity, pursuit of accommodation, and a long tradition of peaceful compromise? Much of the commentary since the end of the Oka crisis in September 1990 has concentrated on specific, local, immediate factors. The Mohawk Warrior Society is either a collection of righteous militants pursuing a sacred constitutional principle or a band of goons. The local residents of Oka and Châteauguay are long-suffering neighbours or red-necked hooligans. The Sûreté du Québec are uniformed thugs or inexperienced law-enforcement officers trying to mediate in a hopelessly polarized situation. Quebec is either the most tolerant and generous of provinces in its treatment of aboriginal peoples or the home of a nationality becoming increasingly unwilling to permit dissent by distinctive ethnic and racial minorities. Ottawa is to blame, either for mollycoddling the Mohawk with promises of accommodation after their claims were rejected or for failing to act decisively after the rejection of the second, specific claim in 1986 to acquire and transfer to the Indians enough lands to accommodate their wishes. Where in this welter of charges and counter-charges do the roots of the exceptional and lamentable eleven-week standoff at Kanesatake lie?

The origins of the events of the summer of 1990 at Oka lie in none of the immediate and local factors on which attention has fastened since late September of 1990. Rather, the violence over the land dispute at Oka is the product of an attitude or disposition on the part of the government of Canada that stretches back at least a century and a half—an outlook that it knows best what serves the interests of indigenous peoples and that it alone can solve their problems. The implication of this, of course, is that the same sort of confrontation and possibly violence that disfigured life in Kahnewake and Kanesatake in 1990 can—and are likely to—happen elsewhere. If the real reason for the trouble is a longstanding approach by the federal government to relations with native peoples, if the origins of the violence lie not in specific and local factors but in national policy, then obviously there is great potential for a repetition of the Oka tragedy in other parts of the country where there is competition for land and resources between the First Peoples and the newcomers. To understand better both the general nature of the Oka problem and its potential to recur elsewhere, it is necessary to consider the aged, extensive, and alarming roots of the conflict.

Prior to the invasion of the valley of the St Lawrence by Europeans in the sixteenth century, the territory near what the intruders would call the Lac des Deux Montagnes or Lake of Two Mountains was used by some of the indigenous people who are known to scholars as the St Lawrence Iroquoians. In the opinion of the Assembly of First Nations, there had been an aboriginal presence at Kanesatake since at least 1000 years before the birth of Christ and in the seventeenth century the Five Nations "took the land from the french [sic] in retaliation for Champlain's raid on their territory."[7] Non-native scholars hold that sometime in the latter part of the sixteenth century, between the explorations of Jacques Cartier and Samuel de Champlain, the so-called St Lawrence Iroquoians withdrew from the St Lawrence region, abandoning the area to a variety of Algonkian peoples. These dwellers of the Ottawa River valley, being nomadic hunter-gatherers, extensively used the territory in which Oka was later established. They travelled over it, fished in its waters, and hunted in its nearby woods. In general, there was little or no permanent occupation of the lands on the north side of Lake of Two Mountains by Indian groups.

By a grant in 1717, confirmed in 1718, a tract of land three and one-half leagues in front and three leagues deep was set aside by the French crown for the Gentlemen of St Sulpice of Paris as a refuge for a mixed group of Indians to whom they had been ministering since the 1670s. (The parcel of land was augmented by an additional grant by the crown that was made in 1733 and confirmed in 1735.[8]) The combination of Algonkians and Iroquoians (specifically Nipissing, Algonkin, and Mohawk) in the Sulpician flock had reluctantly transferred from the Mission de la Montagne near Ville Marie to the Sault au Recollet on the north side of the island in 1696 as settlement of the future Montreal began to present obstacles to successful evangelization. But even the more northerly Sault au Recollet eventually fell within the pernicious ambit of European influence, and the Sulpicians once more became anxious to move their charges to a more remote and less morally menacing location. Again with reluctance, the Indians relocated, being persuaded by the missionaries that the move was for their own good. The French, whose concept of divine-right kingship entailed a belief in the crown's ownership of all lands in New France, purported to grant the land on Lake of Two Mountains "in order to transfer there the mission of the said Indians of Sault au Recollet" on the "condition that they shall bear the whole expense necessary for removing the said mission, and also cause a church and a fort to be built there of stone at their own cost, for the security of the Indians. . . ."[9] In 1743 there were approximately seven hundred Indians—mostly Six Nations Iroquois and Huron, but also including Algonkin and Nipissing—at the Lake of Two Mountains mission.[10]

Title to the lands to which the mixture of Mohawk and Algonkians repaired on Lake of Two Mountains was never free from challenge. After the Conquest, neither the terms of the capitulation of Montreal nor the Royal Proclamation of 1763 provided much protection to the Indian occupants. The capitulation promisingly stated that the "Indian allies of his most Christian Majesty [France], shall be maintained in the Lands they inhabit; if they chuse to remain there; they shall not be molested on any pretence whatsoever, for having carried arms, and served his most Christian Majesty; they shall have, as well as the French, liberty of religion, and shall keep their missionaries."[11] The Royal Proclamation, whose definition of "Hunting Grounds" reserved for Indians did not include the area around the Lake of Two Mountains because it lay within Quebec, also contained provisions regulating purchase of Indian lands within existing colonies. However, this protection did not apply to the Oka lands either, because they were held by the Europeans to have been allocated by seigneurial grant.[12] A brief and ineffective claim was laid in the period 1760–63 by Jeffrey Amherst. The so-called "conqueror of Montreal" argued that these lands should be given to him, inasmuch as the provisions of the capitulation of Montreal, while they guaranteed free exercise of the Roman Catholic religion, explicitly excluded the Sulpicians from their protections of conscience, custom, and lands. But the British authorities saw no more reason to humour Amherst's pretensions to Sulpician or Indian lands than they did his preposterous desire for the Jesuits' estates.[13]

Although Amherst's claim came to nothing, tension soon developed between the Sulpicians and their Indian charges over use of and title to the lands on which natives and clerics resided. By 1781 a disagreement over division between the priests and Indians of revenue from non-Indians who kept their cattle on the lands at Oka led the Sulpicians to state bluntly that the Indians had no right whatever to the lands. The resulting confrontation led the natives to present their claims to the British authorities in 1781, 1787, and 1795.[14] The Indian case rested on several bases. They had once possessed, they said, a document granting them the lands on the Lake of Two Mountains, but they had surrendered it for safekeeping to the priests who now denied all knowledge of it. Moreover, during the Seven Years' War their representatives had met with British Indian superintendent Sir William Johnson at Oswegatchie to promise not to fight the British and to receive confirmation of "our lands as granted by the King of France." They had a wampum belt that recorded their possession of the lands. When Governor Guy Carleton on a visit had asked who owned uncultivated lands on the north shore of the lake, the Indians had told him "that they belonged to the Indians of the Lake." No one contradicted them. Finally, they had been told during the American Revolutionary War that if they fought with the British they would "fight for your Land and when the War is over you shall have it." All these facts—missing deed, their own record of taking the land, Johnson's assurance, the lack of contradiction when they said that the lands were theirs, and British promises during the American revolution—constituted good and sufficient "title" for the Indians on the Lake of Two Mountains.

The Indians' position and other factors began seriously to cloud the Sulpicians' title to the properties at Oka. In particular, in the early decades of the nineteenth century the view increasingly took hold that the Sulpicians' legal position was weak for a technical reason. The original seigneurial grant of 1717–18 (expanded by an additional grant in 1733–35) had been made to the Sulpicians of Paris, who transferred their rights to the Sulpicians of Montreal in 1784.[15] But since the Canadian missionary body had no legal existence—that is, it was not legally incorporated by positive law—the order was legally barred from possessing estates in mortmain, or inalienable tenure. A challenge was raised in 1763 to the Sulpicians' title by an Indian's sale of property to a newcomer, but on that occasion the governor upheld the order's claim and dispossessed the would-be purchaser.[16] In 1788 the Indians of Oka themselves raised the issue directly with the crown, claiming title to the lands on which they were located. However, Governor Guy Carleton's Council concluded on the advice of the colonial law officers "that no satisfactory Evidence is given to the Committee of any Title to the Indians of the Village in Question, either by the French Crown or any Grantee of that Crown."[17] No evidence was adduced, however, that either law officers or councillors had made any effort to ascertain what the bases of the Indians' claim were. The abrupt rejection of the Indians' case did not deter them, and the dubious quality of the Sulpicians' title was regularly highlighted by a number of petitions from the aboriginal inhabitants of Oka for granting of title to them.[18]

Further complications developed in the nineteenth century, especially during a period of heavy settlement following the War of 1812. Often lands were granted to non-native settlers in the lower Ottawa valley without consideration of or compensation for the longstanding use of the territory for hunting by Algonkin and Nipissing with ties to Oka.[19] These encroachments led the Algonkin and Nipissing of Lake of Two Mountains in 1822 to register a claim to land on both sides of the Ottawa River from a point above the seigneurie on the Lake of Two Mountains as far north as Lake Nipissing.[20] The claim was rejected by British officials in 1827 even though the superintendent general of Indian affairs, Sir John Johnson, strongly supported the natives' position, and again by the Executive Council of Lower Canada in 1837.[21]

Still, the Sulpicians were obviously worried. In June 1839 the superior of the seminary made a proposal to the Indians that was designed to regularize the order's claim. The Indians' right of use, expansion, and disposal, as well as their right to build on the particular plots, would be guaranteed, and the Sulpicians would continue to provide the Indians with wood though it might be cut only where the priests said. The Indians of Oka accepted this proposition.[22] Nonetheless, in order to resolve any technical difficulty and remove any cloud on the title, the legislature in 1840 (reconfirmed in 1841) passed "an Ordinance to incorporate the Ecclesiastics of the Seminary of Saint Sulpice of Montreal, to confirm their title to the Fief and Seigniory of the Island of Montreal, the Fief and Seigniory of the Lake of the Two Mountains, and the Fief and Seigniory of Saint Sulpice, in this Province; to provide for the gradual extinction of Seigniorial Rights and Dues within the Seigniorial limits of the said Fiefs and Seigniories, and for other purposes."[23] The fact that the representative assembly had been suspended following the rebellion of 1837–38 in Lower Canada meant that the critical measure could be passed by a small, appointed council. No doubt the authorities wished to reward the Sulpicians for their ostentatious and vocal loyalty during the troubled times in the Lake of Two Mountains region. No one bothered to note that the Indians at Oka had refused to join or aid the *patriotes* though pressed to do so.[24]

Legislative disposition of the question of title did nothing to still the rivalry and tension between Indians and priests at Oka. One basis for the quarrel was the Indians' view that the land was truly theirs and that the Sulpicians were merely a trustee for their lands. This fundamental difference was exacerbated by friction over access to resources in and on the territory that worsened steadily through the nineteenth century because of the increasing pressure of settlement in the area. A further complication arose from the fact that different Indian groups at Kanesatake used the territory differently. While the Iroquois at Oka were inclined towards agriculture on lands made available to them by the Sulpicians without charge, the Algonkin and Nipissing tended more to rely upon a hunting economy for which they extensively used a large area of the Ottawa valley, returning to the Oka area only for two months in the summer. Not surprisingly, then, it was these Algonkian groups that felt the negative impact of inrushing settlers and lumber firms more severely. Their petition to the governor, Lord Dalhousie, in 1822 began by noting "that in Consequence of the Increase of Population and the Number of New Settlements on the Lands in which they were accustomed to hunt and the Game getting Scarcer in Consequence thereof" they were being hard pressed.[25]

The depletion of furs in the region severely affected the economic position of the Algonkians.[26] General Darling had observed in 1827 that Algonkin and Nipissing presented "an appearance of comparative wealth and advancement in civilization" while the conditions in which the Iroquois lived "bespeak wretchedness and inactivity in the extreme."[27] By the 1840s the condition of the Iroquois was still "far from prosperous" because of their reliance on an uncertain horticulture. But that of the Algonkin and Nipissing had become "still more deplorable":

> their hunting grounds on the Ottawa, which were formerly most extensive, abounding with deer, and other animals, yielding the richest furs, and which their ancestors had enjoyed from time immemorial, have been destroyed for the purposes of the chase. A considerable part has been laid out into townships, and either settled or taken possession of by squatters. The operations of the lumbermen have either destroyed or scared away the game throughout a still more extensive region, and thus, as settlement advances, shey [*sic*] are driven further and further from their homes, in search of a scanty and precarious livelihood. Their case has been often brought before the Government, and demands early attention.[28]

The Algonkin responded to these adverse changes in some cases by migrating to the Golden Lake area west of Bytown, and in others by shifting into a trade in wood for local markets.[29] Their increasing utilization of the forest resources brought them into conflict with the Sulpician seigneurs, who eventually prohibited free access to wood for commercial purposes.[30]

Denominational conflict soon exacerbated the situation. The Mississauga Methodist minister Peter Jones visited the Lake of Two Mountains settlement in 1851 at the request of his church to try to convert the Indians there to Protestantism.[31] Jones's mission did not enjoy immediate success, but the Methodists continued to proselytise in the area by means of itinerant missionaries. After the Methodists established a mission at Oka in 1868 a large number of the Iroquois in particular converted to Methodism in a symbolic act of rejection and defiance.[32] (Such behaviour has parallels elsewhere: the Catholicism of the Micmac in the eighteenth century was a badge of their alliance with the French, as well as a creed.) Not surprisingly, given the Sulpicians' view of themselves as owners of the lands and the strong religious feelings of the time, the order attempted to stamp out Protestantism among the Indians. As early as 1852 Bishop Ignace Bourget of Montreal had excommunicated four of the leaders of the Mohawk Indians.[33] In the 1870s the Sulpicians applied pressure by demanding that the Methodist chapel the Indians and their supporters had erected be torn down and and the ringleaders among the Indians arrested. By court order the Methodist chapel was dismantled in 1875. Bad feelings degenerated to the point that in June 1877 a fire of mysterious origins destroyed the Catholic church at Oka. The ensuing criminal prosecution of Methodist Indians embroiled the mission inhabitants and large numbers of non-natives in Quebec and Ontario in bitter controversy for years. The quarrel even attracted the disapproving attention of the Aborigines Protection Society in London and led to inquiries from the Colonial Office.[34] The destruction, threat of violence, and growing political complications finally pushed the government of Canada towards action on the troubled Oka situation.

By the 1870s there was a well-established governmental tradition of trying to solve the Oka problem by either or both of two means: relocating the Indians or resolving the dispute by litigation. In 1853 "16,000 acres of land, in Dorchester, North River, in rear of the Township of Wexford [were] set apart for the Iroquois of Caughnawaga and Two Mountains," and similar provision of new lands was made at Maniwaki for the Algonkians from Oka in 1853.[35] Many of the Algonkin, seeking new lands for hunting and trapping, removed to the Maniwaki area, but the Iroquois stayed at Oka.[36] As the Oka problem heated up in the late 1860s and 1870s, Ottawa was tempted to repeat such a "solution" elsewhere. Neither the federal government of Alexander Mackenzie (1873–78) nor that of Sir John Macdonald (1867–73, 1878–91) wanted to grapple seriously with the issue. There were many reasons for their attitude. First, Canadian governments of the nineteenth century could not conceive of Indians having title to lands once Europeans had intruded into an area and begun to use the resources. Furthermore, by the mid-1870s Ottawa was experiencing considerable difficulties in dealing with the settler society of British Columbia, which was recalcitrant and obdurate in its refusal to honour its pledges in the agreement by which it united with Canada in 1871 to appropriate land for Indians in that province.[37] No federal government wanted quarrels with other provinces, especially the large and powerful province of Quebec, with its French and Catholic majority and its prickly sensitivity on questions of religion and provincial rights. Consequently, federal governments avoided dealing with the Oka issue head on.

Remonstrances by both the Algonkin and Iroquois at Oka in 1868 quickly turned Ottawa's thought to the possibilities of removal.[38] The Indians' demand in a petition that they "should have the same privileges as enjoyed by white people" evoked an interesting response, one that captured perfectly the government's thinking about Indians:

> the Indians cannot have the same privileges as the white man, as long as the law remains as it is, but it is the intention of the Department to submit a scheme by which Indians could, under certain conditions and with certain qualifications, obtain their emancipation, and become, to all intents and purposes, citizens, as the white men are. But in order that such a measure may obtain the sanction of Parliament, and become law, Indians must not violate the law of the land, nor throw, otherwise, obstacles in the way. They must respect property, be content with their present condition, and be sure that the disposition of the Government is to improve their condition, elevate them in their social position, and prepare them for a complete emancipation.[39]

The petitioners were told that their complaints against the Sulpicians were not well founded, and an Order in Council reconfirming federal government support for the seminary's title was passed.[40] The under-secretary of state also informed the Indian complainants that "the government has your welfare at heart."[41] The removal in 1869 of some of the Oka Indians to the upper Ottawa eased the problem temporarily. However, the increasing religious animosity of the 1870s, which threatened to bring on an extended Catholic-Protestant clash as white Methodists rallied to their red brothers' cause,[42] made it tempting to get the Methodist Indians away from Oka.

By 1877, with the Indians at Oka claiming that they owned the land and resorts to violence becoming increasingly common, matters had come to a head.[43] The government launched an investigation by the Reverend William Scott, a Methodist clergyman and father of a future deputy superintendent general of Indian affairs, that upheld the position of the seminary.[44] The Department of Indian Affairs also in 1879 initiated steps to remove many of the aggrieved Indians from Oka to the Muskoka district of Ontario. The establishment of the Gibson reserve and removal of Oka Indians to it turned out not to be the total solution that the government sought. Agreement was reached in 1881 for the province of Ontario to supply and for the Sulpicians to pay for sufficient land in Gibson Township to settle 120 families numbering about 500 persons, and in 1882 some of the Oka Indians settled at Gibson.[45] However, nothing like the expected number relocated. Only about one-third of the Oka Indians moved, and not all of those stayed for long at Gibson.[46] The stay-at-home remained obdurate even though the ever-helpful Reverend Scott remonstrated with them: "By moral suasion alone the Department endeavours to accomplish what is deemed best for you."[47] Since most of the Indians remained on the lands near the Sulpician mission, the Oka land dispute continued to fester during the 1880s and 1890s. Through this period the continuing interest in the issue from Canadian Methodists in an era in which there was a sufficiently large number of other irritants concerning creed and language ensured that successive governments remained sensitive to the matter, even if they did nothing effective about it.[48]

Sporadically throughout the 1870s and 1880s Ottawa explored the possibility of resolving the Oka dispute by its other preferred method, litigation. As early as January 1873 federal Cabinet minister Joseph Howe extended an offer to a Methodist clerical champion of the Oka Indians to have the government "pay the cost of the Defense" of "the Indian to whom you refer as having been imprisoned for cutting wood at Oka." The government, according to Howe, was "prepared to carry the case if necessary before the highest tribunals in order that the questions in controversy between the Two Mountains Indians and the Gentlemen of the Seminary may be judicially investigated and set finally at rest."[49] Apparently nothing came of this proposal, nor of another effort of the Department of Indian Affairs in 1882 to settle the dispute with a test case before the courts. Although Ottawa offered to pay the costs, in 1882 the parties could not agree on facts to submit to the courts.[50] And so, amid bickering and sectarian strife, the Oka question lumbered on, unresolved, through the 1880s and 1890s.

By 1903 the government of Sir Wilfrid Laurier had tired of the dispute and its attendant political liabilities. Religious passions remained strong in the new century, and during the first decade the dispute at Oka over wood-cutting continued to cause friction and political embarrassment for the government. In 1902, for example, Prime Minister Laurier arranged to have an Indian Affairs officer despatched to Oka, where the "Indians are becoming threatening," because "I am under great obligation to the Superior of the Sulpicians, Father Colin."[51] Petitions and confrontations continued steadily. Finally in 1903 a representative of the government suggested to prominent Toronto lawyer N.W. Rowell, who represented the Methodist legal interest in the Oka affair, that "they were anxious that the matter should be settled, and were prepared that a stated case should be agreed upon between the Seminary and the Indians, and the matter referred to a Court for adjudication, the Department paying the expenses of the litigation." Official thinking was that "the Indians have a certain right of possession or use in the property," but the precise nature and extent of those rights or interests were not clear. Best therefore to refer the contentious and complex matter to the courts at public expense.[52] Not for the last time, Indian Affairs opened its files to counsel for both sides, and not for the last time Indian land-claims litigation proved a boon to the historical-research industry. The Rowell firm, no doubt making good use of taxpayers' dollars, despatched a legal researcher to Paris to uncover documents that might strengthen the Indians' argument that they were the true owners of the lands at Oka.[53]

Thus began the celebrated case of *Angus Corinthe et al.* v. *The Ecclesiastics of the Seminary of St Sulpice of Montreal*, which eventually emerged from the bowels of the Judicial Committee of the Privy Council in 1912.[54] The Indians' argument combined a number of propositions. The Sulpicians' interest in the lands was only that of a "trustee for the Plaintiffs"; the Indians "have from time immemorial" enjoyed the right to use the commons, cut firewood, and pasture stock. As their formal argument to the Privy Council put it: they were "the absolute owners by virtue of the unextinguished aboriginal title, the Proclamation of 1763, and possession sufficient to create title by prescription [tradition]. Alternatively, [they] claimed qualified title under the French grants." The respondents, the Sulpicians, relied "mainly on these statutory titles and claim that under these titles, they are the absolute owners of the Seigniory of the Lake of Two Mountains and not merely the owners in trust for the Indians." In the unlikely event that the high court found that eighteenth-century Indians had possessed some form of title or interest, the present Oka claimants "could not be their representative as the Appellants are the chiefs of the Iroquois tribe only, and the Iroquois tribe's territory was far from the Island of Montreal and the Lake of Two Mountains." The Algonkin, who were closest to the land in the eighteenth century, were not, the seminary's factum pointedly argued, suing.

The Corinthe appeal to the Privy Council epitomized the principal features of land claims, which at the beginning of this century were in a most rudimentary state. The Indians relied both upon an embryonic notion of aboriginal title ("from time immemorial" they had used the resources of the tract) and British common law (the Sulpicians exercised title "merely as trustee" for the Indians). The latter argument was buttressed with their oral tradition, which in many instances was supported by documents recently unearthed in Paris. Counsel for the Sulpicians similarly argued a two-part case. The order was the proper owner by virtue of the original grant, and, in the event that there could be any dispute about that point, their title had been clarified, recognized, and confirmed by legislative action in 1841.

The judgment in favour of the Sulpicians similarly represented the limited nature of indigenous peoples' legal title eighty years ago. Speaking for the Privy Council, the lord chancellor, Viscount Haldane, ruled that "their Lordships thought that the effect of this [1841] Act was to place beyond question the title of the respondents [Sulpicians] to the Seigniory, and to make it impossible for the appellants to establish an independent title to possession or control in the administration. . . . neither by aboriginal title, nor by prescription, nor on the footing that they were *cestuis que trustent* of the corporation, could the appellants assert any title in an action such as that out of which this appeal had arisen." However, the court did note that a condition of the 1841 legislative confirmation of Sulpician title had created what in common-law parlance would be a charitable trust, an obligation to care for the souls and instruct the young of the Indians at Oka, and that there might be means by which the Indians through governments could force the priests to honour those requirements. In the opinion of the Methodists' legal adviser, given the unlikelihood of the province of Quebec's interesting itself in the matter on behalf of the Indians, serious consideration should be given to pressing Ottawa, "the guardian of the indians [*sic*] of Canada," to compel the Sulpicians to honour their obligations.[55]

The Privy Council's ruling, though perhaps appearing odd after the Supreme Court of Canada's finding in the 1990 Sparrow case, is understandable in the context of its times. Legally the negative finding rested on the propositions enunciated in the important St Catharines Milling case of 1889. In that instance the Privy Council had ruled that there was such a thing as aboriginal title, but that it constituted merely a usufructuary right and that it was "dependent on the goodwill of the Sovereign."[56] This was a view of indigenous people's rights that, like the federal government's decision to remove some of the Oka Indians to Gibson Township, might reasonably be summed up as the view that the Great White Father knew best what was in the interests of his red-skinned children. It assumed that aboriginal title was limited to use because title inhered in the crown, and it posited that the head of state could remove what it had graciously granted ("'dependent on the goodwill of the Sovereign'"). The implication of this latter point, obviously, was that parliament and the legislatures, of which the crown was a part of course, could also unilaterally extinguish even this limited aboriginal title. And, with very few and limited exceptions, Indians could not vote for representatives to sit in those chambers.[57] That is what the Privy Council held had occurred in the case of the Oka lands by the 1841 statute.

The entire doctrine of a limited aboriginal title that was dependent on the will of the majority population's political representatives was consistent with the approach that Ottawa took in Indian affairs. The government's assumption was that Indians were in a state of tutelage, were legally "wards" of Ottawa, and were to be encouraged and coerced by a variety of policies to grow into full Euro-Canadian adulthood. In the meantime, they were legally infantile; Great White Father knew best. The Privy Council decision in the Oka land case in 1912 was completely consistent with these legal and policy positions.

Needless to say, the Indians of Oka accepted neither the ruling nor the doctrine of aboriginal infantilism that underlay it. In the immediate aftermath of the court ruling, their chief warned that "it will not be possible to restrain the people longer, as he has been holding them in check pending the judgment of the court in the matter."[58] Methodist petitioning of the federal government resulted in no observable consequences,[59] and at Oka conditions reverted to the state that had prevailed before the decision to take the Corinthe case through the courts. The principal reason for Ottawa's inaction was the fact that the legal advice it received was that the Privy Council decision placed no particular obligations on either the Sulpicians or the federal government.[60] The Indians kept complaining to Ottawa after 1912, especially when the Sulpicians from time to time sold off part of the disputed lands.[61] For example, when the Sulpicians were unable to repay $1 025 000 they borrowed in 1933 from the Province of Quebec, the order handed over one hundred lots to the province, which much later transferred some of the plots to the municipality of Oka for one dollar.[62] In the 1930s the Sulpicians sold their rights to a considerable area, including lands the Indians considered theirs, to a Belgian company that began to enforce its proprietary rights on the Indians with consequent friction.[63] As a result of these occasional sales, settlement at Oka came to resemble a racial checkerboard: whites and Mohawk lived side by side. Moreover, since the lands at Oka that the Mohawk occupied were not a formal or legal "reserve" within the meaning of the Indian Act, Indian control was even more tenuous than it otherwise would have been.[64]

The next phase came to a head in 1945. Sulpician land sales having occasioned considerable Mohawk disquiet during the 1930s, Ottawa intervened in a fumbled effort to resolve the dispute and lower the tension between Indians and clergy. Again without consulting the Indians involved, the federal government negotiated an agreement with the Sulpicians, who were nearly bankrupt, to purchase land for the remaining Mohawk at the mission.[65] Although this had the immediate effect of lowering the temperature of the quarrel, it by no means cleared up the underlying dispute over ownership of the whole tract. Non-Indians assumed that the sale meant that Indians in future would confine themselves to their small, scattered plots, which totalled 1556 acres.[66] The descendants of Indians who believed they once had possessed more than sixty-four square miles now found their holdings reduced to two and one-half square miles. As a western member of parliament observed in 1961, "They certainly did get gypped, did they not?"[67] Moreover, since the government failed to follow the terms of the Indian Act by setting the purchased lands aside by Order in Council as a reserve for the benefit of the Indians, this newly acquired parcel still was not legally a reserve. In law it remained merely a settlement, an anomalous status that did nothing to reassure the Indians.

By the end of the 1950s, as noted at the outset, the dispute was becoming troublesome once again. In 1959 the municipality of Oka used a private member's bill in Quebec's legislature to establish a nine-hole golf course on some land that the Mohawk claimed as their own.[68] The town knew that such action was a legal possibility because Indians Affairs had thoughtfully announced in 1958 that the Indians' land at Oka was not an Indian reserve. "These lands do not comprise an Indian Reserve. . . . The right to occupy the individual parcels became involved over the years, and the Indian affairs branch has been attempting to straighten these matters out. The work is nearing completion."[69] Oka's ability to secure the special legislation was perhaps explained by the fact that the municipality and the tract in question lay in the premier's constituency.[70] Perhaps the same factor also explains why the Indians who resided at Oka were given no notice of the private measure and no opportunity to argue against it.[71] In any event, the private member's bill transferred some "common lands" that the Indians had long used for wood-cutting and cattle-grazing into land destined for recreation. "What was once reserved for Indian use and profit is now reserved for golf," noted their lawyer.[72] As the Indians said themselves, "We also consider the building of the clubhouse directly adjacent to our graveyard a desecration and an insult to our sensibilities."[73]

Once the private member's bill was passed, the Kanesatake Mohawk tried to resist. The Indians asked Ottawa to disallow the Quebec statute, but the government of John Diefenbaker refused.[74] The Mohawk remonstrated about the unsatisfactory status of their limited holdings before the Joint Parliamentary Committee in 1961, telling the parliamentarians that "we want tribal ownership of land, not the individual ownership which the white man favours."[75] Once more their remonstrance had no apparent effect.[76] Not even a recommendation from the Joint Committee that an Indian claims commission such as the United States had should be established to deal with the British Columbia and Oka land questions could move either the bureaucratic or political level to action.[77] In any case, whatever Ottawa was doing in an attempt "to straighten these matters out" was overtaken and rendered irrelevant in the 1970s.

As a result of the Nisga'a or Calder case in 1973, a new chapter on Inuit and Indian land claims opened. Prior to the court's finding that there was such a thing as aboriginal title and that it extended well beyond the limited version that the Privy Council had defined in the St Catharine's Milling case, Prime Minister Pierre Trudeau had rejected the notion. In Pierre Trudeau's view, "We can't recognize aboriginal rights because no society can be built on historical 'might-have-beens.'"[78] However, in the Calder case six of seven Supreme Court justices gave powerful support to the concept of aboriginal title, while rejecting the Nisga'a's suit. Three of the judges found that legislative action in British Columbia had extinguished aboriginal title, while the other three did not agree. (The seventh judge found against the plaintiff on a technical point.) In the wake of the Calder decision Trudeau had to recognize that, on the issue of aboriginal title, he faced a much more powerful adversary than some mere historical might-have-been. He reportedly responded, "'Perhaps you had more legal rights than we thought you had when we did the white paper.'"[79] Given the fact that the ramifications of aboriginal title were enormous in an era when the Cree of Quebec were battling the James Bay hydroelectric project and a variety of native groups in the Mackenzie valley were voicing opposition to northern energy development, some concessions were essential. Trudeau and his government, already battered by the First Peoples' united and vehement rejection of the White Paper of 1969, backed away from the prime minister's rarefied individualist notions and prepared to deal with Indians and native land claims on a collective, systematic basis.[80] In August 1973 Indian Affairs Minister Jean Chrétien announced that a new policy would soon be forthcoming.

Beginning in July 1974 Ottawa set up a claims-resolution process. Government now recognized two categories of Indian claims, comprehensive and specific. Comprehensive claims were based on the contention that the claimant had an unextinguished aboriginal right through possession of a territory since time immemorial. The Nisga'a case would have been such a comprehensive claim. Specific claims, which might be about a variety of topics including land, were demands for redress based on an argument that commitments for legal obligations on the part of the government to Indian groups had not been carried out fully and properly. The government would assist in the development of claims cases by funding research by Indian organizations. And the new Office of Native Claims would become the focal point in Indian Affairs for the claims-resolution process for both comprehensive and specific claims. The ONC would investigate claims lodged by Indian organizations and advise the Indian Affairs minister on their strength. If it so advised and Indian Affairs accepted the advice, the claim could then be negotiated. In these negotiations the ONC would represent the federal government, and, following conclusion of an agreement, it would help to implement and monitor compliance with the claim settlement. Finally, the ONC was also responsible for formulating policies covering the native-claim area.

The claims-resolution policy of 1973–74 had a chequered history, largely because it was—and remains—seriously flawed. First and foremost, it was, as usual, the product of the Ottawa bureaucracy. Since it had not resulted from consultation and negotiation, it was the object of suspicion and contained elements that were unacceptable to the native organizations. Some of these problems concerned the criteria by which Ottawa decided if claims were valid. For example, for comprehensive claims it was necessary to demonstrate that the claim emanated from an organized group, that the group had occupied the territory in question exclusively and continuously from pre-contact times (from time immemorial) to the present, and that the claimant could demonstrate that it was the legitimate descendant and representative of the original occupiers. Such criteria ignored both pre- and post-contact migrations of native groups in response to environmental, economic, and military factors. It appeared to rule out, for example, the claim of the Inland Tlingit to the territory in northern British Columbia and southern Yukon that they occupied in the late twentieth century because that group had migrated there in the nineteenth century.[81] And, or course, it worked against the arguments of a group such as the Oka Indians, who had been contending since at least 1781 that the land they occupied was theirs, because those Indians had taken up residence on the land they now claimed well after the Europeans arrived.

Other difficulties stemmed largely from the legalistic approach that the Ottawa bureaucracy took to the claims-resolution process. The governing principle in the ONC's evaluation of specific claims was the doctrine of "lawful obligation," a narrow gate through which not all worthy cases could squeeze. And government representatives proved themselves prone to argue technical objections, such as the invalidity of oral-history evidence and the doctrine of laches (barrier to litigation by passage of time). Such approaches were to be expected from a bureaucracy, but they caused enormous problems. As early as 1980 it was noted that bands and organizations were choosing litigation over negotiation with the ONC.[82] Since Ottawa limited the number of comprehensive-claims negotiations in which it would engage at any one time, a logjam quickly developed. In 1981 a review of the comprehensive-claims resolution process noted that the James Bay and Northern Quebec Agreement was the only such dispute that had been resolved. Thirteen others were in various stages of negotiation.[83] By 1985 a task force set up to review the comprehensive-claims process noted that there were six comprehensive claims under negotiation, another fifteen (thirteen of them in British Columbia) had been accepted by the department and awaited negotiation, seven claims were under review, and several more were expected. As the assessors noted, "In spite of more than a decade of negotiating, little progress has been made in the settlement of claims." The task force chair, Murray Coolican, pointed out that "at the current rate of settlement it could be another 100 years before all the claims have been addressed."[84] Things were no better in the area of specific claims: at the end of December 1981, twelve specific claims had been resolved, and 250 more awaited resolution.[85]

The problems with the claims-resolution process stemmed from more than just the slow pace and consequent frustration. Many Indian groups objected to the two-fisted role played by Indian and Northern Affairs after the process was formalized in 1973–74. The bureaucracy that granted funds for claims research was the same body that decided how much money would be available to bands and other organizations for a variety of social, political, and economic activities. Many suspected that the arrangement was designed to discourage claimants from pressing their cases too aggressively. Moreover, since the ONC both decided which claims were to be accepted for negotiation and then bargained on behalf of the federal government, the process was clearly in contravention of a major tenet of natural justice. If it was true that no one should be judge in his/her own cause, what could one say about the Canadian claims process? More generally, all the high cards were dealt to the government in this unequal game:

> Without exception, an aboriginal party has few resources other than the intelligence, commitment, and skill of its leaders, who must sit across the table from the representatives of the Government of Canada, with their apparently overwhelming resources and power. The government decides which claim is accepted, how much money will be made available to the claimant group for research and negotiation, when negotiations will begin, and the process for negotiations. Except where court action threatens a major development project, the government's patience for negotiation appears unlimited. It is hardly surprising that aboriginal groups have little confidence in the fairness of the process, or in the government's desire for early settlements.[86]

Delay, the double role of Indian Affairs, and lack of progress all added up to a claims process that engendered suspicion and opposition in equal parts.

Because of these discontents, the claims-resolution process has been under scrutiny through most of its existence. As early as April 1975 claims issues were part of the agenda of a joint National Indian Brotherhood (NIB)-Indian Affairs committee, a consultation that ended abruptly in 1978 when the NIB pulled out in protest.[87] A review of the comprehensive-claims procedures led to a restatement of policy under the title of *In All Fairness* in 1981. This document showed little evidence of influence from the native community, and it embodied no new thinking in any event.[88] In December of the same year *Outstanding Business*, a revised statement of specific-claims policy, modified arrangements in this area slightly. Although this document observed that "Indian representatives all stated, in the strongest of terms, that Indian views must be considered in the development of any new or modified claims policy," there were few signs that Ottawa paid much attention.[89] The adoption of the Charter of Rights and Freedoms, with its clause recognizing and affirming "existing aboriginal and treaty rights," caused more uncertainty in the native community about the land-claims process.

Above all, Ottawa's constant search for and insistence upon extinguishment of all aboriginal rights as part of claims resolution became particularly ominous. As the report of the Task Force on Comprehensive Claims Policy (the Coolican report) noted, there were other aboriginal rights—such as self-government, for example—that were not necessarily integral to a land claim. Why should Inuit and Indians give up whatever other aboriginal rights they had to get their comprehensive claim settled?[90] When a parliamentary committee, known usually as the Penner committee, supported First Nations' views on self-government in 1983 by advocating *recognition* of that right, the arguments against accepting extinguishment of aboriginal rights in order to get a comprehensive-claims settlement were strengthened still further.

An abortive attempt to come to grips with these objections was made in 1985 in the Task Force on Comprehensive Claims Policy. Although Chief Gary Potts and the Teme-Augama Anishnabai noted that this inquiry "marks the first time since 1763 that government has made an effort to hear from the First Nations of Canada" concerning treaty-making and claims, there was little evidence that hearing led to acceptance.[91] The task force condemned the slow pace of comprehensive-claims negotiations, blamed government insistence on extinguishment for much of the problem, and called for a new comprehensive-claims policy that would speed up the process and largely shunt aside the troublesome extinguishment issue. However, the *Comprehensive Land Claims Policy* that emerged in 1986, though it claimed later to have dropped its aim of "blanket extinguishment," offered nothing concrete to avoid the problem. When all the verbiage was stripped away, Indian and Northern Affairs still had not committed itself to drop extinguishment, persisted in talking about "granting" rather than "recognizing" self-government, and continued to reserve for itself the role of judge of whether or not a comprehensive claim was worthy of proceeding to negotiation.[92] By the later 1980s the major difference in Ottawa's claim-resolution process was one of structure: the ONC had been replaced by a Comprehensive Claims Branch and a Specific Claims Branch in the middle of the decade.

In light of the unsatisfactory nature and evolution of the federal government's land-claims procedures after 1973, the bitter disappointment of the Oka Indians is easier to understand. They, after all, had always been treated like credulous and dependent children for whom others—

Sulpicians, politicians, Methodist clerics, the Privy Council, and certainly Indian and Northern Affairs Canada—knew best what was in their interest. After 1974 they found themselves enmeshed in a claims-resolution process that was unilaterally created and largely operated by the Great White Father in Ottawa. Given the history of Oka-Kanesatake, it was not surprising that the comprehensive land claim that they launched early in 1975 was rejected a few months later.

On the advice of the Department of Justice, the ONC found that the comprehensive claim of the Mohawk of Akwesasne (St Regis), Kahnawake (Caughnawaga), and Kanesatake to a large portion of southwestern Quebec did not rest on an unextinguished aboriginal title. If the Mohawk had possessed the land being claimed when Europeans arrived (and the expert in Justice was inclined to doubt that they had), they had lost it or given it up since. "If the claimants ever did have aboriginal title to the land in question, this title has long been extinguished by the dispositions made of the land under the French regime, by the decision of the Sovereign, after the cession [Conquest], to open the territory to settlement and by the grants made over the years pursuant to this policy." Justice also believed that the lands the Mohawk were claiming had not been protected by the Royal Proclamation. In short, "the native title alleged by the claimants, if it ever existed, was extinguished, first by the French Kings at least with respect to the grants made by them, and, after the cession, by the Sovereign by the exercise of complete dominion over the land adverse to the right of occupancy of the Indians." However, the same opinion that dismissed the extensive Mohawk comprehensive claim explicitly stated that it did not apply to any "specific claims which the Mohawks of Oka, St Regis, and Caughnawaga may have with respect to lands contiguous or near their existing reserves."[93]

Such reasoning, which showed that in some respects the federal government had not advanced beyond the 1912 Privy Council rationale that was based upon the 1889 ruling in St Catherine's Milling, ignored several facts. Iroquoians had undoubtedly ranged through and extracted resources from the region at the time of European contact. Particularly the Algonkin and Nipissing at Oka had until the 1820s at least regularly hunted, trapped, and fished in the lower Ottawa valley from their base at the settlement. Finally, Ottawa has accepted or seems prepared to accept claims from other groups whose records of occupation are no lengthier than that of the Indians at Oka. For example, the Golden Lake band of Algonkin in Ontario are proceeding with a comprehensive claim despite the fact that many of them are the descendants of migrants from Oka.[94] Nevertheless, Ottawa rejected the Mohawk comprehensive claim that included lands at Kanesatake-Oka.

The Kanesatake Indians' specific claim fared no better. Lodged in June 1977, it languished until October 1986, when its contention that the Kanesatake Mohawk had an interest in the territory that should be addressed was rejected. Since "the Oka Band has not demonstrated any outstanding lawful obligation on the part of the Federal Crown," Indian Affairs would not accept the claim for negotiation. However, Ottawa "recognized that there is an historical basis for Mohawk claims related to land grants in the 18th century," and "I [Minister Bill McKnight] am willing to consider a proposal for alternative means of redress of the Kanesatake Band's grievance...."[95] As noted earlier, efforts to carry out a land-consolidation scheme at Kanesatake failed in 1989–90. This last attempt at resolution fell afoul of fears that Ottawa was not willing to go far enough to meet Mohawk needs, of divisions within the Kanesatake community, and of the impatience of a municipality and a golf club that wanted to expand the existing course by annexing lands that the Mohawk considered theirs. The result, of course, was the violence of the summer of 1990.

Subsequent to the eleven-week confrontation at Kanesatake, Ottawa behaved in its usual consistently inconsistent fashion. While speaking to the Federation of Saskatchewan Indian Nations in August on the error of using confrontation and violence, the minister of Indian affairs, Tom Siddon, observed helpfully that "while our specific claims process *is* working, it is *not* working to the satisfaction of Indian people or myself."[96] In September 1990 Siddon lectured Indian leaders assembled in Ottawa on how they would have behaved during the crisis had they been responsible, good little Indian leaders.[97] Having twice rejected Mohawk land claims, the minister announced during the standoff at Kanesatake that Ottawa would purchase and hand over to the aggrieved Indians the terrain in question. Once Ottawa acquired some, but not all, of the disputed land in the autumn of 1990, the minister's representatives proceeded to become embroiled in a frustrating round of talks that led nowhere. By February 1991 the minister, appearing before the Commons Committee on Aboriginal Affairs, argued that the villain in the Oka story was the traditional system of government by chiefs selected by the clan mothers, a system that one of his predecessors had agreed to have restored in 1969. "Since 1986, clan mothers have appointed six different councils at Kanesatake," with resulting instability. The indecisiveness that resulted from traditional Mohawk governance, said Siddon, had made it impossible for the federal negotiator, in spite of eighteen meetings with band council and municipality after 1989, to reach an agreement. That was why there had been violence, destruction, and death at Oka in the summer of 1990.[98]

The real explanation of the Oka tragedy is not clan mothers. Rather it is the Great White Father, or more precisely the attitude that has long prevailed in Ottawa that it is a paternalistic and benevolent agent that knows better than anyone else what is best for its red children. This attitude is indistinguishable from that of the Sulpicians and French government officials in the seventeenth and eighteenth centuries who shifted

Algonkin, Nipissing, and Mohawk groups from La Montagne to Sault au Recollet to Oka. It underlay the rejection of repeated demands from the Indians at Oka to regularize their title from the 1780s to the 1830s. It accounted for the legislative fiat of 1841 that registered the Sulpicians' title to the disputed lands, a unilateral declaration that was upheld in the Corinthe case in 1912 and, in part, in Ottawa's rejection of the comprehensive land claim of the 1970s. The assumption that Ottawa knew best accounted, too, for the repeated efforts to resolve the controversy at Oka by removing some or all of the Indians—to Maniwaki, to Gibson, anywhere away from the political flashpoint of the moment. And, finally, these attitudes explained the repeated failure of bureaucrats and politicians to respond to Indian petitions to the governor in the nineteenth century, to the joint parliamentary inquiry of the 1940s, and to the inquiry of 1961 that something be done to clear up the mess of the land dispute at Oka-Kanesatake.

The Great White Father in Ottawa is responsible for the Oka crisis, as it is for the larger mess that is the land-claims resolution process across the country. Procedures decided upon in Ottawa and imposed upon aboriginal organizations have responded to bureaucratic imperatives and ignored native needs. The continuing, futile attempt to impose a doctrine of extinguishment of aboriginal rights in the comprehensive-claims process is the clearest, most egregious example of that attitude. In spite of repeated demands of Indian and Inuit organizations, in spite of the collapse in 1990 of the tentative Dene-Metis comprehensive-claim agreement, in spite of the Sparrow and Sioui decisions of 1990, and in spite of the 1982 Charter of Rights and Freedoms, Ottawa refused to drop a requirement that stands in the way of clearing up an enormous backlog. Why? Presumably because Ottawa—the Great White Father—knows best.

Just ask the people at Oka.

Notes

[1] I am indebted to the Social Sciences and Humanities Research Council of Canada and to the Messer Fund of the University of Saskatchewan, both of which funded parts of the research for this paper. I am also appreciative of the advice and information provided by Robert S. Allen, deputy chief, Treaties and Historical Research Centre (THRC), Indian and Northern Affairs Canada (INAC). He is responsible for saving me from many errors, but not for the ones that remain in spite of his counsel. I have also benefited greatly by a paper by John Thompson entitled "A Brief History of the Land Dispute at Kanesatake [Oka] from Contact to 1961" and from a compilation of copies of documents by Mary Jane Jones called "Research Report on the History of Disputes at Oka/Kanesatake." Both these helpful reports have been mimeographed by the THRC under the title *Materials Relating to the History of Land Dispute at Kanesatake (Oka)* (Ottawa, February 1991). Where documents cited in the notes have been examined in the corpus of material assembled by Ms Jones

rather than in the original location or on microfilm, this is indicated by an asterisk (*) at the beginning of my citation. First published as "Great White Father Knows Best: Oka and the Land Claims Process," *Native Studies Review* 7, 1 (1991).

[2] Emile Colas, legal counsel for the Oka Indians to the Joint Committee of Senate and House of Commons on Indian Affairs, *Minutes of Proceedings and Evidence*, no. 1 (Ottawa: Queen's Printer 1961), 15 (14 March 1961).

[3] The contemporary designation, Indian and Northern Affairs Canada, is used in this paper to refer to the department or branch that has been known by various titles since 1880. Occasionally I shorten the name to Indian and Northern Affairs or merely Indian Affairs.

[4] THRC, document 0–44, "Land Title at Oka [1973]."

[5] INAC, press release 1–9029, 27 July 1990; and ibid., press release, July 1990, "An Overview of the Oka Issue."

[6] Canada, House of Commons, *Minutes of Proceedings and Evidence* of the Standing Committee on Aboriginal Affairs, Fifth Report to the House, *The Summer of 1990* (Ottawa, May 1991).

[7] Assembly of First Nations, "Kanesatake (Oka) Update," 20 November 1990, "Kanesatake Background & Chronology," (mimeo).

[8] THRC, document K–59, "Oka 1881–1950." According to M. Trudel, *Introduction to New France* (Toronto/Montreal: Holt Rinehart and Winston 1968), 221, a common league equalled 2.76 English miles, while an official league was 2.42 English miles. This paper assumes that the measure of the eighteenth-century grant was in official leagues.

[9] Title of concession, 27 April 1717 (translation), document K–59, "Oka 1881–1950."

[10] R. Cole Harris, ed., *Historical Atlas of Canada*, Vol. I, *From the Beginnings to 1800* (Toronto: University of Toronto Press 1987), plate 47 (B.G. Trigger).

[11] A. Shortt and A.G. Doughty, eds., *Documents Relating to the Constitutional History of Canada, 1759–1791* (Ottawa: King's Printer 1918), 33 (article xl of Capitulation of Montreal, 1760).

[12] Peter A. Cumming and Neil H. Mickenberg, *Native Rights in Canada*, 2nd ed. (Toronto: Indian-Eskimo Association 1972), 85–6.

[13] R.C. Dalton, *The Jesuits' Estates Question 1760–1888: A Study of the Background for the Agitation of 1889* (Toronto: University of Toronto Press 1968), chaps. 2–4.

[14] Speech of several Indian chiefs to Col. Campbell, 7 February 1781; speech by principal chiefs to Sir John Johnson, 8 February 1787; and letter of Indians to Joseph Chew, 7 August 1795; in Great Library, Osgoode Hall, Privy Council vol. 32, containing factums and supporting documents for *Angus Corinthe et al.* v. *The Ecclesiastics of the Seminary of St Sulpice of Montreal* (hereafter cited as factums). The cited documents are in the first part (labelled vol. 1) at 93–6, 99–102, and 132–4 respectively.

[15] Richard H. Bartlett, *Indian Reserves in Quebec*, Studies in Aboriginal Rights no. 8 (Saskatoon: University of Saskatchewan Native Law Centre 1984), 6.

[16] *Decision of General Gage, Military Governor, 4 November 1763, G.M. Mathieson's "Blue Book," RG 10, vol. 10 024.

[17] *Report of a Committee of the Whole Council, 21 April 1789, ibid.

[18] INAC, press release, July 1990, "Comprehensive Land Claim of Kanesatake Indians."

[19] Daniel Francis, *A History of the Native Peoples of Quebec 1760–1867* (Ottawa: Indian and Northern Affairs Canada 1985), 14.

[20] National Archives of Canada (NAC), RG 10, Series A3 (Administrative Records of the Military 1677–1857), vol. 429:30 248–51, claim of Algonkin and Nipissing chiefs, Lake of Two Mountains, 22 July 1822, in form of petition to Lord Dalhousie.

[21] *John Johnson to Colonel Darling, April 1823; Darling to Oka Indians in council at Caughnawaga, 5 October 1827; and Report of a Committee of the Executive Council, 13 June 1837—all in Mathieson's "Blue Book."

[22] *"Propositions made by Messire Quiblier, Superior of the Seminary of Montreal, to the Iroquois Tribe stationed at the Lake of the Two Mountains, and accepted by them . . . 11 June 1839" by Father Quiblier, enclosed in D.C. Napier to governor general, 18 July 1839, ibid.

[23] 2 Vict., c. 50, 8 April 1839; 3 Vict., c. 30, 8 June 1840; 4 Vict., c. 42 (1841) of *Consolidated Statutes of Lower Canada*, 1861. See Memorandum regarding "Oka Indians" by A.E. St Louis, Indian Affairs Branch, 26 May 1948, in THRC, document K–59, "Oka 1881–1950."

[24] Thompson, "Brief History," 20–3.

[25] NAC, RG 10, Series A3, vol. 492: 30 251, petition of 22 July 1822.

[26] J. McCann-Magill, *The Golden Lake Land Claim: A Case Study for the Comparison of the Litigation and Negotiation Processes* (honours thesis, Carleton University; printed by THRC, Summer 1990), 11.

[27] Quoted in Report on the Affairs of the Indians in Canada 1845, *Journals of the Legislative Assembly of the Province of Canada*, 1844–45, appendix EEE, section 2, part 3.

[28] Ibid. Similarly, see the testimony of James Hughes, superintendent, Indian Department, 16 January 1843, in Report on the Affairs of the Indians of Canada, *Journals of the Legislative Assembly of the Province of Canada*, 1847, appendix T.

[29] THRC, document K–19, A.E. St Louis, Memorandum on "Early History of the Algonquin Indians of Golden Lake" (1947).

[30] Concerning Indian complaints over wood, see Chief Joseph Onasakenrat and fifteen others to Joseph Howe, superintendent of Indian affairs, transmitting petition of 26 July 1868, in Canada, *Sessional Papers (No. 55), 1870*, 32–3.

[31] Donald B. Smith, *The Reverend Peter Jones (Kahkewaquonaby) and the Mississauga Indians* (Toronto: University of Toronto Press 1987), 217.

[32] NAC, RG 10, Red Series, vol. 2029, file 8946, petition of 19 August 1871.

[33] Thompson, "Brief History," 25.

[34] NAC, CO 42, vol. 753 (reel B–590), despatch 30, "Relations existing between Seminary of St. Sulpice & Protestant Indians resident at Oka," 9 February 1878.

[35] Report on the Petition of the Iroquois Chiefs of the Iroquois Tribes of the Lake of Two Mountains, 9 October 1868, Canada, *Sessional Papers (No. 55) 1870)*, 42.

[36] R.C. Daniel, *A History of Native Claims Processes in Canada, 1867–1979* (Ottawa: Indian Affairs and Northern Development 1980), 78; McCann-Magill, Golden Lake Claim, 12.

[37] Robin Fisher, *Contact and Conflict: Indian-European Relations in British Columbia, 1774–1890* (Vancouver: University of British Columbia Press 1977), chap. 8.

[38] Joseph Onasakenral [*sic*] and twelve others to Sir John Macdonald, 10 December 1868, in Canada, *Sessional Papers (No. 55) 1870*, 4–5.

[39] Report on the Petition of the Algonquin Indians of the Lake of Two Mountains, 26 October 1868; ibid., 41.

[40] Report on the Petition of the Iroquois Chiefs of the Iroquois Tribes of the Lake of Two Mountains, 9 October 1979; ibid., 42; Daniel, *Claims*, 78.

[41] Etienne Parent to Joseph Onasakenrat and other chiefs, 15 March 1869, quoted in Thompson, "Brief History," 29.

[42] See, for example, the Reverend John Borland, *The Assumptions of the Seminary of St. Sulpice* (Montreal: Gazette Printing House 1872).

[43] NAC, RG 10, Red Series, vol. 2035, file 8946–4, #200 285, Memorandum of Solicitor General 25 December 1897, annex "a" to P.C. 1727, 1 July 1898.

[44] NAC, RG 10, Red Series, vol. 725, the Reverend William Scott, *Report Relating to the Affairs of the Oka Indians, made to the Superintendent General of Indian Affairs* (Ottawa: MacLean, Roger & Co. 1883) is the published version. It is curious that the published report's preface (3) claims that the pamphlet was printed at the author's expense because in August 1883 the deputy superintendent general of Indian affairs indicated that Scott's financial situation was not good. See NAC, MG 26 A, Sir John A. Macdonald Papers, vol. 289, 132 681–3, L. Vankoughnet to Macdonald, 4 August 1883. Similarly see ibid., vol. 290, 133 064–6, same to same, 28 April 1885; ibid., 133 068–70, same to same, 4 May 1885; RG 10, Red Series, vol. 2203, file 40, 584, Scott to Sir John A. Macdonald, 28 November 1882 and 18 April 1884; ibid., L. Vankoughnet to Sir John A. Macdonald, 27 December 1882 and 23 April 1883.

[45] Donald J. Bourgeois, "Research Report on the Mohawks of the Gibson Indian Land Claim," 21 April 1982, 6. I am grateful to Professor Donald B. Smith, who provided me with a copy of this report.

[46] NAC, Secretary of State Correspondence, RG 6, A1, vol. 54, #7539, the Reverend L. Colin, superior, Seminary of St Sulpice, to J.-A. Chapleau, 6 November 1883; Daniel, *Claims*, 79.

[47] Scott, *Report*, 63, appendix 2, W. Scott to chiefs of Oka Indians, 18 December 1882.

[48] For example, *Christian Guardian*, 17 September 1884, 31 August 1887, 7 September 1904; NAC, MG 27, II B 1, Lord Minto Papers, vol. 10:11, "Subjects

brought before Lord Minto by the Indian delegation from St. Regis and Oka, 1901"; the Reverend John Borland, *An Appeal to the Montreal Conference and Methodists Generally* (Montreal: Witness Printing House 1883) and Norman Murray, *The Oka Question* (n.p., n.d. [1886]); RG 10, Red Series, vol. 2034, file 8946–3, newspaper clippings 1890.

[49] NAC, RG 10, Red Series, vol. 2029, file 8946, (draft) Joseph Howe to the Reverend Borland, 24 January 1873.

[50] *Ibid., vol. 2035, file 8946–4, unidentified, unsigned memorandum, 13 October 1890; Daniel, *Claims*, 79 and 172n5.

[51] NAC, MG 26 G, Sir Wilfrid Laurier, vol. 791G, 225 747, (copy) W. Laurier to Clifford Sifton, 17 November 1902.

[52] United Church of Canada Archives (UCA), A. Carman Papers, box 11, file 59, N.W. Rowell to the Reverend Dr Henderson, 1 August 1903; enclosed with Rowell to the Reverend Dr Carman, 1 August 1903.

[53] I.S. Fairty, "Reminiscences [1947]," the Law Society of Upper Canada *Gazette* 12, 3 (September 1978), 257–8; Daniel, *Claims*, 82.

[54] Unless otherwise noted, this treatment of the case relies upon: *Dominion Law Reports*, 5, "*Corinthe et al. v. Seminary of St. Sulpice of Montreal*," 263–8; and Factums (see n.14).

[55] UCA, T.E.E. Shore Papers (accession 78.093C), box 3, file 57, N.W. Rowell to the Reverend T.E.E. Shore, 2 October 1912.

[56] B. Morse, ed., *Aboriginal Peoples and the Law: Indian, Metis and Inuit Rights in Canada* (Ottawa: Carleton University Press 1985), 58 (Lord Watson).

[57] The 1885 Franchise Act extended the franchise in federal elections to Indians east of Manitoba. The provision was repealed in 1898.

[58] Shore Papers, box 3, file 57, N.W. Rowell to T.E.E. Shore, 2 October 1912.

[59] Ibid., (copy) T.E.E. Shore to Col. S. Hughes, 26 November 1912.

[60] NAC, RG 10, Red Series, vol. 2032, file 8946X, part 3, E. Lafleur, "Opinion as to the Rights of the Iroquois and Algonquin Indians of Oka," 21 June 1916.

[61] *Records of Indian Affairs, file 373/1–1, Bernard Bourdon to W.M. Cory, January 1951.

[62] *Ibid., file 373/3–8, Memorandum by G. Boudreault, 18 April 1969.

[63] *Ibid., file 373/1–1, Royal Werry to W.J.F. Pratt, 16 March 1938. The federal minister did criticize the seminary's disposal of property that the Indians used at one point, but the context suggested that the protest was a bargaining ploy aimed at reducing the amount that the Sulpicians wanted for their lands at Oka. See T.A. Crerar to Sulpicians, 10 December 1941, in *Minutes of Proceedings and Evidence*, 31–2.

[64] Although Bartlett, *Indian Reserves in Quebec*, 6, refers to the "reserve at Oka," it was not and is not now a reserve because the lands have never been "set aside by Order-in-Council as a reserve for the benefit" of the Indians. Daniel, *Claims*, 83.

[65] Their lawyer later claimed that the Indians were not informed of the 1945 transaction until 1957. See *Records of Indian Affairs, file 373/30–2–16, Emile Colas to Ellen L. Fairclough, 9 February 1960.

66 Emile Colas, counsel for Oka Indians, *Minutes of Proceedings and Evidence*, 14, 34.

67 Mr F.G. Fane, ibid., 34.

68 *Statutes of the Province of Quebec*, 8–9 Elizabeth II, c. 181, An Act respecting the Corporation of Oka, 18 December 1959.

69 Minister of Citizenship and Immigration to attorney for the Oka Indians, 27 May 1958, quoted in *Minutes of Proceedings and Evidence*, 15.

70 Assembly of First Nations, "Kanesatake Background & Chronology"; Joint Committee, *Minutes of Proceeding and Evidence*, 14.

71 Oka Chiefs to Joint Committee of Senate and House of Commons on Indian Affairs, 20 April 1961, *Minutes of Proceedings and Evidence*, 319.

72 Ibid., 14.

73 Oka Chiefs to Joint Committee of Senate and House of Commons on Indian Affairs, ibid., 319.

74 Ibid., 18; *Records of Indian Affairs, file 373/30–2–16, Guy Favreau, assistant deputy minister of citizenship and immigration, to Emile Colas, 9 August 1960.

75 Joint Committee, *Minutes of Proceedings and Evidence*, 14. Their lawyer also took pains to explain that the Indians did not regard themselves as Canadian citizens, did not recognize Canadian law, and especially did not accept the validity of the Indian Act. Ibid., 23–5.

76 Ibid., 14; Document 0–44, "Land Title at Oka [1973]."

77 Joint Committee, *Minutes of Proceedings and Evidence*, 614, 615.

78 Don Purich, *Our Land: Native Rights in Canada* (Toronto: Lorimer 1986), 52.

79 P.E. Trudeau as quoted by Flora MacDonald, MP, 11 April 1973, House of Commons *Debates*, 3207.

80 On Trudeau, aboriginal rights, and land claims see J.R. Miller, *Skyscrapers Hide the Heavens: A History of Indian–White Relations in Canada* (Toronto: University of Toronto Press 1989), 224, 254–6.

81 Catharine McClellan, *My Old People Say: An Ethnographic Survey of Southern Yukon Territory*, 2 vols. (Ottawa: National Museums of Canada, Publications in Ethnology no. 6, 1975), 1:45–50.

82 Daniel, *Claims*, 227.

83 *In All Fairness: A Native Claims Policy—Comprehensive Claims* (Ottawa: Supply and Services Canada 1981), 29–30.

84 *Living Treaties: Lasting Agreements*, Report of the Task Force to Review Comprehensive Claims Policy [Coolican Report] (Ottawa: Indian Affairs and Northern Development 1985), 13, "Three claims have been rejected on the basis of their having been superseded by law." As of 15 March 1991, according to the deputy chief of the THRC, nineteen comprehensive claims await settlement. During the winter of 1990–91 the federal government "announced the lifting of the six-claim limit on the number of comprehensive claims the government will negotiate at any time" and moved to set up a task force on "how tripartite negotiations" with native groups and provinces might proceed. INAC, *Transition*, special edition, February 1991.

[85] *Outstanding Business: A Native Claims Policy—Specific Claims* (Ottawa: Indian Affairs and Northern Development 1982), 13. "Twelve claims had been settled involving cash payments of some $2.3 million. Seventeen claims had been rejected and five had been suspended by the claimants. Negotiations were in progress on 73 claims and another 80 were under government review. Twelve claims had been filed in court and 55 others referred for administrative remedy (e.g. return of surrendered but unsold land)."

[86] Coolican Report, 78.

[87] Daniel, *Claims*, 230–1.

[88] *In All Fairness*, esp. 17.

[89] *Outstanding Business*, 16. The document claimed, however, that Indians' "views have been taken into consideration by the government in developing new policy initiatives."

[90] Coolican Report, iii. 30, 40, 43. See also 14 regarding impact of the constitution of 1982.

[91] Ibid., ii.

[92] *Comprehensive Land Claims Policy* (Ottawa: Supply and Services 1986 [the title page nonetheless bears the date "1987"]), 12, 18, 23. For the minister's claim that "blanket extinguishment" was dropped as a requirement in 1986, see his statement to the House of Commons in September 1990 in *Transition*, 3, 12 (December 1990), 3.

[93] Paul Ollivier, associate deputy minister, Department of Justice, to P.F. Girard, Office of Claims Negotiation, INAC, 26 February 1975. A photocopy of this document, which was obtained by means of an application under the Access to Information Act, is in the possession of the author.

[94] McCann-Magill, *Golden Lake Land Claim*, esp. 11–12.

[95] INAC press release, "An Overview of the Oka Issue," 3; Bill McKnight to Grand Chief Hugh Nicholas, 14 October 1986, and R.M. Connelly, Specific Claims Branch, to Chief Nicholas, 10 May 1984. Photocopies of the McKnight and Connelly letters were obtained via the Access to Information Act and are in the author's possession.

[96] *Transition*, 3, 9 (September 1990), 1.

[97] *Globe and Mail*, 11 September 1990.

[98] Ibid., 20 February 1991.

Select Bibliography

The literature on aboriginal land rights and claims in Canada is extensive. In addition to the material cited for the individual chapters, readers are encouraged to consider the works cited below.

Asch, Michael. "The Economics of Dene Self-Determination." In *Challenging Anthropology*. Ed. David Turner and G.A. Smith. Toronto: McGraw Hill-Ryerson, 1979.

———. *Home and Native Land: Aboriginal Rights and the Canadian Constitution*. Toronto: Methuen, 1984.

Barsh, Lawrence, and J.Y. Henderson. "Aboriginal Rights, Treaty Rights and Human Right: Indian Tribes and 'Constitutional Renewal.'" *Journal of Canadian Studies* 17, 2 (1983): 55–81.

Bennett, Gordon. *Aboriginal Rights in International Law*. London: Royal Anthropological Institute, 1978.

Berger, Thomas. *Northern Frontiers, Northern Homeland*. Ottawa: Department of Supply and Services, 1977.

Boldt, Menno, and J.A. Long, eds. *The Quest for Justice: Aboriginal Peoples and Aboriginal Rights*. Toronto: University of Toronto Press, 1985.

Brody, Hugh. *Maps and Dreams: Indians and the British Columbia Frontier*. Vancouver: Douglas and McIntyre, 1981.

Brun, Henri. "Les droits des Indiens sur le territoire du Québec." *Cahiers du droit* 10 (1969).

Canadian Arctic Resources Committee. *Aboriginal Self-Government and Constitutional Reform*. Ottawa: CARC, 1985.

Cassidy, F., ed. *Aboriginal Self-Determination: Proceedings of a Conference held September 30–October 3, 1990*. Lantzville, BC: Oolichan Books, 1991.

Cassidy, Frank, and Robert Bish. *Indian Government: Its Meaning and Practice*. Lantzville, BC: Oolichan Books, 1989.

Cassidy, Frank, and Norman Dale. *After Native Claims? The Implications of Comprehensive Claims Settlements for Natural Resources in British Columbia*. Lantzville, BC: Oolichan Books, 1988.

Clark, Bruce. *Native Liberty, Crown Sovereignty: The Existing Aboriginal Right of Self-Government in Canada*. Montreal: McGill-Queen's University Press, 1990.

Cumming, Peter, and N. Mickenberg. *Native Rights in Canada*. Toronto: Indian–Eskimo Association of Canada, 1972.

Dacks, Gurston. *A Choice of Futures: Politics in the Canadian North*. Toronto: Methuen, 1981.

Daniels, Harry. *The Forgotten People: Metis and Non-Status Indian Law Claims*. Ottawa: Native Council of Canada, 1979.

Department of Indian Affairs and Northern Development. *In All Fairness: A Native Claims Policy.* Ottawa: Queen's Printer, 1981.

———. *Living Treaties, Lasting Agreements: Report of the Task Force to Review Comprehensive Claims Policy.* Ottawa: DIAND, 1986.

———. *Native Claims: Policy, Processes and Perspectives.* Ottawa: Queen's Printer, 1978.

———. *Outstanding Business: A Native Claims Policy, Specific Claims.* Ottawa: DIAND, 1982.

———. *The Historical Development of the Indian Act.* Ottawa: DIAND, 1975.

Dyck, Noel, ed. *Indigenous Peoples and the Nation-State: Fourth World Politics in Canada, Australia and Norway.* St. John's: ISER, 1984.

Flanagan, Thomas. "From Indian Title to Aboriginal Rights." In *Law and Justice in a New Land: Essays in Western Canadian Legal History.* Ed. Louis Knafla. Toronto: Carswell, 1986.

———. "The Case Against Metis Aboriginal Rights." *Canadian Public Policy* 9, 3 (1983): 314–25.

Frideres, James. *Native People in Canada,* 3rd ed. Scarborough: Prentice-Hall, 1990.

Fumoleau, Rene. *As Long as This Land Shall Last: A History of Treaty 8 and Treaty 11, 1870–1939.* Toronto: McClelland and Stewart, 1975.

Gaffrey, R.E. *Broken Promises: The Aboriginal Constitutional Conferences.* Fredericton: New Brunswick Association of Metis and Non-Status Indians, 1984.

Goddard, John. *Last Stand of the Lubicon Cree.* Vancouver: Douglas and McIntyre, 1991.

Gormley, D.J. "Aboriginal Rights as Natural Rights." *Journal of Canadian Studies* 4, 1 (1984).

Green, L.C. "Aboriginal Peoples, International Law and the Canadian Charter of Rights and Freedoms. *Canadian Bar Review* 61, 1: 339–53.

Green, Leslie, and Olive Dickason. *The Law of Nations and the New World.* Edmonton: University of Alberta Press, 1989.

Harding, Jim. *Aboriginal Rights and Government Wrongs: Uranium Mining and Neo-Colonialism in Northern Saskatchewan.* Regina: Prairie Justice Research, 1988.

Hawkes, David. *Aboriginal Peoples and Constitutional Reform: What Have We Learned?* Kingston: Institute of Intergovernmental Relations, 1989.

Hodgins, B., and Jamie Benedickson. *The Temagami Experience: Recreation, Resources, and Aboriginal Rights in the Northern Ontario Wilderness.* Toronto: University of Toronto Press, 1989.

Inuit Tapirisat of Canada. *Nunavut: A Proposal for the Settlement of Inuit Land Claims in the Northwest Territories.* Iqaluit: ITC, nd.

Lester, Geoffrey. *Aboriginal Land Rights: Some Notes on the Historiography of English Land Claims in North America.* Ottawa: CARC, 1988.

Little Bear, L., M. Boldt, and J.A. Long, eds. *Pathways to Self-Determination: Canadian Indians and the Canadian State.* Toronto: University of Toronto Press, 1984.

Long, J. Anthony, M. Boldt, and L. Little Bear, eds. *Aboriginal Rights: Toward an Understanding.* Lethbridge: University of Lethbridge, 1983.

Long, J.A., M. Boldt, and L. Little Bear, eds. *Governments in Conflict? Provinces and Indian Nations in Canada.* Toronto: University of Toronto Press, 1988.

Lysyk, K. "The Rights and Freedoms of the Aboriginal Peoples of Canada." In *The Canadian Charter of Rights and Freedoms.* Ed. W.S. Tarnopolsky and G.A. Beaudoin. Toronto: Carswell, 1982.

Manuel, George, and Michael Poslums. *The Fourth World: An Indian Reality.* Toronto: Collier-Macmillan, 1974.

McNeil, K. *Native Claims in Rupert's Land and the Northwestern Territory.* Saskatoon: University of Saskatchewan Native Law Centre, 1982.

McNeil, Kent. "The Constitutional Rights of the Aboriginal Peoples of Canada." *Supreme Court Law Review* 255 (1982).

Metis Association of Alberta. *Metis Land Rights in Alberta: A Political History.* Edmonton: Metis Association of Alberta, 1981.

Moore, K.A. *The Will to Survive: Native People and the Constitution.* Val D'Or: Hyperborea, 1984.

Morris, Alexander. *The Treaties of Canada with the Indians of Manitoba and the North-West Territories.* Toronto: Belfords, Clarke & Co. (Reprinted Toronto: Coles, 1979).

Morse, Bradford, ed. *Aboriginal Peoples and the Law: Indian, Metis and Inuit Rights in Canada.* Ottawa: Carleton University Press, 1985.

Odjig, Alfred. *Aboriginal Rights in Canada.* Ottawa: National Library of Canada, 1985.

Opekekew, D. *The First Nations: Indian Government and the Canadian Confederation.* Saskatoon: Federation of Saskatchewan Indians, 1980.

Ponting, J.R., and Roger Gibbins. *Out of Irrelevance: A Socio-Political Introduction to Indian Affairs in Canada.* Toronto: Butterworths, 1980.

Purich, Donald. *Our Land: Native Rights in Canada.* Toronto: Lorimer, 1986.

Raunet, Daniel. *Without Surrender, Without Consent: A History of the Nishga Land Claims.* Vancouver: Douglas and McIntyre, 1984.

Richard, C.D. *A History of Native Claims Processes in Canada, 1867–1979.* Ottawa: DIAND, 1980.

Richardson, Boyce, ed. *Drumbeat: Anger and Renewal in Indian Country.* Toronto: Summerhill Press, 1989.

Salisbury, R. *A Homeland for the Cree: Regional Development in James Bay, 1971–1981.* Kingston: McGill-Queen's University Press, 1986.

Sanders, D.E. "The Rights of the Aboriginal Peoples of Canada." *Canadian Bar Review* 61, 1 (1983): 314–38.

Sawchuck, Joe, P. Sawchuck, and T. Ferguson. *Metis Land Rights in Alberta: A Political History.* Edmonton: Metis Association of Alberta, 1981.

Slattery, Brian. "The Constitutional Guarantee of Aboriginal and Treaty Rights." *Queen's Law Journal* 8 (1982–83): 232–72.

Smith, Derek, ed. *Canadian Indians and the Law: Selected Documents, 1663–1972.* Toronto: McClelland and Stewart, 1975.

Swartz, Brian. *First Principles, Second Thoughts: Aboriginal Peoples, Constitutional Reform and Canadian Statescraft.* Montreal: Institute for Research on Public Policy, 1986.

Tanner, Adrian, ed. *The Politics of Indianness: Case Studies of Native Ethnopolitics in Canada.* St. John's: ISER, 1983.

Tennat, Paul. *Aboriginal Peoples and Politics.* Vancouver: University of British Columbia Press, 1990.

Tobias, John. "Protection, Civilization, Assimilation: An Outline History of Canada's Indian Policy." In *As Long as the Sun Shines and Water Flows: A Reader in Canadian Native Studies.* Ed. A.S. Lussier and I. Getty. Vancouver: University of British Columbia Press, 1983.

Vachon, Robert. "Traditional Legal Ways of Native Peoples and the Struggle for Native Rights." *Inter-Culture* 15 (1982).

Wadden, Marie. *Nitassinan: The Innu Struggle to Reclaim their Homeland.* Vancouver: Douglas and McIntyre, 1991.

Watkins, Mel. *Dene Nation: The Colony Within.* Toronto: University of Toronto Press, 1977.

Weaver, Sally. *Making Canadian Indian Policy: The Hidden Agenda, 1968–1970.* Toronto: University of Toronto Press, 1981.